# Myself: In Pieces

A True Cautionary Tale
By
JRH
New York, New York

# Myself In Pieces

Jennifer Rose Hersh

Published by Jennifer Rose Hersh, 2024.

© 2023, Jennifer Rose Hersh

While every precaution has been taken in the preparation of this book, the publisher assumes no responsibility for errors or omissions, or for damages resulting from the use of the information contained herein.

MYSELF IN PIECES

**First edition. February 23, 2024.**

Copyright © 2024 Jennifer Rose Hersh.

ISBN: 979-8224165193

Written by Jennifer Rose Hersh.

# Myself: In Pieces

<u>**Prologue**</u>

We are all made up of various stories, just as a painting has multiple shades and colors. Our history and our experiences make us who we are in the present. If you recall all the stories and try to recall all those memories that made you, you might see yourself as others see you. Where we were then and where we are now might allow us to gain insight into the direction in which we are heading. It's as though we have been creating our road maps. Our stories are pieces of an elaborate, unending puzzle. We can gather as many pieces as possible to see the whole picture of ourselves. These pieces are buried deep in our memories because we cannot always recall our nightmares from our conscience. Sometimes, they are just too ugly or too disfigured to touch, so we try to leave them out. We think we will accidentally cut ourselves on their deep edges if we try to touch those memories. Then there are the pieces of memories that we cannot forget the shape and textures of. We always carry them in our purses and back pockets. These are our favorite pieces-the ones we can't wait to show off, like a favorite outfit we have put together from scraps from the back closet. Although some pieces need to be hidden from public view, we fully know their presence. It's like hiding our dirty underwear under the bed. These pieces have sharp edges, are sometimes rigid, or are often embarrassing to bring to family functions and brunch with friends. You know the pieces I'm talking about. These are occasionally collections of dirty secrets and bad life choices. After you gather most of the pieces of yourself - the pretty, the embarrassing, the ones we try so hard not to look at if you're lucky, you - might see yourself for the first time. Be warned. You might not like the picture you created from all the scraps you collected. You might realize that even though they are connected, you might not be able to display them all for public viewing.

These stories I am about to share are my pieces. I'm unsure if I want to use the word "story" because it makes what I'm about to say fake, like I'm making it up. I don't like to give the impression that I'm talking out of my asshole. I should say that these are some of my pieces (hence the title), the ones that are in my back pocket, under my bed, and in the backseat of my car. There are a few pieces buried somewhere in a dirty sandbox in Starrett City, under broken glass and dog shit. There were a dozen pieces that I struggled to recall. You know when you remember being somewhere but are unsure why or even where you were? For example, I sometimes have a nightmare that my dad is trying to come into my bedroom, and I often wake up crying. I am trying to remember whether that nightmare stems from actual events.

There might be an actual memory somewhere, but I haven't managed to recover it, nor do I plan to. The pieces I recall are the ones I can, at least, somehow reflect on. I am very aware of the details involved in those pieces. I thought I could gather as many of them and try to assemble myself as a whole piece. Writing about them in a collection of pieces, I would gain a better insight into who I am or, at the least, an idea of myself. Maybe I'll be able to see why I'm a bit fucked up. However, trying to display every piece is a huge undertaking. No one needs to know about every Christmas or every time I fucked up. So, I gathered the ones I don't talk about or don't talk much about. These are pieces that I don't share, but I am about to share with the world because I know the people in my life would not be happy to learn how dysfunctional I am. Like they say, 'Be careful of the quiet one.' Most of these pieces have jagged edges and have stayed hidden from my friends and family. They were complicated to write about because I had to be in tune with some memories that were not pretty. Some pieces are very recent, like freshly baked cookies with an unpleasant bite.

This project began years ago when I just needed to write stuff down because my head and heart would explode if I didn't. I'd write small pieces here and there of events I've gone through. I found old letters I'd written to people, which now invoke some intense memories, and I have included them. While reading this, you might feel a different voice is telling the story because fifteen years ago, when I did write them down, I was somewhat of a different person. Most of these stories were about memories I could not discuss with anyone due to their dark nature. Maybe you could call it some sort of therapy to let out some of the pain as well as some of the absurdity I've created for myself as well as experienced. These small pieces weaved in together as I would add more detail here and there, ending up with many pages. It was like finding a shoe box of random fabric scraps, some with scratchy textures, some solid in grim, some new but secret, others in far worse shape even to consider touching. Then, I try to sow these scraps together to create one thing: a complete picture or at least a fuller picture.

For the sake of anonymity and privacy, I will change almost everyone's names which matter or would be able to prove I just wrote some shit about them. The last thing I need is a bunch of goddamn lawsuits. I also felt like weaving the present, well, the present of my present when I wrote it, with the past. I will try to indicate the year or my age so readers don't get lost in this mess. One person I will try not to include as much as possible in any of these pieces is my son. I feel I need to separate him from these pieces. He is too important to me to be affected and tainted by my dysfunctional behaviors. I will barely mention him.

**Ithaka**
BY C. P. CAVAFY[1]
TRANSLATED BY EDMUND KEELEY

As you set out for Ithaka
hope your road is a long one,
full of adventure, full of discovery.
Laistrygonians, Cyclops,
angry Poseidon—don't be afraid of them:
you'll never find things like that on your way
as long as you keep your thoughts raised high,
as long as a rare excitement
stirs your spirit and your body.
Laistrygonians, Cyclops,
wild Poseidon—you won't encounter them
unless you bring them along inside your soul,
unless your soul sets them up in front of you.

Hope your road is a long one.
May there be many summer mornings when,
with what pleasure, what joy,
you enter harbors you're seeing for the first time;
may you stop at Phoenician trading stations
to buy fine things,
mother of pearl and coral, amber and ebony,
sensual perfume of every kind—
as many sensual perfumes as you can;
and may you visit many Egyptian cities
to learn and go on learning from their scholars.

Keep Ithaka always in your mind.
Arriving there is what you're destined for.

---

1.  https://www.poetryfoundation.org/poets/c-p-cavafy

But don't hurry the journey at all.
Better if it lasts for years,
so you're old by the time you reach the island,
wealthy with all you've gained on the way,
not expecting Ithaka to make you rich.

Ithaka gave you the marvelous journey.
Without her you wouldn't have set out.
She has nothing left to give you now.

And if you find her poor, Ithaka won't have fooled you.
Wise as you will have become, so full of experience,
you'll have understood by then what these Ithakas mean.

**Hurt**
Song by Nine Inch Nails (Johnny Cash's cover is better)

I hurt myself today.
To see if I still feel
I focus on my pain
The only thing that's real
The needle tears a hole
The old familiar sting
Try to kill it all away
But I remember everything
What have I become?
My sweetest friend
Everyone I know
Goes away in the end
You could have it all
My empire of dirt
I will let you down
I will make you hurt
I wear this crown of shit
Upon my liar's chair
Full of broken thoughts
I cannot repair
Beneath the stains of time
The feelings disappear
You are someone else
I am still right here
What have I become?
My sweetest friend
Everyone I know
Goes away in the end
And you could have it all

My empire of dirt
I will let you down
I will make you hurt
If I could start again
A million miles away
I would keep myself
I would find a way

## PART I: HAVE TO BEGIN SOMEWHERE
### <u>Pieces of Joas - Spring 2008</u>

So, let's start in Portugal! Ok, I bumped into a guy from Portugal via Facebook in the spring of 2008. I was familiar with the concept of social media. I had a Myspace page for maybe a couple of years before getting a Facebook page. The power of meeting strangers with like-minded interests seemed enormous to me. When I joined Facebook, I already had double digits of friends on Myspace, who were now my Facebook friends. I loved social media and feeling popular or having the digital illusion of being popular in a world I had difficulty connecting to.

Let me set the story better so you can see where I was coming from. During the spring of 2008, I was married with a small child. We lived in our first and last house with my newly retired father. My father was not an easy person to live with, and I didn't want to live with him. However, I didn't have much of a say in the matter. To afford a house, we needed my dad's income to make it work. My husband reassured me that we would eventually get a home with a basement. For my dad, the basement could be turned into an apartment. We found a house with a basement, but it never got renovated. I was stuck living with my dad. My husband's lack of follow through and sometimes manipulation was a series of events that I had little say about or just lied to for my husband to get his way. My husband was an expert in manipulation to get things he wanted, while I had little to no voice. By then, I was well-trained in doing things I didn't want to. My presence on social media was one of the few things I had any control over. At least, that's what I think I felt when reflecting on that time.

This app was attached or part of Facebook when FB was still a baby in the social media world. I don't remember the app's name, but it was swiping on various pictures of people and clicking on if you liked them or thought they were acceptable to exist in society.

You judge people from the picture they provide by clicking 'Like' or 'Unlike," and they won't judge in return. Yes, how fucken middle school but a few hundred adults are clicking away. You would find the same or similar interface on most dating sites. I know I was bored, and I didn't think anything would result from it. It was before or during the same time Farmville was a big rage. So, while waiting for my berries and corn to grow to save enough online coins to buy a limited-edition cow or windmill, I click and swipe pictures of strangers on this app.

Everything changed when I got a random message from a young man from Portugal. I honestly don't remember how old he was. I want to guess the mid to late twenties. Joas, a deep-thinking socialist soul who I now recognize might have suffered from depression. I'm not saying all socialists are depressed, but this individual was. Yet, the internal rose-tipped shaded glasses create an illusion of someone from pieces offered in emails and instant messages. How easy it is for me to get lost in the vortex illusions. I don't want to give the impression that he was full of shit by any means.

I interrupted things how I wanted to interrupt them and understood things how I wanted to understand them. Let's just say Joas, and I existed in a fantasy world I created. If there was any reality to who he was or even who I was, I didn't want to see it. Joas was a profoundly poetic soul, and in my delusional mind, I truly believed he understood how somebody could have a range of emotions and sensations readily evoked over such long distances with a stranger I met over the internet. You would think a grown married woman would know better, and maybe I did. I guess I was gullible then. Perhaps I was just desperate to believe in fairytales. Looking back, I just had a load of open wounds inside me that were too quickly filled with any random act of kindness from a stranger at the time. Denial was often my best friend, and it was easy for a stranger from Portugal to sink in under my skin.

With this crash of new emotions from Joas and my ongoing communication, I began to write a flux of poetry. I was overwhelmed with so many intense new feelings that I had to express through poetry and writing. Since I was a young teen, I have tried to write down the interior of my heart and soul. Communicating my feelings like an average person never came easy to me. Growing up, I needed to hide under metaphors because I felt using the typical spoken language was never entirely safe. Unfortunately, this hasn't changed much since then. Joas was my poetic muse. Words of desire, love, and desperation were pouring out of me like an endless faucet that someone forgot to turn off. I would sometimes attach photos and drawings I'd either create or find online with poems to create a visualization. He was super flattered and let me use some images with poems I wrote about my feelings for him. I poured my heart out in lines as though I wanted to cry all the passion and pain inside me to the world.

What is the best way to express all these emotions and desires that can only be expressed through writing? My dysfunctional warped answer to that question is you don't. You're stuck pining over a person who is not available, no matter how many fun fantasies you come up with. You were fucken screwed with taking off your pants. All writing did not even come close to releasing the storm deep under the surface. Writing helped create a temporary relief to my neediness. I would get frustrated and feel abandoned by a stranger hundreds of miles away who didn't do anything wrong but give me the particular attention I was craving. Joas never made promises to me. This relationship I was mainly having occurred in my head.

Joas was a geologist, gopher, and map maker. He was in love with the shapes and the movements of land masses on the planet.

One of his jobs was to travel through Europe, taking calculations and measurements of various changes in land masses, which meant he traveled a lot. His job also meant he was on the move often and sometimes rarely had access to the internet. I occasionally went to get his emails for days, if not a whole week. I felt ignored, abandoned, and hurt. I would write these heartfelt emails that rarely got answered. Trying to maintain a delusion of a romantic relationship is heartbreaking. I never said I was the most stable person hours in this story, which led us to my first sex tape.

Ok, it was more like a sex CD. Back then, technology to record our most embarrassing and intermittent moments was not as readily available as today. Today we can record sticking dildos up our asses and drop them quickly on various sites or just share them among loved ones. Youporn and other websites alike prove how much the sexually exhibitionist culture has evolved since then. We had a small camcorder that saved our cherished memories on tiny CDs. God only knows where CDs of birthdays and various celebrations are now. What seemed like moments of family memories are barely thought about now. It was not enough to even reflect on the mild family milestone then. Being a film student back in college helped me record my act of masturbating for a guy on the other side of the planet. I hooked the camera on the TV to see what the camera saw and what Joas would eventually see.

Even though the technology was brutal compared to our smartphones and editing apps, I believe I created something that was just erotic but well-filmed. Yes, it's bizarre even to feel any pride in recording twenty minutes of masturbation for an almost stranger. However, the difficult part wasn't creating a sex CD but getting it delivered to someone who didn't stay in one place. Imagine throwing a pebble at a moving target on the Atlantic Ocean's other side. Trying to give this CD took a lot of coordination on both sides of the pond. Joas told me where he would be staying for at least a few days to get this thing delivered. For some reason, I used DHL. Maybe it was because it was the cheapest or something to do with shipping. I don't remember, but it was frustrating on both ends. The DHL office of wherever he was in Europe, the DHL office was nowhere near the hotel he was at.

With a shit load of frustration on his end, he finally managed to retrieve my recorded self -sex- escapades, and he, of course, loved it. However, the situation was highly frustrating and left me with overwhelming thoughts and feelings. I adored this online stranger, and I wanted this online stranger. I knew we were never going to meet. It would not happen, no matter how many stars I wished for. Reality is reality, no matter how many daydreams and fantasies you can weave in. Eventually reality just bites you on the ass and or just laughs in your face. As things move forward, people move in and out of our lives rather unexpectedly, and I did not expect George to pop into my reality. However, I was somewhat grateful for George's timing.

**Thursday, April 24, 2008,**

**The following are several letters written a week apart:**

**Dear Joao,**

**I'm not sure how close I should stay. Sometimes, I question your sincerity because this could be one big game that you have been mastering before you even poked me. I was just foolish enough like a collection of other women to take your bait. Even so, who am I to make any judgments? I have no fucken right at all and none of my business. Really, why in the world wouldn't you be scoping the field? You're young, attractive, and in-depth in more ways than one, and you have a fantastic package in your shorts. Who's to put a restriction and make it a one-ringed show? I'm more willing to play a good game of let's pretend than anyone, but it has never been taken to this high a level of sexual energy before. It's not even remotely close. To feel**

physically starved for someone I have never met and will never meet is one of the purest forms of torture I have ever experienced.

Then, there is a question of sincerity between static strangers. I know that I feel a connection toward you, which is just as cruel as sexual hunger. Hunger makes me hate time, fate, passion, love, and space. Sometimes, no, most of the time, I was hoping that this was just some fucked up game to get lost in the want and the definite emptiness it was leaving. It is easier to accept a role as a collected plaything than to undergo everything.

I have mixed emotions about the 4500 (approx.) miles of water that separates us. For obvious reasons, I hate it. Yet, at the same time, I am grateful for it. It isn't a secret that I have thought about so many various situations. There are the safe and highly unrealistic ones that bend space and time. Then there are the more realistic ones that are dangerous, if not cruel. I find myself living in a world of constant scenarios; during these scenarios, I, in a different email, think that I can feel and hear you. It is very pleasurable and, at the same time, creepy.

Right now, I'm waiting to hear from you about some address to send something. No, that was an understatement. I'm currently obsessing over hearing from you and the location to send this damn thing. It's only been just over 48 hours since I last heard from you, which is not a big deal except for my insides ache. Again torture.

Love,

JRH

Friday, May 02, 2008

Dear Joao,

It felt so good to hear your voice yesterday, even though the line was terrible and we got cut off. I was fighting the urge to call since you felt it, but I finally gave in. I'm weary of expressing myself over the phone because the lines are so bad. Nothing is worse than getting cut off in the middle of an emotional sentence, and being unable to bring back to writing to you allows me to get to the point with no interruptions, even though the sound of your voice melts my insides. I wish I were sitting while looking up at the stars.

Right now, I feel like I'm in package hell. What seemed to be a simple idea appears to be uncontainable. The screwed-up part is that I finally figured out how to transfer the file to upload (yeah, a bit too late!!) You said that it was under control, that you'd get it, so I will trust you or lie to me that you have it. When I get another private moment at home, I'll work on a new one without all the drama. But it will never satisfy my needs.

Beyond the fact that I will never fuck you, kiss you, or even touch you in any way, I will never see you move or sit and have a long conversation about orange trees and ideology while watching your facial expressions. I will never make you laugh or get downright pissed off. All have fragments of sounds and images in secret places in my heart. Now I feel like some sort of whiny child. It's funny how this madness started with an electronic poke. Do you usually have this effect on people? Be honest!

As I mentioned, you are not 100% secret in a different email. I guess to prevent my brain from exploding (just me; it came close at many moments), I had to talk about the methane in the atmosphere and this weird, crazy, lust-love affair-a-far thing to a couple of friends at work. One of them convinced me to give in to the urge to call you yesterday because I've been freaking out about the package. I guess part of me doesn't want to intrude on you, while the other part of me fights not getting on a plane, finding you, and devouring you. That's one of the many scenarios in my head that I live off.

In the afternoon, on my lunch break, I will watch Easerhead. It is one of the things I do from time to time to feel connected to you. Last week, it was 12 Monkeys and La Jetee. What should it be for next week?

If you keep this dreadful job and go back out of contact again, we are getting you a texting device. You have very little say in this matter, young man! Don't argue with me! You brought me addicted, so now you're going to have to deal with it..like it or not.

Love,

JRH

# Pieces of George

The way I meant George is the same way I met Joas. The only difference was George lived on Long Island, which isn't down the block but is still somewhat accessible. Another difference was I didn't feel anything more than morbid curiosity about getting to know him. George was a lot younger. I forget exactly how old he was, but I want to say he was maybe in his early 20s. I was about 37, and in my mind, George was a hot piece of forbidden fruit. He was also a manipulative little fucker with ninja flirting skills. This young piece of fruit knew precisely how to penetrate under my vulnerable skin. I would be surprised if he had plenty of practice under his belt. After my irrational emotional ordeal, I just was trying to shed with Joas and the insanity at home. I was vulnerable and an easy target for anyone who spoke the right words. Trust me, it didn't take much back then.

After maybe a couple of weeks of flirting back and forth, George finally convinced me to meet him in person. My naive understanding of "meet" completely differs from what this "word" implies. When someone you meet online in this sort of capacity, the word "meet" basically means "to fuck" or "to fool around." It does not mean just saying 'Hi' and shaking hands. I perfectly understand the word "meet" today and what it implies. Fifteen years ago, I was perhaps a bit too naive, but I also know I was in the land of denial. We agreed to "meet" in the "middle," meaning the middle of our locations. George was coming from Long Island, and I was traveling from Staten Island. The "middle" ended somewhere between Brooklyn and Queens and a touch off the Belt Parkway.

The way my work schedule was back then, I could 'meet' quickly without anyone questioning my location. The "meet" occurred on some weekdays from the late morning - to early afternoon before being scheduled to work in a parking lot at the

Gateway shopping center. The Gateway shopping center happened to be one exit from where I grew up in Starrett City. There was no shopping there when I lived in Starrett City. Instead, it was vacant ground. I could easily see the vacant area from our 17th-floor apartment. About a year ago, I realized that this once vacant location and now where I was to 'meet' George had a distressing history. These are many memories of adolescent events that a good therapist would love to sink their teeth into. However, that is an entirely different chapter down the road. Let 'say life is sometimes a disturbing fucked up circle.

Knowing I should not be driving over the Verrazano Bridge on the belt parkway, I turned off my moral compass once I got into my car. Parts of my brain went silent. My soul felt hollow, and my body was in control. I went into automatic mode once I got to the Gateway. I got out of my car as soon as George got out of he was his car. We said hello. This is a 'meeting', right? He was young, slim, and attractive. I don't know if the greeting between them ever passed the basic hello before he opened the door of the back seat of his car. This is a 'meeting', right? I do remember he had on sunglasses. I'm unsure if he even said "get in" or if his body language implied it. I got in. He got in. This is a 'meeting', right? I can't recall the series of physical actions in any particular order except the act of penetration and the fact George never took off the sunglasses. 'It' was quick. 'It' happened.

I don't remember feeling much of anything. Maybe I felt excitement more than I remember feeling sexual pleasure. The excitement came from doing something I was not supposed to and doing something with that someone. It was like stabbing the words "suppose to' in the fucken face. There were no romantic gestures or even that much foreplay. A stranger I met online was inside me. This is a 'meeting', right? I remember the gold chain he wore hitting my forehead repeatedly while grinding his body on top of me. I wondered if I should feel annoyed about the chain constantly waking me in the face. I think he grunted like some men do when they are climaxing. All I knew was that his mess wasn't inside my car and, therefore, not my mess to be concerned about. If there was a mess, would George even notice with the sunglasses on?

It didn't take me long to know it was time to get out of his car. I didn't require a cue or a grand gesture. Instinctively, I learned it was time to leave this person's car. The 'meet' was over. There was an exchange of a brief peek on the lips before getting back to our vehicles and parting ways. As soon as I was behind my wheel, reality started slipping through. A few random tears were falling down my cheek. There weren't tears of regret. I just cheated on my marriage by fucking a stranger in their car in a parking lot in board mother fucking daylight. They were tears of the morning. I just murdered a piece of myself and left the body to decompose in the back of George's car. There was a little shock to fight, but that tiny shock crept in. Yeah, I just did a horrible thing. A blanket of numbness also began creating a shell around me. A cascade of emotions, such as exhilaration, remorse, and shame, was trying to flood through my system, but also a blissful nothingness. I began to cling to the nothingness. One thing for sure was that any raw emotions I felt for Joas evaporated into that void of emptiness. I drove home.

George and I "met" a couple of weeks later. It's the same spot at Gateway, same car. The same sunglasses and chain pounding my forehead partnered with the acceleration of being where I should not be again. Doing the same I was not supposed to do with a person I should not be with, and my house's button floor was pathetic, but my primary intention was not to get laid. It was the numbness that I craved most of all. It was the closest I could bring to experimenting with heroin, cutting myself, and jumping off a bridge. This insane act of self-harm was the beginning of how I learned to thicken my skin and quiet my heart.

This memory of what took place with George became my temporary shield from domestic chaos and absurdity. At the time, I was married for about five years with a four-year-old son living in a white-saturated neighborhood on Staten Island. The area's population was a mix of Italians, Irish, Russians, and a little in between. I remained a domestic loner in the sea of white work-middle class. The house was too huge for me to handle with its three floors, two flights of stairs, and, of course, the other people I lived with a husband, a son, and my dad, who thought cleaning up after them was my goal in life. Being the only working adult in the house and coming home to a sink full of dishes, loads of washed clothes, and a small child demanding my attention made me resentful. There would be times I'd walk into the house and not even be given a chance to take off my coat before the various demands and complaints came piling on from these men.

The four years, being four, had a good excuse for not maintaining various household duties, but what were the other two adults' excuses? My dad was at least good at taking out the trash regularly, even though the concept of which types of garbage or recycling go in its perspective garbage cans was a battle I never won. However, everything else about living with my dad was a complete shit show, and I mean this literally. My dad had a natural talent for leaving behind his DNA in the bathroom. No toilet seat was safe from his regular shit stains. My dad also had a weak stomach but also managed to miss the toilet often. I also cleaned the toilet seat from his various waste products, door handles, and light switches. Gross would be a fucken understatement. Even though his bedroom was the closest to any bathroom when he got older and too lazy to get up to go pee, he'd use coffee mugs as makeshift urinals.

It was not my choice to live with my dad. He was used as a financial tool to buy a house. The original plan and the reason I finally agreed to this agreement was that my husband would renovate the basement into a tiny apartment for my dad. All his nasty habits would stay on the house's button floor and never make their way up to the rest of the house. My husband never renovated the basement into any sort of livable space. My opinions are perhaps the fuel to many of my internal protests because these steps for any life improvement had to be shut down by some ecological explanation given by my husband. My husband had a way of lying and manipulating to get what he wanted. Then, when things didn't work out, it was everyone else's fault but himself. It took me a while to understand how he worked and to emotionally detach from this sort of control he had. Living with my dad was a job within itself. Much later, he would blame me for choosing to live with my dad and many other things. I learned that if I take full responsibility when things don't go the way he wants, I should end the arguments. I have no problem pushing myself under the bus before anyone else can do it themselves.

**Nightmare**

In a petrified stillness in bed, I hear muffled rumbling down the hall. It's inaudible, and it's moving closer to my bedroom door. "Please don't let it come in here!" The sounds become closer as though it is about to cross the threshold through the doorway. "Don't come in. Don't come in, I struggle to say, but no words come out of me. If I could just turn over to face the door, maybe, just maybe, I can stop it from coming into my room. My body won't move. A feeling of disgust bares down on my body. I wake in the blurriness of the real world, screaming, "No!"

# Pieces of JC (maybe 2009 or 2010)

My husband visited his brother in Florida for a week in late spring and early summer. Even though I was left to hold down the fort and care for the two other humans, it was peaceful without his over-controlling presence. I remember it being hot outside, and I wanted to set up a kiddy pool and sprinklers for my son in the backyard. For some reason, my husband made hooking up the water for the outside hose a bit complicated. You couldn't just turn the faucet and Wa-La, there would be water. Instead of a direct faucet-knob hook-up outside, the ones you just turn and out pop water. No, you had to go into the basement, turn a few levers, and turn on the faucet outside. You might risk flooding the cellar if you moved a lever incorrectly or went out of sequence. My husband had this as some sort of mission-impossible hookup way to prevent someone from coming to steal our water, even though I'm sure that isn't probable. So, before flooding the basement due to uncertainty, I called my husband for help.

Now, calling someone, especially your husband, for help with something this basic shouldn't be an issue. Well, it was. He might have been drinking because he wasn't making too much sense. He assumed my left was his left or something. I asked him to clarify his directions, which was a huge mistake. The verbal abuse and the yelling I received cut into me so deeply. He was screaming at me over a faucet. I was, of course, too stupid for not understanding his mangled directions. My husband is one of the few people in my life who have this effect on me, but I felt so belittled. He could ultimately reduce me to nothingness. Back then, I didn't know better than to avoid these situations with him. Even now, I'm learning to keep most of my inner pieces away from him because they will be used against me if not trampled on. I often forget. I'm unsure if I waited for him to hang up before throwing the phone across the yard. With my body trembling, tears and snot flowing. Whatever shield I had gained from my brief involvement with George was gone. I felt raw and broken.

At the time, I was browsing various online sites for hooking up. My mind geared up to create some sort of escape plan from any hemorrhaging emotions that might occur. Instead of running to a liquor store or finding a local drug dealer, I came across fing.com. The thought of that particular site finding blissful emptiness and its possibilities calmed me down. All I needed to do was create an account to get the ball rolling. The shield of extra skin I gained at the Gateway Shopping Center parking lot required replacing something just as dark or even a few shades darker. My goal that week was to find a random guy that held some acceptable parameters of attractiveness to come over and fuck me in my husband's classic Benz that was in the garage. It would be my torment "fuck you" gesture to my husband, the world, and the shit stains on the toilet left by my dad.

My handle on Fling was titled "Sexual Insurrection" because I was about to begin my rebellion against the bullshit surrounding me. However, my newly declared rebellion was not as simple as it might sound. It is not a simple thing to find a male who is willing to bang a thirty-five-year-old while there's a kid and senior at home. My parameters where they had to be cute and younger than me. No older than thirty but at least 21. Maybe wanting someone younger than myself, I feel some sense of control. It was not like I wanted to dominate anyone, but I didn't want an authority figure who saw themselves as father figures. Also, I realized I had a bit of a fetish with younger men, too. Getting someone over while hoping everyone was asleep was a colossal task. Although some men said they were into it, they never showed up. First, I had to wait until everyone was sleeping, and I had a kid who had a talent for not falling asleep quickly by himself and, of course, barely before midnight. This request appeared not an easy task, and what seemed like a simple request to the male horny population was not as simple as one would expect.

While I acquainted a few guys here and there, there were possibilities, but there were no winners. Time was running out. My husband would eventually be home from Florida soon. I felt pathetic and stupid that my plans of rebellion were fizzing out. On the very night, my husband was due home, a young JC wanted to step up and was more than willing to finish the job. JC was about to turn 21 on July 4th, only a few days away. He was decent-looking and had that 'go with the flow' personality, which I appreciated. That night, I thoroughly appreciated JC.

While my husband was on his flight to Newark Airport, I met JC just outside the side entrance of our house that led to the basement and the garage. He wasn't bad looking at all and looked older than 21 but still young enough to meet my selected parameters. He looked like the stereotypical big biker and rode a Harley. JC is not too tall and a bit chunky but not obese. He wasn't what I'd call the ideal of perfect, but he would do as time was running out to complete my rebellion. We started making out in the grimy basement. I felt a cold void beginning to rot as heat emerged from my inner core. JC began to grab my breasts roughly. It's strange how certain painful sensations can be confronting. I'd probably have found solace lying on a bed with broken glass. Specific pain can force you into peacefulness as if one was accepting death.

I led JC into the attached garage, where the old Benz stayed dormant like my husband had purchased many things. JC noticed another of my husband's Harleys in the corner of the garage, just another expensive thing purchased to stay dormant. As an actual biker, JC was concerned that he was about to fuck a fellow biker's wife. I reassured him that my husband had only purchased the bike about a year ago, was rarely ridden, and wasn't staying long. I also reassured him that the act of fucking me would be no betrayal of the kin of actual hardcore bikers. I continued to lead the way to the Benz. The fucking car and the history of all fucking vehicles, bikes, and boats was ongoing. We could barely make the monthly mortgage on the fucken house or pay all the bills, but we could afford these useless objects that eventually remain dormant in storage instead of being used.

Continuing to kiss JC, making sure his cock would be ready to go, I opened the backseat door of the car and assumed the position of lying on my back. JC pulled down my shorts and underwear. With my legs wrapped around someone who I had just met fifteen minutes ago, JC dropped his pants, made some apologetic remark about his cock size being a result of being half Irish, and slid ejection into me. I couldn't care less about his cock size as long as it did its job. Although my intention was not to find sexual satisfaction, it felt exciting. Experiencing pleasure wasn't my goal. I wanted to replace the numbness lost. JC didn't take long to find his release and shoot a load outside or on the car. I didn't bother to check the evidence of cum stains. I'm not even sure if I gave a shit.

Mission fucken accomplished. We, the sex, were done dressed, and I escorted JC out of the garage and back outside. We briefly kissed and said our goodbyes. I didn't know or even care if this was a one-ride-per-a-person encounter or if I'd see JC again. I didn't care either way. I don't think I cared about much about anything after the car fuck. I got what I wanted, how, and where I wanted. As detached as the encounter seemed, I felt I gained some control. I got what I liked. As soon as JC left, I received a text that my husband had just landed and was on his way home from the airport. There was plenty of time to change into regular pajamas and crawl into bed. I lay there in the dark, silent, until I heard the door open downstairs. I remained still with my newly enforced shield running through my veins.

Even though I got what I needed that night, I kept my Fling account open. So, let's discuss this website where people are on it to hook up. The site is crawling with cocks everywhere. Once you're on the site, the exposure to a variety of cocks. Big cocks, small cocks, black cocks, white cocks, and the variety in between. Cocks just randomly pop in your inbox. The male-female ratio is mostly horny ass men and tons of fake female profiles trying to get men to go to some high-paying live video sites or just encouraged to pay for some webcam action. Many of horny men are often victimized and sometimes conned. It's pretty sad. Then comes along me, a natural female who is not out to entrap some poor horny soul's credit card—a complete, living, and breathing female who is not too gross to the general eyes. I'm there for the exact reasons they are: to get laid. I was one of the very few fucken unicorns every man in a 30-mile distance wanted.

I got to know a handful of men via this site. My pick of wanna-be Wild Stallions was vast. My inbox was bursting with various men who wanted to get laid. Old, young, white, black, tall, short, and some scary-looking mother fuckers too. Not for nothing, I believe I might have run into a couple of serial rapists here and there as well. With this massive selection of cocks, I had the freedom to be a bit picky. I was aware that I had a younger guy fetish, wanting them young, like anywhere in the mid-20s. Men in my age range or older did not appeal to me whatsoever. I called them Dino -dicks, and I wanted my meat to be a lot fresher for the picking. Somewhere along the lines of maintaining a comfortable void, I became this cougar on the hunt.

I never considered myself famous before, and I'm not some hot Victoria's Secret babe either. I'm short, weigh a few extra pounds, and I'd say pretty average and maybe even cute. I wouldn't classify myself as hot or even desirable, but to the cocks roaming on Fling, my private parts were prime real estate to them. Everybody wanted an opportunity to get a piece of the action. Who knew? There was a tidal wave of responses and chat exchanges. It was a bit of a colossal undertaking going back and forth, trying to weed out whom I thought were the undesirables. At some point, going through this rather bizarre process of attempting to find someone I'd consider fucking, I felt I could have had my reality show ``Who Wants to Bone the Somewhat Attractive, Yet Emotionally Dysfunctional Librarian Chick?".

So with this instead fucked version of a reality show in my head, I had three winners or possible contenders. JC, who boned me in chapter two. Tim was slightly older and slightly farther than in my required parameters, and S. There is another young gentleman who also cut, but being the terrible person, I was, and probably still am, I forgot his name. 'Sorry, cute young skinny dude from New Jersey, but there were too many missed connections and cancellations. Also, not following what I thought were clear directions on where to meet in Clove Lake Park was less than impressive.'

During this glorious time of discovering how fucked up I can be, It would not have been a usual thing to catch me emerging from the bushes at a local park. They were free, and if one takes the time to explore these various areas before a 'meet,' you will find some secluded areas fitting enough to pull down one's pants and pull up one's skirt. I think the correct term for this is called recon. There's a risk of ticks, mosquitoes, and bees getting caught by unsuspecting strangers on their journey to seclusion. Another public location that was doable was one of the JC Penney's men's dressing rooms. I strictly advise not to use the women's or any female dressing room. The men's dressing room often works out if you are caught or suspected; the looks you will get if caught will differ considerably.

Women will look somewhat disgusted as men will give you a high five or nod in approval. One of these days, I want to try the Primark dressing rooms since they are co-gender. I wonder what looks I would get from there?

Then, there is the faithful semi-privacy of the parked car. It all depends on where you park, of course. There are many places to park and fool around without witnesses at night. However, if parking in a park at night, be aware that that location closes at dusk. The employees of the local park department are just trying to do their jobs and, from my experience, are flexible in knocking on car doors. The Parks Department Security people mostly beep their horns and shout that the park is closed and you must take your vehicles elsewhere. Parking at boardwalks appears to be open year-round, but it does get super chilly in the winter.

Lastly, the hotels/motels are very resourceful locations, although not cheap or clean. The Staten Island Motor Inn, off the expressway and near the Verrazano Bridge, appeared to have the most reasonable prices for short-stay visits. The rate was 50-65 for 3 hours of possible bed bug infestation privacy. I had and still have this rule that everyone involved pays exactly half for the room. Now, the Staten Island Motor Inn was an extremely sleazy-looking place. It was well known to be regularly occupied by hookers and drug dealers. The rooms were sad, but they had the necessary beds and bathrooms. Some cheaper rooms had slightly broken mirrored ceilings, which was a plus. When you use a place regularly, it ends up as I did just in one month; it feels like a second home. I never brought home any bed bugs or other free-loving creatures.

I saw JC a few times after that first encounter in the garage. It made sense to go with the cock I knew before exploring other options. JC was the second person I slept with outside my marriage. The second time we met was at his house. Well, at age 21, it was his parents' house, and they were out. I remember I wore a short coral print dress with a matching coral choker around my neck. I thought I looked rather hot but not over the top. Just your average MILF fashion that you would find anywhere at your local Rainbow store.

My body often experiences a reaction to the nervous excitement and dread before meeting someone new and someone I've met prior. There's always discomfort in my lower abdomen, and sometimes, I end up having a horrible bowel movement. I know no one wants to hear about the amount of toilet paper I occasionally go through before meeting someone—also, the word "meet" has been fully established. My body is protesting my actions and doing its best to prevent any 'meet.' it's as though your lower abdomen knows you should not be there, and it gets angrier and angrier when you choose not to listen. You acknowledge it. You ask it to settle. You tell it you know what you're doing, but you have no clue. Maybe you convince yourself that you have everything under control, but you understand it's a lie. You're there trying to play a part you've created in your head in a most unusual story. At least that's the bullshit you want to sell yourself.

Luckily for JC and me, I didn't need to go to the bathroom to attend to an overprotective lower digestive tract. He must have smoked before I tasted the last Marlboro; we didn't require much conversation. This sensual spirit that I didn't know existed within me took control of my limbs, my mouth, and the moisture between my legs. Who was this person whose body intermingled so willingly with this young stranger? Was this person not me, or was it? It was as if I shut the door on my reality and existed in a dream I could participate in. Opening up pieces deep within me along with my body, I gave no resistance to JC's touch as he slid my dress off. Maybe I forget the joy and thrill of being unwrapped like that. My limbs pulled at his body as if begging to be utterly claimed. All the sounds that generally echoed in my head fell silent as he entered me, followed by repeated thrusts.

For some reason, I've noticed most men having sex with strangers causes them to ejaculate sooner than later. Maybe it is the thrill that overcomes them as well. I never discussed quick shooting with any of them, so I have no idea what's going on in any of their heads as they have no clue what is in my head. Or maybe it's urgent to get this done. Maybe it is a fear of getting caught? It wasn't like he was the married person, but perhaps fucking an older married woman while your parents are out can be overwhelming? Again, not in anyone's head. JC did not finish inside of me. However, his load hit the low slope of the attic ceiling over his bed a bit. I don't remember if there was much of a conversation after. Maybe there was some brief small talk.

I remember feeling sated even though I knew I did not have an organism. I felt "mission accomplished." My skin felt like it had grown an extra layer as I left his house. I was not doing this for sex. I wanted to feel blissful emptiness. JC's scent was on me, or was that what sex was supposed to smell like a lingering foreign substance? The rest of the day was pretending that I just didn't get fucked by a 21-year-old biker. Those are the moments when you feel your walls go up a little stronger than before, and the outside world will not penetrate, at least for now. For a moment, the loud eruptions of family and the nuances attached to that reality become quieter. Life becomes a bit lubricated, even if that's probably the worst metaphor I could develop. I had a secret, and it gave me a brief internal power.

I saw JC a couple of times after. Once, he was in his truck between Bay St. and the ocean. It could have been close to Front Street, but I'm unsure. When there's a raging heat inside the depth of your skin, you don't pay too much attention to street signs. These actions might be actual for drug addicts as well. A primal need diminishes that sense of judgment and essential awareness. That need, no matter how complex, just possesses you as you find yourself straddling a person in the front seat of their SUV. My sense of judgment was most definitely impaired as I could see the reactions of passengers of other cars driving by in the distance. I could not see their faces to identify them, nor could they identify me. However, I could see their gaping mouths and pointed fingers as they drove past us. I remembered wondering if I should feel ashamed or not. Jimmy swung me off him as he quickly found his release and got the car's interior roof. He had a knack for hitting low ceilings. No condoms. No birth control. I was playing with fire without actually orgasming myself, but I was getting off in my strange way. It was the rebellion I was feasting off.

I can't say that I was wholly attracted to JC. I'm not saying he's not attractive. He was a bit on the heavy side and often would prophesize that he wasn't going to make it past thirty due to what he referred to as his 'hardcore lifestyle.' At the time, he worked as a para in a particular ed school. Maybe he thought he'd die from one of the bites from an autistic student or a drunk driving experience on his bike. We both agreed that our attraction existed due to our mediocre looks and convenience. JC took care of a need that seemed important at the time.

We had a couple 'meets' somewhere within the tree and bushes of Clove Lakes Park, which was just as thrilling but orgasmically lacking. However, our last encounter in his bedroom was highly memorable, although not in a good way. This experience might be the furthest, most opposite plane of good. I made it clear that during my period, JC didn't seem to care. His lack of concern was because JC wanted to try anal. About ten years before that, I experimented with anal sex with this guy I was dating. To be honest, it first hurt like a bitch. It took a bit of time until I eventually enjoyed it. The trick was learning how to relax my body.

My body remembered how to relax. I have become limp. We were enjoying it until, I guess when JC looked down and saw the reason why having anal sex with me is best with some warning.

In this sequence of events, I remember JC, with terror in his voice, saying, "Oh my God." He immediately stopped what he was doing, pulled out, stuck a bunch of Kleenexes on my ass, and ran into a shower. Left there standing in confusion, I removed the Kleenex off my ass and saw in absolute horror why the previous event just mollified me. I stood there waiting, unsure what to do except feel disgusted with myself. JC finally emerged from the bathroom in a towel and, without saying a word, indicated that I had to go into the bathroom next. I was not going to shower in his house, and I don't even think he ever offered it as an option. I cleaned up the best I could with the sink and toilet paper. I used a shit load of toilet paper and properly flushed over ten times until I felt it was safe enough to put back my underwear and pants.

I left. I don't remember how we said goodbye or even if we said anything. That was the last time I ever saw JC. For a few years, he tried to arrange a 'meet' with me, and I would turn him down. It was impossible not to think about that horrific shared moment. JC has lived well into his thirties. He still rides his bikes and thinks he has found Jesus. We follow each other on Instagram with no conversion or even a like on our posts. The last time I heard from him, he told me he was working with the Parks Department in Clove Lakes Park and remembers the good times. I remember them, too, but I also remember the Kleenex stuck to my ass.

# Pieces of Tim

Just like JC, I met Tim through Fling. Tim was the exception to my parameters of age and location. He was from New Hope, Pennsylvania, in his early thirties. To be honest, I wasn't sure about Tim at first. It took time for him to worm his way into my vagina. I found him to be a bit cocky and arrogant for my liking. His arrogance was why I tried to avoid this particular age group on Fling. They seem to be a bit overconfident and lack any effort beyond their cocks. I started as a bit of a bitchy pain in the ass and would only agree to meet in public. I gave off that 'interested but not interested' vibe because, to tell you the truth, I wasn't sure if I'd be into him. Tim just presented himself as a hard pill to swallow.

One weekday morning, Tim came down from New Hope, Pennsylvania. He worked in an expensive bed and breakfast but recently had a career as a flight attendant, which I found interesting. He was well-spoken and full of himself, which I found strangely intriguing. I didn't believe many of his life's unique stories, but I saw it entertaining. Tim wasn't much taller or skinnier than me, either. I could throw him across the room with enough speed and force. I felt no guilt making him drive the hour and a half just for brunch at a local Perkins and nothing else. Tim, on the other hand, was not all happy being sent back to his hour and half-long drive without having the opportunity to use his penis. Maybe I needed to feel somewhat in control of the situation, plus the pompous fuck had it coming.

However, I didn't take long to communicate my interest once he got over his blue balls, the wasted gas, and tolls just for eggs over easy and whole wheat toast. So we made actual arrangements to meet at a Staten Island Motor Inn that charged sixty-five dollars for three hours of bed bug lust. It's not a bad deal if you survive being bed bug-free after. Once we got to our expensive room with a half-mirrored ceiling, it didn't take us more than a minute to get physical. I remember how fascinating it felt to have someone so slender between my legs. It was as though my crotch could swallow him whole. I didn't orgasm. As I mentioned, this age group tends to be extremely lazy when it comes to sex. Tim managed to have two organisms, though. If I had to compare JC and Tim, I'd say JC put in more effort. Their theory was that if they got off, then magically, so did I. I have to say this is not a good theory. Women's bodies won't work that way. It was too early in the game to find my sexual voice to communicate what I liked and didn't like. That voice took time to find itself on the surface into the spoken word.

At the time, I was still hooking up with JC, too. I had multiple partners because I didn't want to get caught up in a one-sided emotional mess with anybody. If I overthought JC, I would think of Tim and vice versa. Each one acted as a distraction from the other. It was my emotional checks in the balance system. I didn't want the repeated emotional whirlwind that I had with Joas. My heart needed to become sheltered from these arrangements involving any emotion. All I cared about was the feelings that went beyond my legs. Blocking my emotions was my survival system, which worked for a while. I also didn't mind if any of them saw other women. The more emotional safeguards, the better.

Tim and I made plans to meet again. This time, we will have a little Red Riding Hood role-play game. I was going to be Little Red Riding Hood, and he had the role of the hungry wolf. Although there was a bit of time until we were to meet and act out our parts, I was super excited. I purchased a cute short red jumper dress and a hoodie for the event. I was going for the schoolgirl riding hood look, but in my mid-thirties, it wasn't easy not to feel corny. There were tons of wolf-themed sexting back and forth with Tim. My skin was crawling with expectations of devourment.

Of course, I was super nervous and excited the day of Tim's and my arranged meeting at the same charming shit hall of a motel. There were some things I knew to expect, but plenty I didn't. Little Red Riding Hood was my first experience in role-playing games. Hoping to pounce, be overpowered, and devoured by a wolf in that exact order as soon as I got in the sixty-five-dollar room. I was, instead, greeted by a tired human who wasn't into it. Talk about bursting a girl's bubble. Maybe after thirty minutes of making out, things would move in the expected direction, so I took the time to dress up. I did my best to hide my disappointment when he couldn't get it up and keep it up after repeated attempts. He warned himself by engaging in sexual activities the night before and was utterly useless. I couldn't care less that he had sex with someone else, but I did care that he completely wasted my time.

Even though we had the room for three hours, I left as soon as the first hour had come and passed. I was annoyed as shit, if not wholly disappointed. Talk about a waste of fucken time and not to mention the energy in putting together a cute yet hot little outfit together. It's not like I could leave my house or work any time to go dress up as Little Fucken Red Riding Hood to 'meet' anyone I wanted any time I enjoyed it. There is so much strategy and planning involved in most of this. Once anyone like that wasted my time, I don't know you anymore. So it was easy to say I was pissed as shit and never saw Tim again.

**Pieces of S**

Of the men I spoke to online, S was the most human. He talked to me like I was a human being, not a piece of meat. From the very start of our conversations, I was dealing with a unique individual. S wrote as though there was intelligent life in the world of penises and horn dogs. He was twenty-two and a local boy. I had no hesitation in arranging to meet him. We agreed to meet in a park near his house on a hot summer weekday in July. Meeting someone who didn't seem to have grand expectations of getting laid then and there was refreshing. S was just above average height with an average build. I found him attractive, quiet, and awkward.

We walked around the park and talked. It was either the heat or his nerves, but he was sweating buckets. The sweat didn't bother me. We walked until I finally suggested finding a bench in the shade to sit on. From the sweat, I thought getting S out of the sun would be a good idea. I didn't want the poor thing passing out on me. We sat and talked while my body language screamed, "Hey, you wanna finger me in the bushes?". He probably thought this meeting was a disaster due to his sweat glands, but I was enjoying his down-to-earth vibe. He just seemed so sweet and not full of himself. He heard my body loud and clear when he asked if he could kiss me. Without hesitation, I said, "Yes," it was perhaps the most sensual first kiss I could remember having. We made out on the park bench for a few minutes before he said he had to go. Of course, being bummed that our brief encounter had to end, but he stated, "I'll give you a call," before heading back to where he came from.

S reached out that night, saying he enjoyed meeting me and hoped we could do it again. How could I say no? We had a couple of clumpy 'meets.' Once, he was somewhere by semi-hidden hiking paths at a park and once in a small attic room in his house while his parents were out. Both encounters were super awkward and very rushed. I wasn't sure what past experiences he had in the past when it came to sex, but I appreciated the effort. I also enjoyed that throughout our encounters, he never put on airs. S was and still is to this day; what you see is what you get in a type of guy. He struggled to figure out who he was and how he fit into the world. It was nice to meet a person who wasn't trying to feed you a load of bullshit just to get between your legs.

Not long after those super awkward encounters, we finally did the sensible thing and met at the motel. It was the same motel I would 'meet' Tim in. I always wondered if the motel clerk would recognize me and judge me for meeting up with more than one man in the middle of the day. Maybe he thought I was a prostitute trying to pay for college. Sometimes, I would allow those assumed judgments to puncture my skin just enough to check if I was still alive. At least we never destroyed any property.

The insurance of absolute privacy was the key to allowing S to find his sexual inner core. Unlike most of the previous encounters, he was keen on satisfying me and didn't assume that his cock was the entire center of female pleasure. Finally, someone had enough sense to locate my clit and use it to the point to ensure a climax would occur. He ensured I reached the various points of euphoria multiple times within the three hours. The room was his canvas, and I was merely his paint. However, he wouldn't reach his release. Biological science was to blame. S was not circumcised, and the tip of the opening of his foreskin was, for some odd reason, too tight to open. The foreskin situation meant he could not experience sexually what other men did so quickly. His experience with pleasure seemed to be on a different level. S simply desired and knew he had the power to satisfy me, and that seemed enough for him. At least, that's what I assumed for some time.

If I was to compare the rotation for men I was fucking, S was my favorite of the lot. He usually had priority over my crotch when

I was available. S was also hot to the touch most of the time, as though his body heat operated for cooler climates. Lying next to his warm skin was soothing. Sometimes, we would just lie next to each other in silence. That silence became a bit too peaceful. The stillness and that peacefulness between us were uncomfortable because I could hear the distant tapping of emotions that I was trying to ignore to avoid knocking on the door of my conscience. Enjoyment is a tricky feeling. I enjoyed being with S, but I was also afraid of enjoying him too much. I did not want to rely on certain feelings that came out of intimacy. These feelings were far from the numbness I was relying on to survive whatever I felt I needed to survive.

Summer drifted into fall, and fall ensured less availability on my part. I saw less and less of S. Our worlds got busy with various adult responsibilities. At least, that's what I tell myself when I try to remember why I need to back off. Maybe I just needed to hit a pause button. If anything, I remember feeling drained from falling off the radar more than once a week and manipulating time. It takes a lot of effort to be in two places at once. I had to portray the life most everyone believes I had and the life you store in your back pocket. It's crucial to keep both lives separated. They can never bleed into each other. A fine line must always be drawn and kept.

**September: To Whom It May Concern:**

**I felt different inside. I guess after weeks of chasing internal numbness, it has its effects. The writing was so distant. It seems as soon as the temperature dropped, so did the sexual rage. The coldness inside matched the coldness inside me. I don't need to commit emotional suicide. I finally settled the score inside me, and all bets paid. At least, that's what it feels like. Operating in such a way wasn't good, but certain things that made me cry no longer penetrated the wall I had built.**

I concentrated on finding photos and photographers for my writing. I'm just trying to find some focus while being dead. I became friends with one photographer who has allowed me to use his work. But something happened. Cracks in my wall began to show. I didn't care if this stranger was being compassionate or just fucking with me. I'm still not 100% sure about that conclusion. How can someone who's 158 miles away make me feel anything? I sort of have some resentment about that. But I began to write again and even dabble in some visual arts. Maybe it's the cushion of distance that allows some walls to crack. I don't know. I'm somewhat confused. I have met this person twice in person and am still confused. To feel is to feel pain and try to break from that.

Why am I telling you this? You are a good person (maybe slightly wicked), but you have a deep and good soul, and I owe the truth that it is horrible as is above. I like to consider you as a friend. I told you my head is in a weird place. However, I'm sure you will come to your own opinions and conclusions now that you have digested all this information. I'm hoping you haven't thrown up yet.

# Pieces of marriage:

At the beginning of my relationship with my husband, I was happy and hopeful. You know what they say after you kiss a shit load of frogs, and boy, there were enough amphibian tongues that found their way down my throat by the time I met my husband. The story of how we met is a fun story to tell. My husband and I initially met when I was nineteen. He was dating a friend then, so nothing happened between us. Moving the clock about ten years later, while browsing through Classmates.com, I found her name and thought it would be perfectly ok for her and me to reconnect. However, my future husband at the time relied. He told me that she, my long-lost friend and also his ex-girlfriend, must have used his email when signing up with classmates.com without his knowledge. Move the clock ahead another couple of months. When I did reconnect with her, she said she never signed up with any sites, and he must have created a profile without her permission. Someone was lying about whoever created or didn't create the classmates.com profile. If there were any red flags at the time, I did them wave in my face.

There were a few red flags that I chose not to pay any attention to before things got serious between the future husband and myself. One was an incident involving him, my nephew, and my sister. My nephew was about ten years old and loved baseball. Due to several mishaps involving a few car windows, my nephew was not allowed to play catch on the street by his house. However, unaware of any such rule, my future husband offered to play catch with the ten-year-old who knew about this rule. It didn't take more than a few minutes to hear breaking glass in the near distance. My sister and her second husband at the time felt my future husband should pay for all the damage. However, the future husband believed he should only be responsible for paying half to replace the car's smashed car window. His rationality was that he was not aware of any such rule, and since the ten-year-old knew fully well he was breaking this no-playing catch rule, the child should be responsible for his actions. Unfortunately, the child's parents disagreed with the future husband's logic. I had already gone home before all the yelling and cursing between both parties occurred, but I was still in the middle of this huge mess I had not created. Both parties denied full responsibility, and I used a colorful array of verbal insults back and forth. My sister called me complaining about the horrible things the future husband said to her that he denied. At the same time, he'd tell me all the horrendous verbal insults my sister said, which she declined. At the end of all this, I paid for the window to hopefully shut everyone up and end this nonsense.

Perhaps the most enormous red flag I ignored was when my future husband picked me up from work. He picked me up in my car, which allowed him to borrow some time. I should also include that he was not working at the time. Within a few minutes of entering the car, the future husband started screaming at me for no reason. I said something the other night in jest that he did not like. Instead of letting me know at the time, I said whatever I said bothered him so I could quickly apologize then and there. He waited for the next day to scream at me. "How dare you fucken say that!" and on and on, he yelled at me in my car. He was driving to my apartment, where I often stayed. I was crying and shaking in the passenger seat. Honestly, I don't remember what I said to trigger his reaction. Even then, I didn't think what I said was a big deal. What was a big deal was that I had my first glimpse that he was a verbally abusive person, and I should not have taken such abuse at the time, but I did.

Even after all these red flags, there was a time when I pretended to be living an everyday married life. We just were blessed with a newborn baby. All these usual social conventions that I was experiencing seemed sparkly new, but one would only have to look remarkably close to notice those fine hairline cracks. Of course, those cracks were already there waiting for recognition, but it's sometimes too easy to try to cover them up with old rugs, fake smiles, and new furniture. Dirt has a way of sipping through, as do lies and deception. Yet, when you start to look and follow the trail of glass shards and tracked dirt, you won't like what is under that new rug.

The same philosophy goes with internet history and the lack of erasing one's tracks. In our first apartment as a new family, we had a Mac computer in the living room. While trying to grasp being a new mom and working full time, my husband was on the computer far more than I had time for. Even if he was working, he always seemed to have more time on his hands than I would ever have. I believe I was on maternity leave and trying to adjust my life to a new baby's schedule, which would often cause me to wake up at strange night hours. I'd hop on the computer to check my email and look for discounted baby clothes. Before Facebook, I had not discovered Myspace yet. Social media was uncharted territory at the time.

During one of my late-night computer moments, I explored various computer features while trying to get the infant back to sleep after a midnight feeding, probably out of sheer boredom and knowing the multiple features of the internet browser and history function. Porn, a shit load of porn, which I later understood that finding youporn or other porn sights in a history of a male user is quite typical. I still found it sort of gross. I also saw a history of searches for local escorts and prostitutes. That caused an icy chill throughout my veins and bile to climb up into my throat. I didn't know if all internet histories were this disgusting. Maybe I was going through the new mom prude vase, becoming highly taken aback by all the links that were for searching for local sex workers.

While we were visiting my husband's parents in the nursing home they lived in at the time, I needed to try to confront him and this seedy erotic history. My husband could tell by my body language that something was crawling up my ass. Maybe it was the look of nausea and disgust. My husband's answer was such fucken bullshit. He attempted to dig himself out of the mess by convincing me that he just got tons of random links to click on, which resulted in various escort listings for the Staten Island/ NJ area. By reading what I just shared, you know that's bullshit. We've all seen those types of click-here ads for sex, improving sex, random sex, etc. I sometimes get them myself, and there is no better way than to delete them from my inbox. These were noticeable search results. Also, I recently finished my graduate degree in which we learned all about the internet, web design, user interface, and other technological aspects to know that I am being bullshited. That was the first day I knew better than to swallow my disgust and negative feelings. There was no point pushing the argument to get the FBI involved. I learned I was being lied to, and my husband assumed I would believe all his explanations. It would be just one of many learning experiences needed to survive.

When I look back to that day, I understand that most people would lie to their significant other about looking for a hooker in a conversation. I mean, could you imagine, "Yeah, I got a weird escort fetish" as his answer? However, the truth is actual, no matter how you want to dress it up and blame it on e-commerce. Soon after our conversation in the nursing home, he either did a better job cleaning up his search history or thought it would be best to leave the hookers alone.

Just as technology has a way of betraying our secrets, history goes on repeat. If you have a family phone plan or activity with several Apple devices under the same account, can you see what someone else looks at on another device? Discovery of a user's history was especially true if you used the default browser, Safari, and your device. You can see the exact websites others are looking at in time. My husband's morning routine was porn videos first and then the escorts on backpage.com. All the escorts were local enough within a 30-minute driving distance.

You probably want to defend him because, as eeky as it sounds, he's just looking. We all have morbid curiosities, and this is true. However, iPhones also have a Find My Phone app. To help us locate our devices anywhere if we misplace them. Also, it allows you to track anyone on the account. So, you can see the location of your device or devices, but you can see theirs, too. You now have a nifty way of tracking that person's whereabouts. Usually, the little green dot representing that person's device would be home, work, the store, and where they told you they were going. Yet sometimes, and I mean sometimes, you'd see that little green dot parked outside a motel in New Jersey. Discovering this new information was an excellent opportunity for a couple of screenshots just in case of a conversation later. Those days, he'd come home with a nasty stomach ache. My stomach often betrays me, too. My stomach symptoms are a primary reaction to guilt. Often enough, our consciences aren't easy to digest.

I had a nice collection of screenshots of browser history and phone locations and saved them for my defense if needed. They are sort of my "In case of Emergency, Break Glass" kit, just in case. At this point, I was no angel but far wiser in my deceptions. I was learning from his mistakes. I always use a secondary browser that would not appear in any shared history. I would turn my location setting off-line and make it clear that I would be at a location with no service, which would be a school. In my line of work, it is very plausible that I would work at a school with that blocked cell service. I mastered the craft of falling off and on the radar in elegance. Lately, I believe my husband has improved his deception operations, too. I can no longer see shared history; his iPhone location is always off. However, I seem to give little fucks about any of his possible deceptions.

**Pieces of Joe**

It was probably a month or two since I hooked up with Stephen or anyone else. The time feels much longer than it was. Deception can be exhausting business, and I needed a break and a moment to catch my breath when the months and the expanse of time seemed to clump together in a mesh of memories. The iTouch was my first 'smart' device, and I had a little world in my hands that allowed me to communicate with the world in privacy. Before, I had to type brief messages on my Nokia flip phone to people, which was a complete pain in the ass.

One of the apps I downloaded was an app called Whohere. In the attempt to look for various social networking apps like Facebook and Myspace, I stumbled upon it. My intentions for downloading it were not sexual at all. My intentions were purely friendly and socially seeking in nature. My woman parts were on a much-needed break. However, being on this app contradicted my innocent intentions. It was a social/hookup app, and once again, being an actual real female made me super famous with the needy penis population. I wasn't in the mood to seek out someone to screw me, but I still craved conversations with anonymous people. That is the app where I stumbled onto Joe.

Joe also wasn't looking to hook up with anyone either. He was using the app to network his artwork. Joe was an extremely talented photographer and thought this random app would help expand his business. I have to say that most of his work, especially his self-portraits, was terrific. The photos were dark, forbidding, and somewhat hot. I would share some poems with him, and as Joas did, he allowed me to use his photos to connect with my work. It's impossible not to feel connected to someone on a personal level while you are trying to communicate on an artistic level. We were becoming close, and I allowed that closeness into my world. Also, he lived in Maryland, and for some reason, the distance seemed, if anything, emotionally safe.

It didn't take long to make the same fucken mistake by opening myself up to someone I didn't know. The error wasn't because Joe was a dumbass or an asshole. He was a nice guy. I just had a bad habit of opening doors to old, dirty rooms in pieces of my life with the concept that having sex with them would heal whatever wounds I had. If anything, I was a dumbass at the beginning of the learning process when it came to controlling my emotions. Of course, I was failing miserably. Like some teenage kid swooning over a rock star, I held Joe high on a pedestal. My view of Joe was due to how he portrayed himself. To be honest, he was extremely good at photography. History was repeating itself as I fell with another man I met online. Reality and fantasy were cascading upon themselves too rapidly on both sides. A prince is always a prince before that prince gives you a reason to shatter that image. Maybe it was because I didn't know Joe well enough to have any reasons for fine hair cracks in the image I was creating.

We took that opportunity to finally meet because Joe had some business to take care of in the area. The meet was to be at one of the parks that were not alien territory anymore when it came to "meeting" these men. I wouldn't have lumped Joe in the 'these men' category or our meet as a 'meet.' There were emotions in play, and I thought our delusional connection differed from anyone else. Our chatting online was beyond the sexual nature of things. I don't believe we were pretending we were reaching the core of our emotions. If anything, we were both just survivors of our past and present. People like us easily cling to any fragment of compassion and what appears to be love.

One excellent function of the Whohere app is that it tells you how far that person is from you. As Joe approached me, I could see the miles decrease every time I hit refresh. The triple digits turned into double digits, and my heart was racing. The miles, then finally, are just the single digits. Finally, he was less than a mile away, and my heart was in my throat. I was going to meet him in the flesh. It took me a while to realize that sometimes, people do not look as impressive as they do in the car with their photos. This fact holds even more true if that person was a professional who knew the art of lights and lenses to make him look like a god. This idealization is how Dorthey felt when she finally peeked behind the curtain. Even without all the use of lighting and filters, Joe wasn't half bad-looking. It would be fair to call Joe average without rehashing the pun. He was tall and just above average weight. So, what if my god's image of him was less holy?

Looks aren't everything. I knew Joe was a nice guy. Then Joe opened his mouth to talk, and that god image shattered a bit more. His teeth were so rotten-looking. The majority of the inside of his mouth was black and decayed. I tried my best not to notice them when we kissed, but I swear I could taste the decay on my tongue. Maybe my mind was just playing a trick on me, like if you see something that doesn't look appetizing, your pallet can't think independently. Beyond his fucked up oral hygiene, he was a charming man who was not assuming that his drive would result in getting laid or sucked off in the bushes. Joe was genuinely happy to see me for me. He didn't seem the type of guy who was full of shit. If anything, he might have been bullshitting himself. Our brief encounter was sweet, and the oral decay didn't kill the romance altogether. After perhaps forty-five minutes of kissing, talking, and hand-holding, Joe returned to where he came from. After he left, I watched the digits in the Whohere app increase from single digits to double and back to triple. Although our encounter wasn't entirely what I expected, I was sad to see the miles increase and increase. It was like watching a tiny part of myself move further and further away.

After the meeting in the park, Joe and I continued to chat back and forth via texting. We were both deluding ourselves that either of us could fill the other's internal voids. Joe shared about his colorful past. He was born in Utah to Mormon parents, who were both drug addicts and prostitutes. Apparently, both his parents sold their bodies often to pay for their drug habits. They would even sometimes bring Joe in the car when he was a child. Can you imagine what it would be like for a little kid witnessing their mom and dad blowing off a stranger in the front seat before shooting up whatever drug they did? How can a child's brain even begin to process that? I don't remember too many details. He joined the military in his early 20s, somewhere between that dark childhood and adolescence. His relationship history had its shades of colors. Joe cheated on his first? Wife with their nanny. He then married the nanny, who then cheated on him. When we met, he was with an older woman he didn't like but stuck around because they had a daughter together.

About a month past that first encounter in the park, Joe and I felt ready to take our relationship to the next level. I wanted to meet up somewhere between his location and mine. Considering he was coming from Baltimore, that middle appeared to be the southern tip of New Jersey. Thanks to the miracle of MapQuest, I found the cheapest motel as close to the middle as possible. Honestly, this middle was closer to me than to him. This drive was the longest distance I've ever ventured in my world of deception. Making sure the tolls and bridges didn't charge my EZpass would be a fully cash-only trip to the shittest motel on the border of New Jersey and Delaware.

As each mile passed, my nerves began screaming for me to make sense of my actions. Each mile I drove took me to the Motel Shit Hole I was to spend a few hours in. For the first time in this saga of causal encounters, I truly believed I was meeting someone

I cared for, and they cared for me just as much. It wasn't just sex this time. There was a connection. Two damaged soulmates finally become one fucked up mess of their own. This relationship was not one-bit fucken ass shit crazy at all. Our choices damaged us, and desperate people were starving to express love and passion. We got to the motel. It was just as cheap and stanky as the Staten Island Motor Inn. We kissed. We got naked. We fucked. It was not the worst sex ever, but not the best. It was as though our bodies were saying, "Ummm, I don't think so," but being so wrapped in each other's illusions of each other, we didn't listen. I don't even think I enjoy kissing him. I still swear I could taste his rotting teeth.

It didn't take long for this long-distance affair to get a bit of a kinky upgrade. Perhaps it was the half-living daydream that we believed we were in love. Our daydreams passed the reality that we didn't have any chemistry. However, due to the illusion of chemistry, Joe revealed a few kinks, which included reverse gender and anal play. The thought of pretending he was a woman and I was a guy was a big turn-on for him. Joe also revealed that he enjoyed using a dildo on himself while jerking off. I'd like to consider myself open-minded, so I quickly complied with Joe's exciting requests. There have been times I wondered what it was like to be the man in an intimate relationship, and here was an opportunity to explore.

Questioning my sexual and gender identity has been a thought in the back of my mind. I never felt like I fit in 100% in the girls' club, but neither 100% belonged in the boys' room. Sexual and gender identity was just a tiny bud in society that people rarely discussed during this time. No sources were available to help anyone discover who they are without feeling like a freak. According to current yet changing sources today in gender identification, I think identity is a "Demi girl." This gender is a gender identity describing someone who partially identifies as a woman or girl. In addition to feeling partially like a girl or woman, demi girls also feel partly outside the binary. That can include anything under the non-binary umbrella-like agender, genderqueer, or xenogenders, for example. Well, that's the closest match I can find that fits me the best. As for sexuality, I'd say I'm Pan-curious, which means I find myself attracted to all genders. Not only does this include men and women, but I have found various transgender and non-binary people attractive, too. These identifications don't mean I'll try anything once or twice. Joe Kinks didn't freak me out. If anything, I was open-minded and intrigued.

Our texting now included gender reversal and how to develop it in planning our next meeting. During our texting, Joe would go all femme on me while I tried to summon the inner dominant male that did linger in me. Joe shared more and more about his anal play fetish fantasies. Many men with this fetish are not gay. I wasn't the type of person who would get grossed out if he confessed he was gay or bi anyway. If anything, I'd be honored that Joe would share something deeply personal. It would not have stopped me from being very intrigued to explore something different. Joe was more than happy to provide the strap-on and the attaching dildo, so I didn't have to try to purchase anything. Who said romance was dead?

We planned to meet at the same beautiful shit hole on the border of South Jersey and Delaware. Joe was running late, leaving me to care for the room. Women who try to rent rooms unaccompanied by men get screwed over. The fuckers at the front desk thought I was a prostitute who would not attempt to complain. I was a bit screwed over. I swallowed my pride and took the room. Joe was still running late, which allowed me to put on my femme/ male persona as requested without feeling rushed. I wear a simple male shirt, pants and a vest. This outfit was the best I could come up with. Joe finally showed up and went straight to the bathroom to put on his femme persona. He took a vee only had two hours. I had, when those rare opportunities happened, a difficult time maintaining the mood required while waiting for him/her to get their ass out of the fucken bathroom.

Joe finally emerged from the bathroom wearing a modest dress and makeup. I could tell he was trying to get comfortable with himself. We were in customs as we began to play our roles. Joe, being a submissive female, I no longer existed as I summoned my mucho identity that was supposed to take charge of the situation. It's easy to dress up and pretend in the play-acting. I tried my best to control the situation as required. Unfortunately, I needed help putting on the strap that Joe provided. "Help me get my cock ready to fuck you." I never wore a strap-on before, so having a cock, although fake, was a new experience. I can't say I felt empowered by this thing attached to me. It was just a tool on loan for the moment at hand. The first thing I noticed was that humping requires specific muscles in the glutes that I was not familiar with. It was a workout. I tried my best, which seemed to be enough. Joe jerked himself off as I thrust into his ass. He came. I did not. That changed quickly.

As an agreement to this particular arrangement, I brought my vibrator. Joe was aware that I would not get off my ass fucking with a piece of plastic attached to me, so he wanted me to bring something that would guarantee my sexual pleasure. He had me straddle his chest as he held the magic wand onto my clit. Even though my pleasure would be as a result of the plugged-in device, he wanted to be in control. Intense clitoral stimulation is my favorite way of achieving a hard orgasm. I tend to puddle. Having Joe in control of the device put me at his mercy to gain a complete, mind-blowing orgasm. Another kink for him is to be covered, if not wholly drowned, by vaginal fluids. I was more than happy to participate in this kink. I soaked the shit out of him, and we both felt "satisfied" in that small niche that time allowed. After our moments of satisfaction, we parted ways and continued texting.

That day was the last time I would see Joe. Again, I experienced the pain of wanting things I could and should not have. I remember the last text he sent me was that he needed to work on his personal life, and who was I to deny someone's need to search the inner workings of their soul.? During these desperate moments, it takes time for the brain to understand the difference between reality and the heart's desire. Eventually, Joe married a belly dancer, but they were divorced maybe a year or two later. I think he married even once again, but it's hard to keep up. He should write his book. It was difficult for me to reflect when we stopped communicating emotionally. Through the years, I've perfected the skill of near surgery, removing unwanted emotions. Like viruses, they no longer exist once they have run their course through my system. I know I did feel many things towards Joe: Love, desire, and abandonment eventually led to a comfortable detachment.

**Rituals**

No different from taking medication or lighting up a joint before bed to relieve stress, the slight incision on my left arm keeps my nerve endings focused as it tingles under the band-aid. Remember to cut under an inch because of the size of the awaiting band-aide. The chosen blade brings me a new sense of calm. Just one straight line under the shoulder of my shirt sleeve, and the blade penetrates the skin just enough to produce the welcoming red to cover up. If anyone notices and inquires, I can easily say it was the cat, and no one will think the wiser.

# More significant Pieces of S

While my heart was still purging the remnants of Joe, I reconnected with Stephen. My memory is a bit foggy on who reached out to whom first, but I remember it was perfect timing during the beginning cusp of winter. I'm pretty sure that S reached out first. Reaching out to anyone first has never been my strong suit. It wasn't hard to continue our 'relationship' as it was before. We would primarily meet at the shit hole motel near the expressway. There was no denying that we had a sexual chemistry that attracted me to him. Our bodies just connected beyond the simplicity of basic intercourse. Unfortunately, at times, it was a bit overwhelming and also a little frustrating because Stephen never could ejaculate. There would be an overwhelming build-up of sexual energy for both of us, but only one of us would find that much-needed release. This issue was because he was uncircumcised, and his foreskin was too tight to allow the natural friction that uncircumcised supposedly enjoy to reach their moments of orgasm. Besides that particular issue, he had no problem performing various functions that I found highly satisfying. S was perhaps the best sex partner I had.

Sometimes, I would come over when his parents were away for the day or the weekend. I cherished those moments of not being in the motel or the back of my car. Those moments allowed me to pretend we were like any other boyfriend and girlfriend. I loved being in his room and bed When those rare opportunities happened. If there's one sensation outside the scope of essential sex that I would associate with being in his room, it would be softness. His bed was so soft. His bedding was soft. His pillows were smooth, and his body felt soft. If lullabies had any texture, they would think like S's room. There would be a tranquil peacefulness that I'd allow to come over me, which was unexpected but welcomed just the same. We managed to find calmness with each other. The world would just go quiet when he would hold me in our blissful shared silence.

One snowy day, I came over while his parents were out for a few days. Mother nature covered the world in thick blankets of white and shoveled pathways. S had a fire going in the fireplace of the living room. S had several blankets laid out in front of the fireplace. The setting he created was nothing less than absolutely romantic. It was probably the most romantic gesture I think anyone ever offered me. This setting was unexpected, and it was impossible to resort to my realm of detachment. S was making it extremely difficult for me not to feel. While our limbs tangled together, this moment didn't just feel like a simple act of sex but something much more. I remember looking up at his eyes while he thrust inside of me. With that moment of eye contact, a profound connection emerged from within. That was the very first moment I knew I was falling in love with S, and that terrified the living hell out of me.

Trust me, it was the last thing I wanted, to fall in love again. S was not Joe. S lived within fifteen minutes, and his mouth did not taste of rotten death. I tried primarily to hide my feelings from Stephen as well as myself. This arrangement was not about love, connecting, or reconnecting. This arrangement is supposed to be just two lost souls attempting to fill the missing gaps in one's life and nothing more than that. I didn't want to feel like a sixteen-year-old, considering I was fourteen years older, married, and with a kid. We managed to meet at the same hotel at least once a month. I'm surprised we never got a discount for being regular patrons. In between the days and weeks, we were not fucking. We managed to fill those spaces in between through so much texting. It felt like he was always near, even though he wasn't.

S suffers and still struggles with deals depression and anxiety. The medication he was on also added to the difficulty for him to fully and completely enjoy sex. It was already rough for him that his tight foreskin prevented him from achieving maximum pleasure. I never knew someone who could retreat within his darkness when he wasn't taking his medication. S's text would often be depressing and sometimes on the borderline of suicide. It was like watching a snowball spiral into an avalanche. All I could do was to be as supportive as possible. I have to say it's so difficult to witness someone go through so much pain and not be able to be there as much as you want to. S would compound his mental state by drinking. Even though I'd try to be supportive, it hurt that I could not be there for him. All I wanted to do was hold him and tell him he would be ok. Imagine someone you love repeatedly standing on the edge of a fifty-story building. Then, you force yourself to watch because this was someone you loved and could not ignore. Yet simultaneously, you were only allowed to watch from a distance.

One night, I received a disturbing and heart-crushing email from S. It was full of a feeling of revolution and resentment towards me. The words were ugly; the tone was ugly. He might as well have wiped his shitty ass with my heart and threw it at my face. My response was close to 'Sorry, I didn't know you felt that way." His words gutted me. I left him alone. I didn't try to reach out to force out some understanding of him. There was nothing to understand. Something triggered inside his head to hate my guts. Of course, I wonder what I've done to deserve his verbal onslaught. My soul and heart had become torn into tiny pieces before flushing them down the toilet. I think I could; those tiny pieces swirling around the bowl before being sucked into the sewers below.

A few weeks later, I heard from S. He was deeply apologetic. He was super drunk and super depressed one night. He didn't ever remember writing any of it at all. He said he was utterly horrified when he read it. Maybe this would be considered an equivalent of when abusers forget to smash their partner's face, only to wake up to a bloody mass crawling up in the corner. We met soon after his written apology at the mall. He apologized even further in person, and I found it impossible not to forgive him. I forgave him because I understood that we were carrying traces of darkness inside. Not only did I love him, but he also became my closest friend. I opened up about parts of my darker past, and he let me in on his darkness. This way, little surprises were going forward.

S tried to give college near an abandoned house one more go. He once tried earlier after graduating high school but also worked full time. It was too much for him to handle. It would be too much for a lot of people to handle. To get his parents off his back, S quit his place of employment and gave college a second go. Since the college was close to where I worked, I sometimes met him there. Again, sitting in a classroom wasn't his thing. S had a difficult time finding where he belonged in this world. For a moment, he wasn't working or going to school. Due to having his life at this standstill, S would be at war with his parents. As a parent myself, I understood where his parents were coming from. Seeing your adult child do nothing with themselves is not extraordinary.

I'm not proud to say that having him not doing anything productive in his life made him highly available to my personal needs. If we weren't fucking in the motels, we would find places in parks behind trees and rocks. A couple of times, we fooled around in the JC Penney's men's dressing room. Any crack of time that would offer us a minute of privacy, I'd jump on in a heartbeat like a person with an addiction to an available drug. S was my drug of choice and was nearly always available for me to consume. Pieces of myself were becoming addicted to not just him but also the thrill of fucking in public places. Even though there was a lot of sex, S never was able to finish due to his fucken foreskin.

At age twenty-five, S finally decided to get circumcised. Somehow newborn baby boys manage to get snipped, cry their ass off, and eventually fall asleep, and that's the end of it. Moms put antibacterial cream on their tiny peckers for a couple of weeks, and life just goes on. Unfortunately, this procedure is not as easy for a grown-ass man. From S's account, it's one of the worst pains a grown-ass man can go through, and it takes longer to heal than for an innocent newborn. His mom was different, not putting any antibiotic cream on the hip-sipped pecker. Eventually, it healed enough to give S's newly snipped pecker a go. What's the point of getting a new toy if you won't play with it? Still, S was not able to ejaculate. Like What The Fuck!! I had a couple of theories about why he was having so much difficulty finishing off. One was I assumed he was terrified of getting me knocked up, and a condom hinders the male experience. My other theory was emotional. Maybe because he didn't feel emotionally connected to me, his heart, mind, and body could not harmonize properly.

One afternoon, we parked near an abandoned house in one of our usual and favorite places in Emerson Hill. I don't remember if it was fall or spring. Most of my memories with S seem to blend in, and I have difficulty separating the memories into a particular year or season. I just remember it not being too hot or too cold. My SUV was often used as my mobile motel when the weather allowed. I stored pillows and an extra blanket. S and I were doing what we usually are doing. Then he uttered the unthinkable, "I'm so close." He'd have a couple of moments in the past where he would be 'close' before with no final happy endings. Since I had just finished up a menstrual cycle, the chances of reproduction were significantly nonexistent. I don't know if it was that knowledge, the angle of the car, or if his body finally began to trust me, but S experienced his first full orgasm that day. After that, there was no going backward in that department. Can I get an AMEN?

Soon after Stephen's triumphant ejaculation, I began to consider getting an IUD. We were using condoms, but I wanted to make the experience for S more pleasurable for him. His new ability to reach ejaculation was also a personal triumph for me. Also, I suffered from massive heavy menstrual cycles, and from the research, getting the IUD decreased my monthly menstruation to nearly nothing. It seemed like a pretty good option. After a regular check-up with my Gyno, I went back to this magic piece of plastic inserted into my uterus. It hurt like a mother fucker. It was like someone punched me from within my cervix. What I failed to read in all my research is that it takes a while for your body to adjust to a foreign object. For about four to six months, I had an endless menstrual cycle. So as an option to birth control, it worked like gangbusters because no one was fucking me due to this infinite visit from Auntie Flow.

When you're having a sexual relationship with someone for a few years, and the levels of trust have developed, you might begin to experiment with different flavors besides vanilla. My body felt at home with S, so trust was a nonissue. We started our kinky fetish journey with some role play. As Halloween approached, S always thought it would be the coolest to get personalized vampire fangs. Some people are called fang-smiths who create customized fangs for those who wish to step up their inner personas. S located one of these fang-smiths in Queens. I journeyed with him for emotional support. He was beginning to emerge out of his comfort zone. Witnessing various moments of personal growth was always an honor, even if it was as silly as traveling to Queens to get fitted for vampire fangs. We met at the Staten Island ferry on a late summer morning, and he forgot to take the copy of directions on how to get to this fang-smith person. Knowing he'd use the forgetting the directions as an excuse not to follow through on this quest, I was able to generate directions on my phone. I wasn't going to allow him to back out. We were doing this. He was doing this. I wasn't going to fail in my duties as emotional support.

We adventured to Queens, taking the M train I never knew existed. With a bit of course correction along the way, we found Mr. Fang-Smith's apartment. A tall, gothy African American greeted us with fangs in his mouth. He was extremely friendly and very focused on the task at hand, taking measurements, sizing teeth, creating casts, and other things a fang-smith goth dude would need to do to ensure you left his apartment within several hours with a set of fangs to wear on your ride home. It took S some time to wear them, but I could tell he was pleased to endure the ordeal.

As Halloween approached, S wanted to test out his less anxious self and tried to find places to go or parties to attend. He liked to test out his vampiric persona, too. Being introverted is not easy when someone is as inverted as he was. He didn't know anyone to be his wing person either, and I was not in the position to lend the support I wanted to give. This arrangement is what sucks about being in secret relationships. You could never indeed be there for that person when you knew how needed you felt you were. I gave most of the support to S through very limited texting.

My husband was away that Halloween weekend, which opened up some vampiric possibilities. I still couldn't join S in his quest for social interaction, but I could sneak him into the garage once he had filled his entertainment with whatever party he would attend. The question remained on how to sneak a vampire into the basement while your child and father are asleep upstairs. I had to wait for unconsciousness to hit them both. My dad was easy because he'd always be cold before 9 am. However, the child, whose sleeping habits were jennever ideal, would be a problem. Add the predicted Halloween sugar rush to the equation. Getting this kid to bed and out cold before S's arrival wouldn't be easy.

Luckily, there is such a thing as a sugar crash after a sugar rush. I got the child in bed enough time to prepare the basement for the upcoming vampiric scene. The preparation included inflating the air mattress I'd hidden in the basement, turning on the electric tea candles to set the mood, and getting into a costume of a long white silk nightgown that was the perfect attire as a virgin waiting for a vampiric lover to devour her. That night was the first time S would be coming over to my house to get smuggled in. He got lost and was running late. While waiting, I worried about what happen if my child woke up looking for his mother while she was engaging in sexual activities with a man with face make-up dressed in all black. Luckily, the basement had a separate door from outside, so if the child were to wake up, he wouldn't find me. The poor child would be alone in the house with his grandfather and two dogs. It's not the worst situation, but it's still not good.

No matter the age difference and varied life experiences, I was madly in love with S. His existence was my entire world that deeply penetrated under my skin and through my bones. Not being able to be an average couple was sometimes extremely painful. I never had the guts even to consider getting a divorce. The thought of dealing with my husband's anger and resentment wasn't worth it. Anyone could tell you that I avoid almost any confrontation like a mother fucker. I was a fucken coward. Keeping everything that made me happy close to my chest was a big part of my survival skills. Also, not wanting to fuckup my son's life was an ample excuse not to throw gasoline amongst the flames: my main reason not to rock the boat.

Our role-playing games didn't end on a vampire note. S and I wanted to explore a sub-dom aspect of this relationship. He felt at home being the top, as I thought the same way about being his submissive. Maybe because I read all three Fifty Shades books and Anne Rice's Beauty series, I'd be well equipped to explore the fetishes described in all the chapters. Also, there are tons of videos if one requires more visual examples. S began purchasing various items and tools for binding a person's arms and legs while punishing them with a paddle or, worse, a bamboo cane. Despite all the resources available, we were stumbling through cuffs. It is a learn-as-you-go situation and, simultaneously, morbidly fun. Strange having your hair pulled and your ass spanked, making you feel even closer to the one you love.

There was this one day when his parents were again away that S would turn his garage into a glorious torture sex chamber. All I had to do was wear something sexy underneath my everyday attire and show up. S went all out by setting the scene with chains and binds attached to the garage ceiling, as well as turning his weightlifting bench into a place to be bound and whipped. It was impressive. I was blindfolded, gagged, and bound to either the ceiling, the newly constructed sex bench, or some other form of furniture. S even had me collared and leashed like a sex pet. There were even nipple clamps that hurt like a bitch once removed after having them on for a while. It was practically an Olympic BSM full-day event which left me with welts on my ass and thighs days after. We didn't know what we were doing. I lost some circulation in my left wrist, which took over a week to recover, and I thought I was going to vomit from the rag being in my mouth too long. If I didn't love him as much as I did, I probably would have given this sexual experimental stage deeper consideration. I think I still have some minor issues in my left wrist.

S became more accessible when he moved out of his parents' home and got an apartment with his brother. At times, I almost felt like an average couple. S would even cook for me, adding to the normality illusion of normality. It's painful to want something so badly that you know you're not allowed to have it. Strangely enough, the thought of a multiverse and other dimensions comforted me. I came to believe that S and I were together for a long time as lovers in the past. I arrived to think that we existed on many levels in different realities. We were high school sweethearts in one reality while married in another. Strangely, one could find survival skills in quantum physics, but it worked. I often thought of these possibilities, which gave me peace of mind. We existed somewhere in many options.

Although I've already experienced having feelings with Joas and Joe, they were just the tip of the iceberg of what I experienced with S. Having a whole new understanding of what desire, love, and pain meant was my endless creative muse. I fed off the array of emotions and wrote. Our relationship, affair, or whatever you want to call it, lasted almost ten years. I honestly lost track of the amount of time we were in each other's life, and I had to look back at past writings, which I found starting in 2008 to the end of 2020 when I began to slip away from him, which wasn't anything really to do with him as much as I was starting to become sick.

I've struggled to remember all the crucial details that would capture our time together. It's challenging to recall so many emotions in a ten-year life span, a decade. I had this letter hidden at work that S gave me a while back, but it shows what we meant to each other.

**July 8th, 2018**

**Dear...,**

**I remember the first day I met you. Many of the extreme specifics escape me now. The day itself becomes recollected as a warm glow. A bright summer day. The kind of memory that is remembered more in feeling than image. I remember shaving in a fury, wanting to be at the park on time. I raced up the hill and crossed the park a minute behind you. Meeting at the bench, I remember the walk we did around the lake, talking. I remember feeling lifted and never more at ease meeting someone new, like I had someone simply turn a kein me, opening a new filter through which the perception of life would be witnessed.**

The times we met after that were straightforward in ways, but what they grew into was he being able to rest my anI struggle to saI struggle to say " don't ones and be with someone who was able to let me feel peace in the simplest of settings, Allowing us to slip away from our worries in life to something private for both of us.

We've been able to share our innermost secrets. I've been able to abandon the facade I held up with other people. They have never been necessary with someone who has always bared themselves wholly to me. We have spent these years in sometimes awkward dances over what we do or don't have. In it, I have never been without affection from you, and I try to carry that positivity, even just representations of it, with me—the Celtic peace charm on my key ring. The Jewish good luck charm is in my work jacket. Your letters and poems were kept in my locked box of essential files.

Over ten years, people can change significantly. I've gone from shop boy to EMT to paramedic. Your sense of humor always lightens some of the dark times. Along the way, you're always there. I doubt I would have made it without you. One can chalk his success to himself, but the truth be told, with all my doubts, you were there all along the way to shield me from capitulation: Not with disconnected drawl of solution ions but with understanding.

There is no one I am in contact with as regularly as you, even if it's a simple "good morning." We are both getting older, hopefully wiser. I will be your friend, counselor, shoulder, and confidant when needed. You are a light in my life. I only want to shine on yours in good and bad times.

—S

Flash forward:

I recently had dinner with S, who is now the same age as I was when we first met. He's been at his job for nearly ten years, if not more. He had one disastrous relationship under his belt after the reality of our involvement faded into memory. He is now very involved in the BSBM scene. He has a regular dominatrix who is in love with him, but he doesn't feel the same for her. I know how she feels. However, he seems at peace with himself. There are still brief hints of that shy twenty-two-year-old, but I see a confident thirty-five-year-old, too, who sometimes gets chained to the ceiling or anal-fisting some guy during public BDSM events. We still speak now and then.

**Nightmare:**

In a petrified stillness in bed, I hear muffled rumbling down the hall. It's inaudible, and it's moving closer to my bedroom door. "Please don't let it come in here!" The sounds become closer as though it is about to cross the threshold through the doorway. "Don't come in. I struggle to say, "Don't come in, " but no words come from me. If I could just turn over to face the door, maybe, just maybe, I can stop it from coming into my room. My body won't move. A feeling of disgust bares down through my body. I wake in the blurriness of the real world, screaming something that resembles "No!"

# Part II: Product of Our Experiences
# Pieces of Apartment 17-G

Sometime in the late 70s, my family moved from Ravenswood Queens to Starrett City in Brooklyn. My mother wanted to escape the violence in our project development. People were constantly getting mugged and raped in the building elevators and staircases. I have a faint memory of seeing an older man's head covered in blood and escorted onto the sidewalk. Even at a very young age, I understood something terrible happened but didn't understand why. I didn't understand why, when I was maybe 3 or 4, people screamed "GET DOWN!" while there was a series of booming sounds around us while playing outside our building.

My parents meet somewhere in a Queen Synagogue. My dad was born in Berlin right at the beginning stages of the Holocaust. Kristallnacht was his family's clue to get out of dodge. For some people, seeing scattered shards of glass scatter onto your sleeping child as they lay in their crib is enough to change neighborhoods. My grandparents, with a couple of aunts and uncles, could hop on a boat headed to Columbia. At the time, Columbia was one of the few countries that would take Jews trying to escape the upcoming nightmare amid WWII. Dad lived in Columbia for about eighteen years. Not only could my dad speak his homeland's language, but he also spoke Spanish. He and my grandparents moved to NYC when he was about eighteen. My mom's family were mostly all born as raised Bronx kids.

Starrett City, now called Spring Creek, was brand spanking new when we moved in. It was close to Carnise, but you'd be in East New York if I walked down two blocks from my apartment building. All you had to do was cross Flatlands to see the worlds of our newly developed neighborhood and old, run-down East

New York. Everything about Starrett City back then looked nearly untouched. This Utopia of Brooklyn was across a street from a landfill, so it smelled like raw sewage, depending on where you lived or how the wind blew that day. It was and still is a massive complex of apartment buildings, some twenty stories high with terraces. It had a shopping center, a recreation center, a pool, and schools. It had its security task force and was deemed the promised land of lower-income families wanting a fresh start.

The buildings got lumped into several sections. There was the A section, B Section, C section, and to the H section. Each section had a group of buildings designated by a number like A1, C4, and H2, and these sections had a four-floored parking garage to accommodate parking for the residence. Each section had one or two playgrounds in the middle with a swing set, monkey bars, and often a sandbox. Each building has its own laundry room and storage facility. We lived in building A1, apartment 17-G. It was a three-bedroom apartment with a terrace. At five years old, our new apartment was a castle amid paradise. My older sister and I would finally have our rooms. Not bad for white Jewish trash.

I know that doesn't sound politically correct, but we were a Jewish white trash family. Being white trash was something impossible not to notice every time we visited my uncle's family in New Jersey. My mom grew up poor Jew trash in the Bronx with her two brothers and mom. Her dad died of cancer when my mom was about twelve years old. At some point, my uncle married a middle-class Jewish princess, moved to the suburbs of South New Jersey, and left all his white trash ancestry behind. Although he always welcomed his nieces to visit him in their lovely four-bedroom home and backyard. My aunt's family treated us like we were all about to steal money out of her purse and OD on Tylenol. They were snotty-ass white folks who rarely traveled to our neck of the woods to visit. We would have to take the city bus to the train to the Port Authority to catch a bus that would bring us there to see them. I would always get motion sickness and throw up each trip there and back. Maybe my uncle was too traumatized from his Bronx upbringing for him to see his roots lingering in our 17th-floor apartment.

It wasn't long before the tranquility and safety of Starrett City quickly declined. Crime slowly crept and seeped into the walls and foundations. The 80s drug epidemic didn't care if the buildings were new. As the neighborhood's utopian promises were slowly becoming harsh realities, my home life quickly disintegrated into shit. Any wrong crowd easily influenced my older sister; she could stumble on. Some people are born with gay-dar, but she was born with drug/booze-ar. I love my sister, but back then, not so much. She was one of many tormentors I had to endure growing up. One of my memories is trying to escape her and her friends by locking myself in the bathroom. Unfortunately, the bathroom lock opened easily by anyone from the other side by inserting a narrow object in the adjusted hole of the lock. I must keep my thumb on the lock button to open it. Knowing I was holding this button by the door, my sister ignited a can of hairspray with a lighter, creating a flamethrower effect. As I heard the lighter flicking, I quickly moved my feet just enough to avoid the flames emerging from underneath the bathroom door without losing my grip on the lock.

It seemed my mom would let my sister get away with almost everything. She would either be smoking and drinking pot with her friends in her room or our apartment. It wasn't as much of my mom letting my sister get away with everything but more like Mom was afraid of losing my sister. My mom was just not equipped with the necessary tools needed to deal with an adolescent narcist. When we first moved in, my sister insisted we exchange bedrooms because mine seemed better. Once, my mom ordered a new wall unit for the living room, which my sister claimed for herself upon its arrival, and my parents moved it into her bedroom. My mom thought saying no to my sister would damage their relationship. My dad was even more absent in acknowledging the dysfunctional situation.

There was loads of crazy shit going on in my sister's bedroom. Such crazy shit activities included some Satanic Rituals, drugs, and a lot of sex. For some reason, my parents thought it was perfectly safe to allow this sadist young teenager to look after me when they were out overnight. These weekends were house party time when my parents went away. My sister filled our apartment wall to wall with teenage debauchery. Not only did some party activities include drugs, alcohol, and sex, but we also went over our terrace to our next-door neighbor's apartment to rob jewelry. When I was eight years old, her party guests, kids ranging from fifteen to actual grown-ass adults who liked to hang out with teenagers, enjoyed shoving vodka down my throat. It was a 'let's get the little kid drunk" game. Otherwise, everyone often ignored me except for one or two creepy adults who liked hanging out with little girls.

As much as I loved my mother, I didn't understand her selective blindness to the shit around her. Yes, we had warm beds and food in our bellies. Besides the bare basics, the neglect was apparent. No one told us to take a bath or change into clean clothes. My mother never cleaned our apartment, and it looked and smelled like shit. We had many cats with litter boxes that no one cleaned, which added to the harsh aromas of my childhood. Roaches infested Starrett City, and if you didn't keep on top of maintaining the condition of our apartment, you had a problem, so we had a huge problem. With my clothes rarely washed and my hair never brushed, I'd go to school wearing four-day-old underwear. Nobody told me I was supposed to change my underwear daily, just like nobody told me to shower, bathe, or even brush my hair.

Throughout childhood, I wore my bird's nest of hair held together in a ponytail.

Did I mention roaches? We had a brown carpet, so those little mother fuckers were camouflaged. They were everywhere. You know, when there's a vast roach problem, it is when you see more than one albino roach more than twice a week. You couldn't open cabinets and drawers in the kitchen without one or two scurrying about. I was terrified that they wouldn't jump on me. I'd be scared to sleep at night. The lights had been on in my bedroom. They would sometimes find their way into our food, the dishes, everywhere. There was this one time we were in the dining/kitchen area. I think it was after dinner that my mom thought it was a perfect idea to spray for roaches from a crack just under one of the kitchen cupboards. It rained roaches, dead ones, live ones, all falling onto the counter. I just remembered standing there frozen, which is pretty much the exact reaction I would have if I saw one now.

I could not eat at home because of the roach and filth situation. Unless it were a pre-packaged sealed item, I wouldn't eat it. Also, you could not find one clean dish or utensil in our house. For some reason, my mom made my dad wash the dishes because cleaning anything was something this woman would just not do. Dad would wash the dishes in greasy water with little to no soap. I grew up with cabinets filled with greasy ass dishes with food particles still attached to the surfaces. I developed an eating disorder growing up. My eating disorder has little to do with my weight and my body image. I was just too revolted to eat dirty ass dishes and risk eating food that might be hiding a roach or two.

Although my dad was an excellent role model when it came to dedication to the workplace was often mentally and emotionally absent from the house. He worked for Con Ed for over forty years, and he drank. My mom resented his existence but not his paycheck. He'd often drink outside the house so he didn't have to hear her scream at him. She would yell at him anyway just for breathing the same air she did. Dad did most of his drinking outside. Usually, Dad would find a nice quiet spot on some grass, away from our view on the 17th floor, and enjoy a couple of 40oz of Budweiser. Then Dad would wander past Flatlands Ave to no man's land, East New York, to drink. I think in the twelve years or so that we lived in Starrett City, my dad was mugged about eight times, give or take so. He'd come home a bit bloody and banged up. Often, he came home in ripped pants because they were trying to get his wallet from the back of his pants. Due to the fact his leisure time was often outside while he would be downing those 40oz on and off, he would feel comfortable public urinating wherever he stood. I would walk with my dad somewhere; he would feel like any place was good to pee. He wouldn't even bother to hide behind anything. It was like walking a dog needing to mark their territory.

Back when we used to live in Queens, my dad would use me as an excuse to go out to drink. We lived within walking distance of a park by the water. On the way to the park, I remembered two stores nearby. One store was blue and the other green. I liked the blue store the best because that's where all the candy was. However, my dad preferred the green store because that one sold beer. We'd always go to the green store and rarely the blue one I liked. The park had a playground, but my dad never took me in that direction. Instead, he'd find a quiet spot on the grass, usually with a good view of the water and drink. I was to sit beside him and stay put while he drank his fill before returning home.

Once, when we moved to Starret City, my dad thought it was an excellent idea to take his daughter to one of the local bars when he was left alone with me. All I remember was going for a walk with him, not knowing our final destination. Once we crossed Flatlands Ave, I knew we were heading to a more dangerous location. I realized I was in a bar when we reached our final destination. It was a dark and depressing-looking establishment with only a handful of customers out for their afternoon alcohol refreshments. I could tell that the bartender was unhappy to see a kid in his business and yelled at him and the bartender to sit back in the booth. I don't remember when we finally left and headed home. I do recall that not only was my dad completely shit-faced, but he nearly started a fight with a stranger while we were walking home. If I weren't there crying and begging my dad to stop, this stranger would punch the shit out of my dad. His choice of leisure activities is a good reason why he got mugged so many times.

# Pieces of Booger Girl:

I have a learning disability. It's through my brain that, on and off, I struggle to understand the sounds letters and words make. I have a difficult time spelling and even pronouncing certain words. I think my learning disability is due to multiple traumas. A good part of the trauma happened in school. Instead of learning, I was trying just to survive each day from my tormentors. The bullying began in the second grade. I was not a good student. I misbehaved like any seven-year-old whose intentions were far from academic. I was a goofball. I'm not even sure I understood the concept of school. It was just a place to stuff little kids and force them to know useless information like reading and writing. As long as I had cartoons, my life was complete. I didn't have many friends, but I wasn't misliked either until one day, one event, one moment changed everything. Whatever change I had in a slightly normally socially acceptable childhood was flushed into a dark, helpless realm.

Second Grade, sitting in the back of the class, we were all quiet and strangely eager to educate. I had a stuffy nose, and basic blowing wasn't getting the job done. I thought it was wise to go finger-diving for the annoying phlegm balls blocking my airways. And that's when the teacher said it. I heard it. The entire class heard it. My soul, to this day, still hears it. "Debra, stop picking your nose!" was followed by an "Eeeww" in unison by the entire class. My teacher might as well have sliced my throat open, which would have been considered more kindness than the brutal force that traveled behind those words. From that moment and moving forward through elementary school, I was called "Booger Girl."

Little kids are horrible creatures with poisonous fangs and claws. They will repeatedly kill you once they see something different or weak. My classmates and the entire second grade were well-trained emotional assassins. They became more skilled at verbal and even physical abuse as each grade went by. I hated them. I hated that second-grade teacher. I hated everyone in my school who had to see the ongoing abuse I was suffering—almost every day. If I had any friends, they quickly abandoned me once they noticed my new title as the school's booger girl. The very few who decided to play with me were only the other social outcasts who endured their daily torments. However, we were all ready to sell each one of us out if it meant being the recipient of what seemed to be positive attention from anyone who wasn't marked. I am not innocent of being a monster myself to a so-called friend if it meant the approval from a more socially accepted child, even if it was just for five minutes. Of course, those five minutes of believing I was like everyone else were always bliss, but the universe was only making a sick joke because, within a heartbeat, I would cast back down to my untouchable status. It didn't help that my mother let me leave the house in the condition I was in. Clothes smelling, hair tangled. I was a living, breathing, walking target.

From 2nd grade to 8th grade, my peers tormented me every day. Most of the abuse was verbal. When there were no adults in the room, the physical abuse commenced. Besides being called 'booger girl,' she was called ugly, stupid, and even retard. As each grade passed, the very few kids who pretended to be my friends, if any, forced me to give away my lunch money or allow a boy to stick his hands down my pants. Those boys were secret friends, and the secret was having either of our hands down each other's pants. Kids usually would play school, house, or doctor, but this was our game. Boys sometimes don't call you names or threaten to punch you if you regularly put their cock in your mouth or show them "yours." These secret games with boys kept my cousin from throwing down the stairs when we visited my uncle in New Jersey and allowed me to draw in the neighbor's son's coloring books. I would sometimes steal money from my parents to buy loads of candy to give out and a tiny bit of peace for the day.

The worst was sixth grade. If our teacher was out and there was a stub. That's when the worst of the physical abuse occurred. Three or four boys would line up at their desks behind me as soon as we all got in the classroom. I was their favorite spitball target. Morning to lunch, spitballs. After lunch until 3:00, spitballs. I look like a fucked Christmas tree with spitballs dangling in my knotted hair. Everyone in the class knew this was happening but never gave a shit to try to stop it. None of them bothered to tell the sub or our regular teacher the next day that this horror was happening under their watch. Even Though it was just a few boys, it felt like the entire class, school, and even the world was using me for target practice. I would just be there crying as silently as I could, wishing I was dead.

Once, I took a Sharpie marker to my desk and wrote "I need to die" and "I need to be dead" or something like that. My desk was clear evidence that I needed help. Writing the hate, I felt for myself got our teacher's attention, the school counselor's attention, and my mother's. When asked to explain my actions, I couldn't. I think I just gave the basic "I don't know. "Grown-ups r translated to just attention-seeking behavior. At age twelve, I couldn't put into words the pain boiling inside me. I now have the talent for expressing pain in some form of art, so I hold onto all the horror. One of my sister's friends, who later was known as a child molester, gave me a peace sign neck charm with a satin ribbon. In class, I would sometimes twist the satin tightly around my neck. I twisted the thick velvet thread around my neck until there was else to twist until my lungs would struggle for air. No one would question the red lines that were on my neck.

This trauma continued through elementary and most of middle school. I was the school's untouchable thing. I was a thing to tease, call names to, and be told lies about. One lie was that I was talking shit about a girl's mother. We were friends one day, and then she jumped after school the next day. I don't think the teachers or the school wanted to notice the violence I was facing daily, or you'd think someone would have put a stop to this fucken hell I had to wake up every day and face. Sometimes I wish I could go back and ask these fucken adults why they seemed to be so selectively blind to what appeared to be so fucken obvious.

Not only did these various childhood traumas affect my ability to understand the English language, but they also made it difficult to make friends as an adult. It took me a while to come out of my social shell and attempt to connect with people. I think I can contribute social anxiety to the mix as well. Crowds of strangers terrify me as though I will drown their unsaid judgments of me.

# Pieces of Camp Sussex (Age 15)

In the summer of 1985, my sister had an incredible experience working for Camp Sussex, located in NJ, and she insisted that I have the same experience. Mind you, she was in her twenties and thought her fifteen-year-old sister would have the same positive experience as her adult ass did. No one questioned that. The commute required me to travel from Starrett City to Flushing Queens on a train for an interview with the camp director. Now, take a moment and look at a NYC subway map. Please tell me how any adult responsible for a fifteen-year-old's wellbeing was a good idea. I think the trip required one bus and three trains to get my fifteen-year-old ass to the NYC office of Camp Sussex. The only position they had for a fifteen-year-old was a waitress.

I didn't know what that meant, and I didn't have an adult with me either. I said yes and became one of their camp waitresses for the summer of 1986 for 100.00 bucks. That's right; I was to make 100.00 for eight weeks of working seven days straight. I made about 1.75 a day. Maybe having an adult present would have helped.

On the first Saturday in July, I was shipped off to Sussex, NJ, to have a positive experience and make my 1.75 a day. I knew no one. I knew nothing about this place, a camp aimed at unprivileged NYC children. Well, I was an underprivileged NYC kid. When I got off the staff coach bus that left Flushing, NY, at 7 am, I had no idea where I was or where I was supposed to go or do. , I wondered about the campgrounds for a good hour until someone directed me to where I was supposed to bunk. The camp had two sides, a boy's and a girl's side; each had about twenty little houses called "bunk houses." Each bunkhouse had about twenty beds. The camp served children as young as six years old. There were a lot of kids. Also, they had older teens and adults from different countries. Some organizations hire young people from all over the world to work in camps and resorts. I wondered if they made the same 1.75 a day, too.

Most everyone in my bunkhouse was about my age. Some were camp servers like me. Some were office helpers or worked in the laundry room, and most of us didn't know anyone here either, but we were on the 1.75 per day payment system, which we would all see at the end of camp if we all made it that far. There was one older girl who was from England. I forgot what her job was. The rest of us were born and raised in NYC. We didn't have too much adult supervision inside our tiny home. Camp directors and senior counselors were around to align us all with the camp's priorities. We had a camp counselor who was assigned to oversee the 1.75 staff. Our counselor was an obese dude named Mark. Most of Mark's family members worked for the camp, too. They were all huge mother fuckers who looked like they probably wouldn't see past age thirty due to heart disease or something similar. He had two female cousins who were counselors for the twelve-year-old girls. They were so huge and required medically enhanced bras to keep their monster boobs in check.

Being a camp waitress or waiter required us to be up before most of the camp before 7 am to report to the dining hall so we could eat before all the campers filled the place. Although I was on time, the woman who supervised the wait staff made me return to my bunk to change my clothes quickly. You had to wear pants, socks, and shoes when working with or near food. I had on shorts and a tank. I only brought two pairs of sweatpants with me. Again, it would have been nice to be told this before packing my little ass to Sussex, NJ. Our crew lump every camp reject over fourteen to work this job for 1.75 a day. I might not have understood social peeking orders before, but it was crystal clear here on the first day.

After the breakfast shift, we had to prepare for the lunch shift quickly. The tasks included cleaning up after over 100 hungry mouths and sometimes helping the kitchen staff and preparing lunch. The kitchen staff were a mix of older born and raised New York City teens and a couple of European foreigners. The kitchen powers-to-be established a pecking order. I learned quickly that the kitchen staff would harass the boys by tripping them or dumping various cooking substances before throwing them in the dumpsters in the back. It was all in the name of camp fun. They never bothered the girls too much, though. I had some flour thrown at me at some point. After we cleaned up after the lunch shift, we were allowed some free time before having to report for the diner shift. We could enjoy the campgrounds for a couple of hours, but most of us would shower and try to catch an extra hour of sleep.

Even though some free time was allowed, there wasn't much to do. After the dinner shift ended, we had to make the dining hall as clean as possible. It felt like it took forever to get this vast dining hall 100% clean after serving over a hundred little mouths, counselors, and senior staff. The carpet of this enormous dining hall required vacuuming, and we all shared two semi-working vacuums to share among the ten of us. It took forever to finish all the cleaning. Once done, there is freedom to enjoy the available camp activities like talent shows, movie nights, and some staff-only locations. There was one house dedicated to staff only, which had a pool table and a snack stand, which required money, which I didn't know I had to bring but later learned how to steal from. The only place staff were allowed to smoke was on the porch of this staff house. If caught smoking anywhere else, you ended up on a couch bus the next day going home. I learned how to smoke on that porch.

My camp waitress career ended abruptly after faking a heat stroke just after the lunch hour when exhausted from working my ass off for 1.75 per hour in this shitty dining hall that lacked AC. My fainting spell didn't require much impression. You just need to allow your knees to bend and gravity to do its job. The key is not to attempt to use your limbs to break the fall. You must appear to take on as much impact even if it means bruising your elbow from impact. For good measure and effect, have a stack of plates so that they can create the required crashing sound as they tumble to the ground with you. Keep your body limb as much as possible and have your eyeballs roll to the back of your head.

Of course, some people assumed I was faking it but could not prove it. Senior Staff took me to the camp infirmity, the only place with AC. They allowed me to drift in and out of consciousness as though fitting a much-needed nap, given a soft, cold bed. I must have slept for a few hours and didn't know various supervisors were looking at me. I was in the camp infirmity for at least twenty-four hours before getting the all-clear to leave. As a result of my acting abilities, they transferred me from the dining hall to the laundry department.

I am still on my 1.75-a-day rate, but now I can wear shorts, a tank top, and sandals. I was now privileged to be part of a four-person team to wash the entire camp's dirty laundry, as well as become privileged to learn some other dirty laundry that was going on throughout the camp. I still had to get up almost as early as I wanted breakfast. The laundry room was dank-looking, with a machine that looked like the camp had purchased in the 1940s. These vast industrial washing machines could clean, or appear to clean, the amorous pounds of camp laundry. However, they didn't have the spin cycle feature we have become used to in our modern domestic appliances. We had to unload soaked and heavy pounds of laundry from these monsters in these rusty-looking colossal metal bins that probably were purchased at the same time as these old ass washing machines. Then we had wheels that soaked mess over to the extracting machines, which looked like they got purchased at the same time as the pre-WWII washing machines. There was just one working extractor machine; it's a bit of a stretch when I say working. The brakes, either a pedal or a leaver, on this thing didn't work. After you made the damn thing spin 90 miles an hour, you then hand to stop it by hand. That's right; by your hand. Stopping the machine that was spinning 100 miles per minute was achieved by pressing a thick towel on the edge and slowly pressing down on the rim without having the towel sucked and having your arms ripped off. Child safety laws weren't in full force in the mid-80s as they are today. After conquering the clothes extractor of death, we placed the clothes in the dryers, which, yeah, you guessed it, were pre-WWII as well.

Summer Loving is no stranger at summer camp. Everyone is trying to find someone to hook up with and hopefully have that excellent summer romance seen on TV. Since I just got my braces off that spring, I didn't know why this should not apply to me. I was just entering that part of adolescence where I was beginning to feel a little pretty. I no longer felt like Bugsy Bunny with Down syndrome. My self-esteem had a slight influx of positivity. Boys and men were beginning to notice me, and I was starting to notice them noticing me. No one knew me as the 'Booger Girl". It was a fresh start, so I searched for that great summer romance.

The first boy I made out with at Camp Sussex was this pretty British boy. I made the error of being too clingy, which ended as quickly as it started. The heartbreak didn't last long as I set my eyes on one of the older boys who worked in the kitchen's camp head baker. Craig was 19, going on 40, and didn't abuse the boy servers with other kitchen staff. However, he'd coned getting us to help him do his job. He played his con to perfection and was happy to volunteer every time. If Craig needed help preparing 100 grilled cheese sandwiches, I was there. If Craig needed help making mini rolls, I was there. Craig knew he was my camp crush, but he stated that he was not having any jailbait issues. Senior staff tried to set Invisible boundaries between them and younger staff. I was never good at boundaries. Boundaries were paper walls I wanted to punch through. And guess what? Craig wasn't too good at his boundaries either.

Whether he planned it or it's just one of those things that just happened in the heat of the moment, or in this case, the chill of the moment, is still a question that remains unanswered. He wanted to share the physical feeling of temperature change by going into the kitchen's walk-in freezer for a bit and then getting out. There was another kid about my age with us at the time, so it probably wasn't planned. We hung out in the freezer, enjoying the arctic relief from the heat and humidity of the summer. We even took advantage of some opened cartons of ice cream sandwiches. When we walked out back into the heat, it felt delicious. It's hard to explain because the drastic temperature changes felt nice. The closest to this feeling would be spending time in a hot sauna and jumping in a cold pool. It felt good, so we did it a couple more times until the other kid left, and I was left alone with Craig with his so-called jailbait boundaries. I don't remember what happened or what was said, but we made out for a few minutes outside the freezer. Feeling his hand go up my T-shirt was a shock. It wasn't a call from a child protective service type of shock. It was more like an omg, my camp crush's tongue is my mouth, and he's fingers are on my tit type of shock.

Waiting for those clothes to dry took forever. After loading most of the clothes into the dryer, we had a little time to relax. Sometimes, we'd crash on the folding tables and catch up on some sleep. Believe it or not, I had a few good naps on those complex wooden tables. The increase in free time also gave me a bit more time to try to have a repeat performance with Craig, but he was back to sticking to his jailbait boundaries again. We were also allowed to smoke in the laundry room as long as the head director did catch us, but since upper management never bothered to check if our arms became mangled from the spinning machines, they never checked if we were smoking, napping, or even making out. On laundry duty, adult supervision meant being supervised by a 19-year-old whose name I forgot. Our laundry supervisor was only concerned that we completed most of our responsibilities by 5 pm. There was some random making out. I made it with my supervisor, the ground crew supervisor, and one or two of the other waiters. It became a game to see how many boys I could kiss before the end of summer. By mid-summer, I'd made out with at least five different boys.

My summer at Camp Sussex was a summer of many firsts. I smoked my first joint at Camp Sussex. It was right before our evening drop-off and pick-bin run. Arthur, about my age and on the grounds crew, was hanging with us right after dinner. He was willing to help lift the overloaded bins in and out of the van. The main reason he and the other boys wanted to help was because there was a handful of female European camp counselors who liked to sunbathe topless in the middle of the girl side of the camp. Arthur also started in the dining hall with me but was able to jump on the opening on the grounds crew. In our laundry van, I sat behind him, enjoying my first high, touching the back of his neck. I'm not sure why I was feeling this kid or exactly where and when I got stoned. I can't say if I was really into him or even noticed much before that evening. I felt like touching something in front of me, and he just happened to be that person at that time in front of me. Arthur didn't mind the touching.

After the laundry run was complete, I don't remember the events or the conversation that led Arthur and me to sit by the lake. The lake area was off limits to all at night, but that was just one rule most didn't follow or oversee. We made out. We lay on the moist grass. He ended up on top of me. Arthur removed my pants. Arthur lowered his pants. My legs were spread. I felt his hardness trying to push itself inside me. It took time for my body to attempt to allow it to open me. I think it hurt, but I also believe the shock of what I was allowing to happen helped to numb the lower half of my body. At some point, I think I left my body and waited for 'it' to be over. It was over fast once the necessary part was in its essential position. Far off in the distance, I heard male voices hollering and clapping. They were probably too far away and could not see who I or he was. They knew what was happening. As soon as I returned to my bunk, I went straight to the bathroom. There was blood. There wasn't a lot, but enough to know that I was no longer a virgin. My feelings lingered between that realm of pride and shame, thinking I was now an adult. I didn't know this kid that I just fucked, and he didn't understand me. We weren't boyfriend and girlfriend. We were nothing. I was nothing.

News travels fast in camp because the following week, this kid Jason, a close friend of Author, takes Author's place at the lake. Jason, a grounds crew member, asked if I'd like to grab a walk. I said yes. He asked if I would want to go near the lake. I said yes. He led me to a different spot that seemed a bit more private than where Author fucked me. Jason asked if I would like to sit. I said yes and sat. He asked if he could kiss me. I said yes. We kissed. We made out. Again, my shorts came down. Again, my underwear came down. His shorts were lowered. Again, I felt the pressure press at my crotch. Although Jason wasn't as thick as his friend, I had to convince my body to comply. Just as before, it was quick but not as painful. There was no cheering from afar. Again, we were nothing. I was nothing. There was no blood this time. I was regularly called a slut and whore in my face by all the members of the grounds crew.

Then there is Michael, or was it Mike, maybe Mark, another kid from the grounds crew but with the same request to walk onto familiar grounds. However, this one was different. Whatever his name was, he couldn't get it up. After a few failed attempts, he gave up. But the word was out. I officially became one of the camp sluts. The easy girl. Craig also heard the word and didn't mind me hanging out in the bakery after the diner crew had left. I still had a massive crush on him now; he was a challenge to conquer. My body language was pretty obvious. A blind and deaf person could have heard and seen that I wanted a moment with this nineteen-year-old that I became infatuated with. Craig got the message loud and fucken clear.

One night, in the bakery, I stayed late with Craig. When he thought the coast was clear, we made out before lifting me onto one of the bakery's counters. As he kept his ear to the door, I felt him wanting to push through his white work pants in between my legs. I was wearing easy-access clothes. I don't know if I wanted him or just him to want me as much as I liked him. However, he wouldn't fuck me. He was too scared to get caught fucking a fifteen-year-old on the same countertop he made camp diner rolls. He pulled me off the counter and brought me to a very secluded gap between the back of one of the enormous baker ovens and a back door. As he pushed me onto my knees, he pulled out his cock. Now, I have never actually given anyone a head before. I've had a cock in my mouth a few times as a kid, but no one knew what we were supposed actually to do. However, a nineteen-year-old has some level of expectations in receiving oral sex, and this fifteen-year-old girl had no clue. With his cock in my mouth, I just sucked on it like it was an ice pop. Little did I know there were some sort of movements with my head, tongue, maybe even hand that played a role in a bare blowjob. Craig quickly realized I had no clue what I was doing and, pretending to hear a noise out the kitchen, rushed back on my feet and out that back door. He made sure I went my way, and he went his.

That was not the last opportunity I would have with Craig. A few days later, he told me to meet him at the parking lot at 8 pm. He always kept his car in the back of the laundry room, and I assumed that was where we were meeting, so I waited and waited, sitting on the steps of the laundry room as it was getting closer to 9 pm, one of the counselor's older male counselors passed by and spotted me. A teenage girl was sitting by herself in what wasn't the safest place to sit. The counselor directed me to walk with him. I didn't know where he was taking me, and for what purpose, and at that point of disappointment with Craig not showing up, I didn't care. He brought me to the primary office but not to report me or even to fuck me. The main office building looked like a living room with others just hanging out, playing board games, and watching movies. This older teen plucked me out of another moment of self-harm into a safe place. So, decent human beings who instantly did the right thing were lingering around us. Even though I'm sure all of the camps know I had a reputation, I sat quickly and quietly with the group and watched Alien 2 and wondering what the fuck happened to Craig. There was more than one parking lot on the campground, but that didn't dawn on me until after the fact. I often wondered what would have happened if I had shown up. Would he have smuggled me in his car to drive to an excluded area to finally fuck me?

My whorish legacy in Camp Sussex didn't end on the campgrounds. I later learned that my second lay, Jason, lived in the building just across the street from mine. On the last day, the camp handed out a directory with everyone's contact information so everyone who made such unique connections throughout the summer could write and call each other. Jason and Arthur, who are close friends of their own, wanted to reconnect with me. On the day that Arthur was visiting Jason, they both wanted me to come over. The term "come over" in my naive brain meant hanging out with the possibility of keeping my clothes on. I 'came over' to Jason's apartment, where both boys had a slight scent of vodka. My sense of smell was validated when they offered me a drink. I declined. I should have accepted.

Jason offered to show me around the apartment, which I thought was strange since most of the flats had the exact layout of rooms. There was nothing to see that I hadn't seen before. Once we got to his parent's bedroom, I noticed the towel on the bed. Why would Jason's parents have a towel on their bed? The door was closed behind me. The term "cover over" and the reason for the towel became crystal clear as Jason told me to remove my clothes. Compliant and without questioning him, I deeply regretted not taking the shot of vodka when I had the chance. Without a drop of alcohol, part of my inner self left my body until whatever was to come was over. Separating myself into pieces to deal with various situations was a natural occurrence by then. As part of myself undressed, part of myself sat in the corner of the room, pretending to be somewhere else.

No matter how much I distanced part of myself in Jason's parents' bedroom, my body was so incredibly tight to the point of frustrating Jason. My body knew this was wrong, but I wasn't listening. My body just knew better than I did that it didn't want this kid's dick inside me. After Jason finished, Arthur came in. Although I understood what was happening and was being 'shared,' I didn't stop it. I obeyed until they finished with me and told me to leave. I was done with me as well.

Camp Sussex eventually closed its doors, bunk house, and dining hall a few years later. The camp director was stealing from the inner-city kids' cookie jar. The minor corruption explains the $1.75 a day pay most of the younger staff received. Not to mention the pre-war laundry equipment and other child safety-labor law issues that were part of the Camp experiences, it hasn't reopened since.

# Pieces of Bruno (age 16)

I told my mom I was sick that day. There wouldn't be much debate about whether she believed me or not. Missing school again isn't the worst thing I could be doing with my life. It's not like I was failing any of my classes. Ok, so I was failing Spanish. Spanish was my most hated class of all classes. Having an undiagnosed learning disability had to be the culprit. Cheating on a test had little effect. I barely made it through basic English as a first language, and they wanted to learn Spanish. Even when I made these tiny little cheat notes that fit under my wrist, I still failed. Oh yeah, then there's math. It's some weird ass math that should be legal to teach. It's like an abomination of math. I don't even know what they call this type of math. It wasn't algebra. I like algebra and geometry. This math class was as if algebra was gang raped by trig and statistics which resulted in some sort of a mutated math unwanted baby. That stuff they were trying to teach me, no thanks, you can keep it. Plus, I sat next to an asshole named Jamal. He's the remnant of the hell of elementary and middle school when I was constantly bullied and tormented. I guess he didn't notice that I'm no longer buck-toothed, fat, and looking like a bug bunny with Down syndrome, as he also managed to be complete and utter shit. I also wondered what would have happened if I went completely psycho on his ass in the middle of math class. Just add that to the list of regrets.

Back then, having a learning disability wasn't as recognized as it is today. No one spoke the word 'inclusion'. Today, there are a series of well-crafted tests to determine a student's various challenges in learning and multiple services to assist any student experiencing various learning difficulties. However, in 1987, those tests and services were limited, so I struggled not to always fall into those forgettable cracks in the education system. Kids like me were labeled 'lazy,' 'daydreaming,' or just a problem.'

Otherwise, I was an average practicing Jewish girl of the late eighties and an average student at the end of my sophomore year who was beginning the nasty habit of cutting school. Ok, I'm lying. The word average never actually comes to mind in describing myself. I was one of those weird, quiet girls who had a rare tendency to be loud when it felt required in whatever appropriate moment. The few friends I had were leftovers from nerds' squads and wanna-be bad-ass heavy metal headbangers. We had to take public transportation to our high school, where we all would sit safely in the front of the bus away from our tormentors in the back of the bus going through Carnise to South Shore High School. The only connection within our group was our desire to fit into the regular clicks that rejected us regularly desperately. My small circle of friends simply sucked at fitting in but pretended to be ok with our low social status. Cutting school now and then to steal a couple of beers from the basement of a pizza place was one of our favorite activities. Stealing the beer was an easy accomplishment. All one had to do was ask to use the bathroom, which was located in the basement exactly where they stored the beers.

Now, I was upgrading the truancy experience by sneaking into the city to see my twenty-one-year-old boyfriend, Bruno. I met Bruno at a Halloween party given to an international service organization my parents belonged to called the Lions Club. Bruno was with his uncle, who was a bigshot in the community. His uncle was a counsel person or one of those elected officials that almost no one ever bothers to vote for when it comes time to vote. My parents allowed their fifteen-year-old daughter to dress as a prostitute or some sort of glam-whore and join them at this community event. My custom seemed acceptable to everyone, and I attracted a twenty-year-old man. I would be lying if I didn't attempt to receive his attention and make all the horror I felt about myself fade into the mist of the dance floor. For what might have been the first time, I felt attractive. I was pretty glam-whore, and my heart belonged to Bruno that night. What topped off that night was winning the basket of top-shelf alcohol at the raffle. I could walk out of the community center gym with a big basket of booze and a heart full of pretty feelings. Win-Win!

Bruno and I quickly began to date in secret soon after. I used babysitting as my cover to sneak out at night to see him. Being a twenty-one-year-old nephew of an elected official and dating a fifteen-year-old was something not to advertise. Plus, I assumed my mom would connect with her motherly duties in protecting her daughter from the clutches of grown-ass men. From my self-education from Camp Sussex, my knowledge of the erotic zones of a man's body became impressive, if not valuable, for this new relationship. I allowed myself to be an active participant instead of the empty puppet shared with Arthur and Jason not long ago.

I would cut school to see Bruno once a week. He worked as a locksmith on Chambers Street in the city. His boss seemed cool enough to allow me to hang out in the back if I didn't get in the way. There were pictures of this thin, sexy blonde by Bruno's workstation. He had photos of his ex-up. I wasn't worth having them taken down. I pretended to care while the insecurity of always seeing them there lingered in the back of my throat. During Bruno's breaks, we would sneak into an abandoned office building next door and fuck. There was this on time; however, I had my period, and Bruno attempted to gain entrance through my back door. My body wasn't having it.

It wasn't unheard of that I'd be asked to sleep over while babysitting. This cover is something I did but also used as the perfect cover to spend the night with Bruno. The first night I would spend with him was at a notorious motel in Brooklyn called the Windjammer. Anyone from Brooklyn knows of this place, even from a safe distance. It was an establishment in which to get laid. My challenge was attempting to look good but not too good because I was supposed to 'babysit.' How does one manage to look presentable to fuck without gaining any parental suspicions? Unfortunately, the wind blew away my attempt while waiting for the bus. My hair looked like noticeable crap. Bruno even made a crappy comment about making no effort to look nice—nothing like having one's ego blown before crossing the street to the sex motel. As Bruno paid for the room, he also paid the extra twenty bucks for the porn.

The second time I was 'babysitting' overnight, I ended up somewhere in the Bronx. We were hanging out with one or two of Bruno's cousins. I don't remember how in the world I got there. I don't know if anyone drove or if I took the train. What I do recall in some clarity is throwing up after drinking too much beer in front of a pizza place. Also, Bruno became highly embarrassed, but I also remember a female who could have been one of the cousins or just some concerned woman who helped me clean up and get my shit together. We spent the night at Bruno's strict aunt's house and slept in separate rooms. I remember feeling cold because they only gave me a thin sheet to sleep under. How I got home is a mystery to me as well.

After months of lying and sneaking behind my mom's back, I got tired due to inviting excuses to ride the L train from Rockaway Parkway through Brooklyn. It's a lot of work to keep a lie going and going. Shit, it's exhausting! It's like a full-time job that requires overtime that you never see in our paychecks. So, one day, I made it easy to get caught. My lies didn't connect. I left too many unaccounted breadcrumbs. There were enough loose ends that yelled, ' 'hey I'm not telling you the truth here!' It was so easy to slip up. Being terrified to face my mother and her wrath, a part of me found peace and some sort of release. The kicker was she wasn't as pissed as I thought she should have been. My mom grounded me for maybe a month, lasting only two weeks. Not having much of a social life anyway, this wasn't the worst punishment. The worst part was she demanded to meet Bruno. "If you ever want to see him again, then you will have invited him to dinner." FUCK!! CRAP!!! NOOO!!!!

This situation brought flashbacks to the time she found out I smoked. She made me stand in front of her and smoke a cigarette, which, now that I think about it, is weird. Was it her way of saying, 'ok, little girl, let's see if you had the balls to do that in front of me?". After finishing what felt like the worst cigarette of my life, my mom permitted me to smoke, and this included inside the house. If I could do it in front of her, I was allowed to do it in the real world. Yeah, I know. My mom's parenting skills are a bit wrapped.

Our apartment was as disgusting as ever. Having my twenty-one-year-old boyfriend see the filth I lived in was not ideal. Included in the filth were roaches we had. If you've seen more than one albino roach in your lifetime, you might have a roach problem. Maybe. Our apartment was as bad as it was a couple of years ago. My parents separated for a year, and my sister temporarily ran to Israel to live in a kibbutz. At age twelve, I learned a few things. Maggots will magically appear in the cat litter box and food dishes if not changed or cleaned after some time. Eventually, I realized how to dissociate myself enough to deal with these situations sufficient to combat the tiny white worms. Dissociation is how I learned and am still learning to survive. However, the apartment has improved slightly since then because my parent's separation didn't take. So I had to clean up maybe a couple of years' worth of grimness before introducing Bruno to my Mom. We were allowed to date under strict guidelines we surpassed months ago when I snuck out with him in the Bronx and had already gone to a motel. We were to have a regular boyfriend–girlfriend relationship from then on. No more cutting school to take the L to the A, and I wasn't allowed to babysit even though I had babysat for months. If I were grounded, dating now had a curfew. Blah, blah, blah.

# Wrong turns (age 16)

So today I'm 'sick' again. But even being 'sick' is boring. I don't feel like traveling into the city to Bruno again. Now that Mom knows about him, those train rides have lost their shininess. There's not much to try to get away with. I have recently discovered Party Lines, one of the few things I can still sneak under the radar. I can kill an hour at least before getting bored and hope something is half-interesting to watch on TV. You call, talk to a bunch of people, pretend to be the coolest shit, hang up, and call again. I've done it a couple of times before—no big deal.

I dial. I hear voices blending into a muddled nothingness. Then, one voice sticks out from the sea of uninteresting words.

"Hey yo! Hello!" a guy's voice says.

"Hey," I say back. It's a harmless interaction through phone wire.

"So, how old are you?" he sounds older. Not my age.

"18" people say I look older, so it's only a technical lie.

"So, was up?" he says.

"Nothing much," I say.

After maybe ten minutes of your typical 'how do you do' conversation. I hung up, got in the shower, and put on a short denim skirt. Somewhere during the introductory talk, I agreed to meet an absolute stranger downstairs in the building lobby. No voice in my head tells me this is not a good idea. And if there is a voice, I attempt to rinse out with the shampoo. It's not like I'm going to meet anyone. I'm just going to walk through the lobby as I am not the person who is about to meet the stranger from the phone. I'll just get my eyes full and just walk past anyone who's there. At least I'll see what he looks like. No harm. It's not like he'll know what I like or what apartment I live in. I'll just walk out of the elevator, glance around, and walk out the front door. He'll probably give up waiting in a few minutes. He might think I lied about which building it is, too.

After the descent of 17 flights down, the elevator door opens. I'm ready to rush through the lobby unnoticed. A voice from a slender, tall man says my name. I stop as though hearing my name spoken aloud forces my feet to freeze in place. He motions to a car. Crap! I give my real name. The owner of the voice inside my head that I thought I'd rinsed off in the shower has already run out of the lobby. Like a deer caught in the headlights, I produce a corny ass smile. Now I've got to go through with the acknowledgment of his existence without coming off like an utterly disinterested bitch.

"Um, hi" Maybe he'll think I'm some retarded girl and make a quick getaway. He's not anything special to look at. He's skinny, and it looks like he doesn't eat much. His eyes seem too big for his head. The left side of his cheek had fine scares that were hard not to notice.

"You wanna go somewhere?" he asks. I'm not prepared for any 'going somewhere' in this scenario. I still have the retarded girl smile, too, but I don't know how to respond. The voice won't come back from outside.

"Just to hang out for a drink," he continued. The fact that I'm underage doesn't faze him. I don't know what to do here or go anywhere but back upstairs. So why do I feel obligated to say yes? Maybe when it comes to guys, I am unable to say no. Perhaps this is why I was the camp slut of the year. I can't deny that someone who sees me notices me, even if it means they will take more than I want to give.

"There's gotta walked place nearby," he says. The only place I had that seemed safe enough was the bar at a Chinese restaurant next to the Pathmark. Why I have determined that this is a safe place is beyond me. It's not like I'll be completely alone. There are always people in the restaurant. There's another bar closer than the one my dad used to take me to when I was younger. There's nothing more pleasant than watching your old man get wasted on Budweiser than go mouth off and challenge strangers who could kill him to fight. Unlike my dad, they had some sense of adult Etiquette not to fight in front of a crying child begging her dad to stop.

"All I know of is a place by the shopping center. It's only a few blocks away, but I can't stay out too long", I answer. I'll just go and get this over with. After pulling out my imaginary fake ID at the bar, we'll get kicked out, and he'll think I'm a big loser and just leave. Great plan. End of story.

"You'll be back in an hour. No big deal".

He motions to a car as we walk out of the building together. I wasn't expecting a car. "Um, you don't have to drive. It's about ten minutes by foot."

"Then it'll only be 2 mins if you get in". My legs are begging me not to walk towards the car. My knees are telling my ass not to sit down. My legs are not listening, and neither is my ass. I got in. I close the door. "You have to tell me where we are going." Ok, at least I'm somewhat in control.

"When you turn out of the driveway. Make a left onto the street. After the second light, make a right into the parking light. It's in the Chinese place on the left of the grocery store", I direct.

Within two minutes of getting in, we get out. The danger is over. This poor choice is almost over. Soon, I will completely embarrass this man for getting kicked out of a bar and leaving forever. He'll probably call me names too, like 'tease' or 'slut' That's nothing new. I can digest the modification and move on. I've been called so many bad names that new ones would heighten my vocabulary skills.

We walked into the dark Chinese restaurant where I had come with my family so many times that it was almost surprising that the manager didn't recognize me. I think I remember him. We go into a red-lit bar with excellent tropical Chinese and Pacific decorations. It dawned on me that I wasn't sure of this man's name. I'm so horrible with names. Well, I'm not going to ask. He'll think I'm complete. But yet again, I don't want to know his name. I don't even like to be here. Only a few minutes and get out of here. I began to wonder if my mom tried to call the house yet. If she finds out that I went out, she'll fuckin kill me. I got to go home.

We got to sit at the bar. The bartender looks at us and asks, "What would you like? What would I like? To get the fuck out of here!". But I don't want to seem rude or lame. I rack my brains on my choice of alcoholic beverages. When I first met Bruno at that fundraiser Halloween party, I couldn't forget about him; there was a raffle. There was a bottle of Malibu Rum, Absolut Vodka, Dewar's White Label Scotch, and Gin. I should know because I was the fifteen-year-old hooker who not just won the booze lute—also, being the fifteen-year-old kid, whose mom let her keep the bottle of top-shelf alcohol in her room. I kept those bottles unopened in my room until my sweet sixteen birthdays. They remained unopened until three of the six friends who showed up puked their brains in the bathtub after the cake. Right after that, my mom thought it was best to give the stuff to my twenty-two-year-old sister.

"Scotch on the rocks" was my poison of choice as I waited for the bartender to request me to produce ID. Instead, the bartender just poured our drinks and walked away. Wow, I do look older!! I enjoyed the taste of scotch. Everything else to me, except cold beer, was disgusting. Scotch is something that tastes warm and cool at the same time. Then, it dawned on me that this plan of ditching this guy was backfiring on me. I wasn't supposed to get the drink. I wasn't supposed to sit with a stranger at a Chinese Restaurant bar.

Halfway through our drinks, he excuses himself and leaves for the men's room. It seems like he's gone for a very long time.

Contemplating running for the door, I regret not being a fast runner. I'm the worst runner ever. What if that pisses him off, and he catches up to me. Or even worse, beat me back home and wait for me there. I sat. I waited. He finally comes back to the bar. He seems strangely wired, almost on edge. I notice there's a little blood on his hand.

"Let's go", he says frantically. He's rushing to get out of here, and I can't blame him for wanting that. Doing this was not one of my best ideas. Maybe he finally realized this, and we can just part ways. Why am I following him to his car? Perhaps the scotch has gotten to my head. Why is there blood? Maybe he cut himself trying to urinate. Is that something that happens in Men's room? I don't bother to ask because I can forget about him when I'm home. Maybe my mom hasn't called. Perhaps this day can be overlooked as just another embarrassing excuse to get out of a day of boredom.

I get in the car and tell him where to turn. We leave the parking lot and down Pennsylvania Ave close to the building. "You can leave me here and drop me at the corner," I say. But he doesn't. He keeps going. Maybe he didn't hear me. If he makes the next left and a U-turn, he can leave me off at the next corner. I told him. He makes the left but no U-turn. Damn, some people can't follow simple directions. Now we have to go around the block. "You're gonna have to make the next two right after this light." He keeps going, and I wonder why he isn't listening to me.

It only takes a few blocks to see that we are no longer in the building or the neighborhood anymore. You can see what resembles half a race track from my seventeenth-floor terrace. Before the cops cracked down, they used to drag races here. We could hear the roar of the engines and the stretch of tires from the terrace, and this was where this stranger I had only met just over an hour ago was driving. There's a tightness around my throat. I feel the goosebumps harden on my skin. I don't know what to do.

Do I hurl yourself out of the moving car? The pavement will hurt. I'd never thought I'd be here, in a car with a stranger. I want to go home. I need to know if my mother has called yet. I'm probably already in trouble. My body freezes as the car stops under an overpass under the highway. I think we are under the Belt Parkway towards the airport. There is nothing else here but a vacant chained-up lot that blocks us from driving further. There's nowhere else to go but back.

Kiss me", he says.

"NO!" I'm saying no. It is a word I seldom use with men, and I'm not just saying it. I'm yelling as though I am walking on fire. Like hell am I kissing him? I'd instead be kissing dirt on the street. He grabs my arms and begins to pull me on top of him. I use every ounce of strength not to straddle him. My legs are like steel iron poles. They do not bend to his will. His grip squeezes my arm like his fingertips are penetrating my skin. I am fighting. My arms are swinging and pushing to get any distance from him. He looks amused. The smirk on his face enrages me even after I made an impact on his jaw. The expression on his face hardly changes. He has managed to have me straddled on top of him. There's a pencil sticking out of the armrest. I grab it, aiming for the point, ready to apply as much force as possible. Before any impact happens, the pencil snaps in half as he takes hold of the other end. Am I next to be snapped into pieces? As I still fought as hard as I could, the driver's side door suddenly opened. He grabs the back of my hair and flings me out onto the dirt. I don't care about the grime. I don't care about blood on my scraped knee. I'm out. The car door slams shut as it begins to move backward. Whatever that was, it's over. It might take me half an hour to walk home, and I have to think of a good reason why I didn't pick up the phone if and when Mom called. It's ok. It's over.

Before my brain tells my feet to move, the car returns and my body freezes as he exits the car. I take steps backward. I don't know what else to do. I walked backward, not turning away, as his long strides quickly caught up to me. He pushes me against the concrete surface of the underpass. With the force of his hand on my neck, he shoves my head against a wall of cement. I make a half-assed attempt to kick him in his crotch. The pressure of fingers around my neck increases as he pushes my legs apart with just one of his knees. My face goes hot as my fingers pull down my underwear, or is it the lack of air going to my lungs? Pieces of my soul break apart and drift off from all existence. My body doesn't know if it should even bother to fight to hold on to my soul as an invasion takes place under my shirt. I would not have noticed the invasion opening me if he had tightened his grip a little trickier and longer. He was breaking me into tiny pieces scattered onto the dirt road. Maybe it will rain soon. A heavy downpour to wash whatever remains away with the surrounding waste.

A sudden rush of dirt air fills my lungs. My body drops like a rag doll onto the ground. The sound of a car stretches away as dust kicks into the air. Behind a chain-linked fence, a dark figure in a guard uniform approach. I didn't notice the small trailer beyond the wall there before. I'm either hysterically crying or just struggling to breathe. Maybe I'm doing both. Perhaps they are the same thing. I get up off the ground. Slowly walking to the fence, the man in his gray suit. It's a uniform. He unlocks an entrance into the fencing and doesn't say a word to me. He barely looks at me. I follow him into the trailer, which looks like a tiny office. He's a security guard. He removes a metal folding chair but doesn't ask me to sit. I sit down anyway.

"Police, I call?" He has a thick African accent. He barely looks at me.

"No, I just want to go home," I answer, barely making the words come out. I can put it all behind me if I can just get home. It never happened. I was never here. The guard leaves me alone. Leave. I should just get up and go. It's probably a thirty-minute walk home. I can do that. Maybe I can make it home before my mom. I can make up some excuse for why I went out. I need cigarettes or something.

A different security guard comes in. He's shorter and fatter than the other guard. He looks right at me and asks in a quiet tone, "Let us call your mom or the police."

I shake my head and find it difficult to look at him. "I just want to go home." Maybe the fact he used the word 'mom' makes me want to run deep inside myself, if not out the door.

The fat guard slowly approaches and kneels on one knee. Though trying to make himself seem less intimidating, he looks at me with his soulful brown eyes that try to tell me, 'It's OK. You're OK. Not louder than a whisper, he says, "Please, let us call your mom or the police." Again, that word 'mom' causes me to tremble and a tear escape. I look into eyes that plead with me. It's as though he is pleading with me just simply to live. A series of numbers emerge from my mouth through my trembling lips. I want to suck them back in, but I can't. Saying numbers just confirms the reality of the situation. No downpour can help me now.

Before long, Mom bursts through the door with my sister and her boyfriend. I don't want to look up. I don't like to see their faces. "Oh my god! Oh my god!' is repeated as mom struggles to catch her breath. Looking at her will only result in acknowledging the reality of the situation. What remains of me sitting on this cold metal chair will break into a million pieces if I don't. More voices follow. The police and EMS are now here. How many bodies can fit inside this trailer office? My sister's boyfriend is a paramedic and acts as if he holds the magic of the 911 system in his hands. I still can hear 'Oh my god' repeated and repeated right next to me, and I still do not look to the source of where it is coming from.

One of the police officers is a female who, like the fat security guard, squats down to one knee. She has her little notepad out.

"What's your name?" she asks. Like I'm on autopilot, I say my name.

"And how old are you?"

"16," I reply, still on autopilot, as though I was programmed with the essential information to give when asked,

"Can you tell us what happened?"

No! Not in front of my mom! Not in front of my sister! Not in front of me! I am not even here. Someone else is sitting here on this cold metal chair. Not me. Not me! NOT ME! Ask them to repeat the events of the last hour. Not me. Not me! NOT ME! Not fucken me! The world around me is not my reality. Why did he loosen his grip? Why didn't he just finish me off? Maybe he did, and this is my death. I'm 16 and dead. I am just a corpse sitting on the cold metal surface. It must be cold because the body sitting on it cannot stop shivering. Not me. Not me! NOT ME! It's not me that these people will know as a full-blown slut. I want to be in a body bag now. Different voices around me say words like "Shock, strangulation marks, hospital, rape kit, injured, Police report."

Recently, maybe a year or so ago, as I wrote and edited these words, I realized that the location where I was raped and nearly strangled to death was in very close proximity to where I met up with George. The shopping center where I opened my legs for someone I barely knew was this overpass. It might not have been the exact spot, but close enough to feel my heart in my throat. It's like when we connect the dots in our lives only that the sequence of dots and lines creates an ugly picture. I cried myself silently to sleep when I saw the bigger picture of myself and some of my unsafe actions. Once done crying, I began the familiar process, detaching from whatever fragments remained floating in the distant oceans of memory. Detachment is my survival skill.

**Pieces After Rape:**

I knew what a rape kit was. I heard about them in school and, of course, from various television crime and medical shows. The kits contain multiple tools and storage for evidence under your nails, hair, and anything inside you, hoping that this collection of physical evidence would lead to some sort of closure from the violent act. Closure does not exist. Closure is a myth. I noticed the facial expressions and body language of all the nurses and doctors attempting to gather as much information as possible when I lied that I was a virgin. Hiding behind the falsehood of childhood innocence separated me from who I was. Camp never happened. Having various family members and older children, exploration of my childhood body never happened. Even Bruno and the sex motel in Brooklyn never happened. Maybe I never happened, either.

Bruno and I broke up a week later. He was angry that I even considered talking to any other man on the phone and agreeing to go to a bar with another man. To him, I was damaged goods, and he wanted a refund. For my family, during this time's sake, I put on a brave face and acted out the stages of recovery. Many recommended that I join a support group and get counseling from a social worker from the hospital. My act of compliance gave everyone, including myself, the illusion that I made a decent rose bush and would be strong and brave and get on with life as usual. I found a support group for teen survivors of 'sexual violence". Saying "I'm a survivor of sexual violence." or "I'm recovering from a sexual trauma." is easier to say of hearing than the word 'raped.' We like our language to be as watered down as possible to swallow its reality. How else can we digest our shame hersh and ugliness?

In the small support group for teen survivors of 'sexual violence' in downtown Brooklyn, I met M. We even went to the same high school. She was a year younger than me, and I probably would never have known if I hadn't met her in this group. While walking in her neighborhood, a man forced her down an alley. He attacked and raped her. She became 'a survivor 'of sexual violence.' M became one of my closest friends in High school. We would refer to each other as twins even though we were a year apart in age and our skin was two different colors. I loved M. She was my purest form of sanity and one of the few who knew what had happened to me.

M and I also began seeing the high school counselor, Mr. Frank Casa, a dead ringer for Father Guido Sarducci from Saturday Night Live. I kid you not. He, too, was part of my sanity. Mr. Casa formed a support group in the school for the teen survivors of 'sexual violence. M and I were not the only ones who carried our nightmare in our back pockets. M and I saw the nuclei of a small cell of violated children. We become each other's lifeline. Mr. Casa, M, and the group probably kept me from leaping off the 17th-floor balcony or slashing my wrists open. I still had nightmares but rarely mentioned them to anyone. I wanted to be the 'recovered' as though it was a race to win and not a road to walk.

I was in drama class performing Beauty and the Beast during this time. I played one of Beauty's bitchy sisters. It didn't take that much effort to capture the typical bitchy teen role and to bring her to life on the high school stage. However, my favorite role in this production was helping to create props. I made a decent rose bush with chicken wire and some tissue paper. Working in creative solitude has always been my happy place. At this time, Bruno and I were very much done, and I started fooling around with one of the kid's friends playing the lead as the beast named Jason. Jason was not very attractive. He had highly messed up teeth. I didn't care because I needed to feel something other than complete detachment. I took advantage of Jason. I emotionally manipulated him to sleep with me. He was a vulnerable soul for me to penetrate and take what I wanted to take.

We were to perform our play for two nights. My family attended the first night, which seemed to go well enough. On the second day, I hung out with Beauty's other bitchy sister and her friends. We got highly stoned about a couple of hours before being on stage. Being stoned before, this particular batch of weed seemed extra potent. I could not remember most of my lines and took to some form of ad-libbing which included using such words as 'asshole' and 'screw it.' While on stage, being mesmerized by all the shiny, bright lights, I could have sworn I saw Bruno standing in the door frame at the back of the auditorium. Then, I gazed at the front rows. Jason was in the second row with a bouquet of roses. No fucken way. There I was, on stage, stoned as fuck, making a complete ass of myself while one guy I broke up with lingered near the exit and another guy who I manipulated his virginity from was ready to give me roses.

When the beast turned into the prince and that curtain fell, I booked it. I wasn't dealing with any of this. Hiding in the dressing rooms of both Jason and what I thought might have been Bruno, I refused to come out. Even after other kids from the play tried looking for me, I refused to emerge into sight. I was no longer there. After a while, when there were no more voices, I left my hiding spot and took the bus home alone. I dealt with the hated stares and wipers the next day in class. From what I gathered from the very few who would talk to me, Jason was devastated by my actions. He went out for dinner with some of our teen cast members and cried through most of the night. I was labeled a slut, a bitch, a whore, and whatever other names by my class after. Jason was my victim. Even though no one caused any violence, there was no violence involved. I caused a tremendous amount of pain to someone who did not deserve it all. I never found out if that was Bruno or not standing in the back of the auditorium that night.

# Pieces of Johnny Weed

Besides most bathrooms, South Shore High School had a few nicks in the hallways where students like me would light up and smoke between periods. There was an exit under a flight of stairs leading to one of the gyms, past the girls' locker room, a popular light-up area. You could spend the entire day hidden in this alcove without anyone checking for bodies. The second popular place for in-between periods was another little nook on the second floor that led to the upper levels of the school auditorium. Of course, there were the bathrooms and locker rooms, but those two places were my top haunts to light up.

By my junior year, all the popular trends of the late 1980s seemed stupid. I couldn't care less if I fit in with the status quo. Everyone looked like they were just copying of each other with their big hair and overuse of make-up. Dressing the way, I wanted to, which was usually all in all black, I might have been goth before goth was goth. I often hung out in the heavy metal or gay creative crowd, depending on who was around then. The more unique someone presented themselves, the people I wanted to be around the most. Categorizing me wasn't easy. Some would call me a druggy hippy one day and a druggy rocker the next. The funny thing about each assessment was, beyond some weekend beer drinking and the rare joint, I barely did drugs. Giving a shit about those with opposing opinions was something I didn't do.

I was one of the students who frequented those smoking areas daily. No matter what cliché you belonged to, if you needed to light up after a surprise quiz, you found yourself in either of these locations. Everyone is welcome to join us for their regular nicotine fix in our alcove. That is where I met Johnny Weed. That wasn't his real name, but that's what people called him for what people assumed were apparent reasons. He was the latest addition to the

Hidden Smokers Club. He recently got kicked out of his Catholic school, so I never noticed him. Johnny radiated a badassness that I found alluring. He was my James Dean in the 11th grade. I couldn't wait for the period bell to ring, so I rushed to one of the smoking spots, hoping Johnny would be there. Sometimes, he wasn't there, and I would be disappointed, or I was so excited when he was. Johnny began to have a weird effect on me. My body would start trembling, and I could not control it around him. I didn't understand why my body felt overwhelmed, shivering in his presence. He even noticed how my hands trembled while lighting up and asked what was wrong with my hand. I didn't have an answer.

I brought the shaking up to Frank Casa, the school counselor. At this point, I felt comfortable disclosing personal information with him, including the uncontrolled shaking when I was around Johnny Weed. Frank, we're one of the few who knew of the trauma of the previous year as well as some of the more colorful dramatics with my family that would cause teenage girls to act the way they acted, sometimes with the opposite sex. There was no softening of blows from Mr. Casa. He was always straightforward with his students, and that's why most of us damaged souls trusted him. Frank bluntly said that my body was reacting to Johnny this way because Johnny was the first boy I was honestly attracted to since the rape. My body just had a difficult time processing this new bit of information.

Writing poetry or lyrics was something I did often back then. I had this uncanny ability to write through another person's skin as though I'd walked in their shoes and could feel what they could feel. My sister once commented that my writing felt like I was writing through her experiences. Maybe I was. Perhaps I could absorb her pain and put it down on paper. Once, I could do this with Johnny by writing a poem that reflected the angst of a seventeen-year-old boy with a severe drinking problem. I gave him the poem When I met him in one of the smoking corners. He read it, and I could see a connection he felt with the words in his eyes and on his face. When Johnny Weed finished reading, he kissed me like he was with me. I caught him in my responsive kiss back.

I remember the first actual date I had with Johnny Weed. After the Bruno shitshow, my mom felt she needed to step up her parenting skills. For me to go on a date with Johnny or probably any boy, they must come to the house first to meet her before being permitted to go anywhere. At this point, I was exhausted from misleading her. I could have easily lied to her that I was going to a girlfriend, which I usually do on weekends. I guess I felt I owed her to finally do things properly after the shit I put everyone through last year. Once again, I scrubbed the house down from its collected grim. Hopefully, Johnny didn't pee after taking at least two buses to get to my apartment. About thirty minutes before Johnny arrived, one of the cats scratched me badly on my upper lip. Mother Fucker!! That was what I fucken needed, a causing bloody lip right before our date.

Luckily, my sister helped to control the bleeding enough that I wasn't an utterly bloody mess when Johnny showed up. There was an obvious gash on my lip that I think he just pretended not to notice, or it wasn't as bad as I felt. We took two buses to the movie theater to see the John Ritter film Deep Skin. However, no more seats were available when we got there, but we could sit on the floor in the back corner for free. Even though this didn't seem ideal, we took the offer anyway and sat in the back corner of the movie theater, laughing our asses off during the glow-in-the-dark condom scene. That's all I remember from the movie was this battle of glow-in-the-dark cocks fighting for domination to win over the leading lady. I ignored the fact that John Ritter's character was an alcoholic. This first date seemed to test us. We could get through bloody gashes and sitting on a sticky movie theater carpet, and maybe we had a shot at having a relationship.

When Johnny Weed cut school, I'd often cut school to be with him when I could pull it off. Cutting class was our version of dating. There were times when I could reach down and touch the inner workings of his soul. While grasping what felt like tangible fragments of Johnny, I wrote and gave him the poem describing what those fragments of himself might look like when I told him beers and drank them behind our school. Most stores never bothered to ID Johnny. Maybe he looked older than seventeen, but back then, alcohol laws lacked much follow-up as they appear to be now. While I nursed one beer, Johnny would put down three, four, five. He was drinking himself silly until he'd puke it all up. He even puked all over himself once. I don't know what to do with a boy I was convinced I was madly in love with, covered in his beer vomit. All those teen romantic comedy movies never fully covered that sort of scenario. Luckily, I had a wad of napkins in my backpack to wipe his face, but that clearly could not clean the entire mess of his clothes. Being with Johnny was a learn-as-you-go moment.

Romance wasn't completely dead. There was a weekend when my parents were going away for a social event or something I couldn't remember. Finally, there is an opportunity to have Johnny over for an entire night. Luckily, the apartment was still slightly clean from the last time when Johnny picked me up on that first date. However, the rest of the house needed massive cleaning, which meant conquering the roach situation fully. Somewhere, I heard that most bugs, including roaches, hate boric acid, which was easy to get from any drugstore then. War was declared on those nasty mother fuckers as every tiny area of that apartment got lined with boric acid. This chemical mother fucken warfare!

The apartment looked civilized once I finished cleaning the shit out of every room. In the afternoon, after my parents had left,

I placed blankets and pillows in front of the television set. I lit a couple of scented, hoping to set a mood. Johnny brought beer and a couple of VHS tapes to watch. One tape was Pink Floyd's The Wall, in which Johnny shared his interpretations of male-female relations from some of the bizarre imagery The Wall had. To be honest, most of Johnny's insightful interpretations went over my head. For a seventeen-year-old wreck loose, he was brilliant. The next movie is called Barfly, starring Mickey Rourke as the alcoholic Henry. Johnny seemed drawn to movies where the male main character lives in an alcoholic downward spiral. Was he trying to tell me something by his movie preferences, or was he wholly drawn to seeing what he just related to? Maybe this was his version of wrapping himself in bright yellow 'warning' tape. We made out, had sex, and passed out in front of the television.

On Saint Patrick's Day of 1989, Johnny and I cut school completely to go into the city to catch the parade. Mike and Darlene, two other kids from school, joined us. By the time we finally got to the City, the parade was just wrapping up, but we were able to catch the tail end of the excitement. We even scored some free green beer. We strolled down Fifth Ave for no more than an hour before heading back. Johnny and I started making out on the fourth train, heading back to Brooklyn. Then Mike and Darlene began to make out even though I knew they weren't dating. Then shit started getting weird. Johnny went to make out with Darlene while Mike tried to make his move and make out with me. I respectfully declined Mike's advances. Ummm, like, what the fuck is happening here. Johnny returned to make out with me again, while Darlene made out with Mike again. Still not making out with Mike, I just stared as Johnny and Darlene rammed each other's tongues down each other's throats. The swap kissing happened on and off throughout the train ride from Manhattan to

Brooklyn. We weren't alone on the train. Several other commuters had a bit of a show.

Things calmed down once we got off the train and onto the bus. We all were going to Darlene's house, but for what? The look on Johnny and Mike's faces hinted at the possible activities involved. Feeling confused and betrayed by what happened on the train, I wasn't up for what I assumed they were all up for. When the three of them got off the bus, I stayed and made whatever excuse required me to bring home. I never knew what happened after they got off the bus. I should have been distraught because my, whom I thought was my boyfriend, just made out with someone else in front of me and went to her house to fuck. Maybe because the entire thing was too insane to get jealous, or I was learning to master how to remove my emotions. I wasn't even upset with Darlene after the fact. Although we were never best friends, we'd hang out occasionally. There was an invisible understanding that we were two damaged girls from the cut from a similar damaged cloth. Darlene got knocked up, convinced her actual boyfriend then that it was his, and they played house. However, Johnny's erratic behavior was a challenge to keep up with. Perhaps trying to be immune to his drinking and crazy behavior, I began to feel numb inside. In our last phone conversation, Johnny was drunk. Maybe that's why I felt little when he told me how much he loved me. Usually, I'd become a fly in a deadly light because someone loved me. Maybe I understood that his affection came out of an unhealthy place or just had nothing inside me to give. I broke up with Johnny Weed without battering out a tear.

**Flash forward to 2017:**

Usually, when I'm at a particular service point at work, I rarely pay too much attention to the names of the people on the screen. For some reason, I noticed the name on the screen as a woman I've seen before. It was the same last name as Johnny. I asked her if she knew a particular John of the same last name. She was Johnny's sister-in-law. Within a few minutes of talking with her, I learned that back-to-back tragedies had filled Johnny's life. In his mid-late twenties, he was in a terrible car accident and suffered severe head trauma. To make matters worse, only a few years back, someone violently mugged John, which only added to the head trauma. Holy Fuck! He currently lives in a nursing home hospital setting. My heart broke for Johnny Weed. His sister-in-law told me where to reach him, so I wrote to him, hoping he'd remember the girl he found long ago smoking her cigarettes.

11/21/18

**Hey John,**

**I'm unsure if you received my last letter. I'm sure I'm writing to an empty void of no one. I just guess I'll write anyway. I'm not used to this concept of writing via snail mail and an electronic world. Even the idea of buying stamps seems foreign.**

**Just in case you forgot from the last letter or didn't receive it, let me recap who I am: 'JRH" from South Shore High School; we briefly dated, and there was an exciting train ride on a 4th July with two other people, I think we met in those hidden corners of South Shore to smoke, I wrote you a poem, and you kissed me.**

**I also have another memory I didn't share in the last letter. I think there was a night you came over, and you wanted to watch this depressing movie called Barfly. Mickey Rourke and Faye Dunaway were in it. The movie was about Hank Chinaski, the fictional alter-ego of "Factotum" author Charles Bukowski, who wanders around Los Angeles, CA, trying to live off jobs that don't interfere with his primary interest, writing. Along the way, he fends off the distractions offered by women, drinking and gambling. It was a very depressing but somewhat thought-provoking film. When I look back, it was a movie**

17-year-old boys would want to watch, but even then, I thought it was autobiographical. I think parts of you relate to the self-destructive struggles of the main character. I guess it's strange to be 17 and incredibly self-aware but unable to know the vocabulary involved. I have a memory of us cutting school, but all we did was hang around the neighborhood, and somehow, we could buy beer. I think it was a 40 oz of Budweiser. (New Budweiser!!- we didn't know better, and Samuel Adams beer was out then) You, put yourself into vomit mode. It didn't' seem to bother you that you vomited all over yourself. I tried to pretend it didn't worry me either. I think I had a napkin or two and wiped your face. Perhaps we were baby barfly lavas buzzing within our environment.

I remember you did have a reputation for being intense. Most of it was just rumors. Kids just like to talk to make their world more extensive and more interesting than it is. One rumor was of you once mashing a kid's guitar during one of the Battle of the Bands. The rumor was that you went on stage and, for no reason anyone knew, smashed someone's guitar I didn't mean long-lost this letter into the most depressing memories of our on-my-phone adolescence. Perhaps the upcoming holidays will bring out all this joy (Enter sarcasm here). Getting together with family is nice, but staying in bed with the cat is nicer. I'm not the most festive person, especially now that my kid is 14 and way past the Santa Conspiracy. And it's not that I don't like my family. I just want my pillow a bit better. We usually have Thanksgiving with my brother-in-law, which brings out all the drama on his side of the family, but the turkey did kick ass. However, that part of our family just recently moved to Tampa. So, this year is a new scene for us as we will be at my nephew's house. His wife seems big into hosting these shining dings.

What are the holidays like for you? Being a Jew born on Christmas and married to a catholic, I pretty much celebrate whatever is going on. My birthday and Christmas used to have a more depressing connection a long time ago when I was dating this guy whose mom passed away on Christmas. Let's just say it was awkward. Also, my mom passed away about 18 years ago on 12/self-aware is getting sad again. Maybe it's because my sinuses are acting up, for it is the season of sinus infections. Both my son and husband are coughing up lungs. My husband has been home three days straight with a cough and a fever. Thank god for Netflix.

Again, I don't know if you're getting these letters if some old nurse is reading them, or if some crazy old Russian lady who thinks she's Betty Davis is reading them. But I will enclose a self-stamped card to get some sign of life from your end. You don't even have to write anything on it. You just have to find a way of getting it into the *__OUTGOING MAIL BOX.__* I believe in you, John!!! I know you can obtain this self-addressed and stamped index card to go out in the mail. I'm not questioning your ability to write or mail stuff, but you might be like me and very attached to your pillow. I want to leave my phone number, but I'm afraid I will miss the call because it's hard to pick up while I'm at work. I don't pick up from numbers I don't recognize, and my husband might take issue with the fact I've reached out and you're reaching back...or maybe not. Don't be discouraged if I don't pick up, but please leave a voicemail and an excellent time to call you back. You don't have to worry about mailing the index card back if you choose to call. However, you may still do both, but only if you feel like it. Please do one. Please, please, please!! It will be great to hear from you.

I might continue to write while I still have stamps left, even if I wait to hear from you.

Be well. Sincerely,

JRH

A few days later, I got a message from this long-lost ghost from the high school halls and hidden corners on my phone. Johnny Weed was living in Ocean View Nursing home. We played a phone tag game, trying to reach each other. I'd attempt to call his unit on the floor he resided on but would only get a nurse telling me he likes to walk around. Then he'd call back, always when I couldn't get to the phone, and kept leaving messages. I would always miss myself when I called back, sometimes by mere seconds. The elevator door would close to bring him wherever he felt he needed to wander to just a second before I'd call. I'd keep writing to him.

12/31/18

Hey John,

We've been like two ships at night trying to get hold of each other by telephone. I missed your call when you called me Friday morning from Brookhaven by a few seconds. I called Brookhaven this morning after you left to go to Wavecrest. And when I called a couple of hours later at Wavecrest, you just stepped out the door to explore the new area. At least you're closer to a few stores now. It looks like we both don't know how to stay still to reach each other. Hopefully, our dumb luck will improve soon, and we can talk briefly. I'm determined to do so even if I must annoy every receptionist and every faculty member you enter. I'll drive to Far Rockaway as soon as you're ready. I must settle for old-fashioned letter writing, envelopes, and stamps. All I can do is hope these words and my thoughts reach you. I promise you my thoughts and warm wishes. I will continue to try to reach out to you. Please do your best to stay safe where you are.

Again, I will enclose a self-addressed and stamped envelope if you wish to write back. If you have never received or lost the first two letters, just let me know, and I can resend them easily. It's sometimes hard to get to my phone when I'm at work, but please leave a message (and talk as much as you want to), and I promise I will try to call you back as soon as possible. And I also promise you I will make it out there to Far Freakin Far as Motherfucker Far Rockaway.

Be well, John. I hope this New Year brings you peace, and also know that someone is thinking of you and wishing you well.

All my best,

JRH

After researching the new facility, a nursing home employee told me he had been moved to Wavecrest Home for Adults, just minutes away. After what felt like weeks, time was finally kind to allow us to be in contact with each other. I don't remember who called who, but I remember the bitter happiness of eventually speaking to Johnny Weed. The boy who once made my body quiver on site who now lived in nursing homes, hospitals, and this group home in Far Rockaway. How does one find fragments of grace in such a tragedy?

Here is my attempt at summarizing Johnny Weed's life. The Navy stationed Johnny Weed in California after he graduated. His time in the Navy did not last long because he fell deeply in love with a woman in California. They lived together for a while until the relationship managed to fail for reasons unknown to me. Around this time, he was writing poetry and attending open poetry readings, and I was doing the same thing on the other side of the country. Johnny had the misfortune of entrusting a friend with his poetry, which this so-called friend ripped him off.

Sometime after that, Johnny moved back to New York to pursue a degree in teaching. During this time, he got into a terrible car accident. The car accident left him in a coma for a reasonable amount of time. When he did regain consciousness, he suffered so much brain damage that he had to learn how to speak, eat, and everything. Once he did recover enough to function in society, he lived alone in an apartment, not doing much of anything. At some point, he was mugged and bashed over the head with a baseball bat. Although the attack was not as severe as the car accident, it added to the already present brain injury. Once again, Johnny had to live under hospital care. During the second struggle to recover from his injuries, his mom passed away. His mom was his only genuine link to his family, who wanted to do anything with him.

I needed to see Johnny Weed in the flesh. I needed to hug him. I needed to apologize for all the cruelty in the world. I need to drive to Far Far Far Rockaway. Finding him in good spirits after everything he'd gone through was a surprise. Maybe all the brain damage didn't allow the expected despair to sink in. Perhaps the grass is slightly greener if you can't process the actual condition of the ground you must stand on.

Wavecrest is a group home that houses similar cases of various mental illnesses and poverty. These poor souls were barely taken care of by the healthcare system. Besides having beds, meals, and access to minimal medical care, they could wander outside as long as they made it back before curfew, unlike the nursing home, which was restrictive in allowing patients to walk out of the facility. Wavecrest allowed their attendance to come and go as long as they returned at some point after dark. Some would wander by the stores asking for handouts, while some would have ongoing conversations with themselves and the air. Like Johnny, these people were abandoned by family and even the system itself. It wasn't surprising that Johnny's daily routine was to head out early in the morning to wander about the beach nearby, drinking cans of cheap beer. Being next to him after so many years, I could see a glimmer of my James Dean underneath years and years of misfortunes.

After visiting him several times, I tried to stay in touch, but it was too depressing to hang out with him. Flashbacks of cutting high school to watch him drink were unavoidable. Watching someone drink the world away before noon wasn't something I wanted to attach myself to. There was not much I could do that could have any realistic impact. We'd try to reach each other on the phone but he'd call at the worst time and never pick up when I attempted to call. I don't know where Johnny Weed is today or if he survived Covid.

# Pieces of Catskills

When I was about eleven, my mom found a small ad in the Daily News advertising a Farm/ranch resort up in the Catskills of NY. Even though it appeared that we didn't have much money growing up, this place seemed affordable for an actual vacation. We didn't have a car, and neither of my parents knew how to drive. My mom and I would travel from Starrett City by bus and train to the Port Authority station to catch a bus that would take us to Golden Acres Farm and Ranch in Gilboa, NY. Traveling by coach bus was something I was already used to. We would hike to Port Authority more than twice a year to visit my Uncle in South NJ. I was one of those kids who never traveled well on these coach buses. Every trip to NJ eventually had my little ass vomiting in the bathroom without fail. The ride to see my uncle was approximately ninety minutes each way. The ride to Gilboa, NY, was roughly six hours. On the ride to Gilboa, NY, I think I threw up at least twice on the ride up. More than halfway through the trip, the bus route left the regular highway to take a more minor road up the mountains. Even though all the twists and turns tortured my stomach, the view from the bus window was spectacular, with endless forests, hills, and even a tiny waterfall.

When we finally got to Gilboa, NY, it felt like I was in the middle of nowhere and I loved it. The tallest building had to be at most three flights. There was a lovely man from the Golden Acres to meet us and drive us a bit further to the farm resort. The beauty of lush trees and undisturbed greenery was so overwhelming that my stomach didn't have a chance to act up during the short twenty-minute ride. In my eleven-year-old eyes, the farm ranch was immense even though the property's size was relatively modest. There was a decent playground in front of the main complex where most of the guests slept. Just past the playground were a dozen goats, sheep, and chickens.

Further down a steep hill were the cows. The stables, horses, and the man made a lake for boat rowing on another side of the complex. Then, there was the side where the outdoor pool and volleyball courts were. There was a smaller in-door pool near the snack bar and the bar across the main complex, and the dining hall and other rooms for guests were adjacent to the playground. I was in paradise.

Golden Acres Farm and Ranch was my childhood oasis. Here, no one knew we were white Brooklynn trash or that I was the 'booger-girl.' Like the clean, fresh air that filled my lungs, I felt new and clean like the clean. I swam in what looked like immaculate water. I rode horses. I fed goats, sheep, and chickens. I had my first kiss on a rainy day. Michael and I were like two peas in a pod that week. On rainy days, Golden Acres was a little boring. Besides the crowded indoor pool, there was a game room, snack bar, and a crafting area, which was also a bit crowded by other guests seeking their money's entertainment. There were very few places that were private on days like that. One was the lobby's second floor, filled with old-looking sofas, books, and board games with pieces missing. The second floor, above the lobby, is where I first kissed before sneezing a lump of snot soon after.

Of course, my favorite thing about the farm was the views of the forest and mountains surrounding me. At the main complex, a porch at the end of the hall offered the most awe-inspiring view of the distant mountains. God knows how I loved being able to see those mountains every summer. Growing up in Brooklyn, the Twin Towers was my only interest. Standing on my terrace or looking outside our apartment window, I stare at those magnificent silver structures. Between myself and those tall towers were often sounding of what I thought as a kid were fireworks but were random gunshots. The sounds between myself in the distant mountains were wind through nearby branches and other innocent random sounds of nature. A sense of stillness centered me from within every time I looked toward those mountains.

We would visit Golden Acres every summer. Usually, the trip would just be my mom and me. Sometimes, my older sister came along too once. As I kept my Brooklyn existence out of Gilboa, NY, my sister brought parts of hers along. She managed to get my mom to buy her alcohol at the bar every night. My dad always stayed behind because someone had to feed the cats. Even though I dreaded the six-hour coach bus and the series of vomiting attached to the journey, I knew that the forest and mountains were waiting on the other end.

One summer, one trip to Golden Acres had a bitter beginning. At this time, we had four cats. Jingles, the oldest, was a tuxedo female we found on Christmas night in Ravenswood. Hence her name. Magic was a black, mischievous male stray with the best personality. It was hard to stay mad at him whenever he knocked over the garbage. My sister found Baby in a bar, a traumatized gray tabby stray who'd been tortured by drunk assholes from the very beginning. I was one of the only ones in the house that Baby went to. Childhood trauma connects us no matter the species. Lastly Sam, a fat ginger tabby someone gave us who stayed high on top of a bookshelf. Before heading out to the Port Authority, I wanted to say goodbye to our fur children. Magic wasn't anywhere. We looked under beds and in closets. Then we heard my mother's scream from the terrace. Looking down the seventeen floors below was Magic's black silhouette on the pavement. Someone must have forgotten to close the terrace door the night before. That someone was my dad, who would often go out for a smoke. I never forgave him for his carelessness. After that, I awoke in tears from nightmares about cats falling from high places.

Like Camp Sussex, Gold Acres Farm, and Ranch, they employ young people worldwide. Some agencies hire young people just over eighteen years of age to work overseas in camps, family resorts, and other establishments. The deal was that after working throughout the summer at whatever assigned location, they would have earned enough money to travel through America for a couple of weeks before returning to their home countries with all warm and fuzzy American memories in their hearts.

At sixteen years old, I got to know the staff of Golden Acres, who were maybe a couple of years older than me. It was fascinating to learn about all the European countries they were from. The staff I hung out with were from England, France, Australia, Ireland, Holland, and New Zealand. There were also people from Spain and China, and probably even more, who didn't have jobs and interacted with the staff because of their English or lack of knowledge. However, later in life, I realized these young European people were probably lovely to me because they relied on tips to spend money. I believe they generally and sincerely like me. In their eyes, I wasn't some white trash kid with luggage of trauma or the camp slut either. I'm still in contact with a handful of these people via social media.

One of the lifeguards from Holland liked me. "A" was glorious to behold, being tall, blonde, fit, and cute. Wanting to find opportunities to hang out when he wasn't on duty was my favorite summer activity the week my mom and I stayed at Golden Acres. "A," and I often played pool, which I discovered I wasn't too bad at. I couldn't break for shit, but I know how to line up a shot to sink in my solids or stripes. The flirting between us was evident to anyone else in the room. Even my mom could see we were into each other. She didn't seem bothered that a six-foot-two poster boy for the Arron race wanted to fuck her sixteen years old Jewish daughter.

The sixteen-year-old Jewish daughter had problems with opening her legs for this Dutch demi-god.

"A," and I only made out during those few days I was at Golden Acres. No matter how much I tried, I could get him to fuck me. "A" excuse for his lack of sexual desire in this spunky sixteen-year-old was because he had claimed there was a girlfriend back home. The fact was he was involved with an older woman in her thirties, which, in truth, trumped my sixteen-year-old ass. We did make out a lot when we were alone. On the night before I was to head back to Brooklyn, I did manage to get some dry humping. This lack of sexual attention didn't stop me from being entirely in love with him. Maybe because this Dutch god was into me enough to find places to hide and fool around, I interrupted as love. In my eyes, he was a sight of pure perfection with his golden blonde curls and ocean-blue eyes. Even after I left the solitude of the mountains, "A" and I stayed in contact. I was even willing to find a job when I got home to pay for a plane ticket to visit him next year in Holland. We would write often and even exchange mixtapes back and forth across overseas. This international teen romance was alive and kicking.

That same summer, my mom scrambled enough to find just enough money for us to go back again to Golden Arches before they shut down for the season. I think she saw how happy and alive I was whenever I was there, supposed to look like the walking dead of Starrett City. She might not have noticed if I wore clean clothes or showered as a kid, but she knew the mountains and this place made me happy. Unfortunately, "A," the lifeguard, had already left that week, which was a bummer but not the end of the world. I still hung around the regular staff, and most of them seemed cool with me as well. They even let me hang out in the bunk house, which is a small, shitting-looking house where they slept and allowed themselves to be themselves instead of always pleasing guests on the resort. They knew I was over being 'pleased' as a paying guest and just wanted to be part of the group. I even got highly stoned with this Australian guy who was also a lifeguard. He had a massive bong. I've puffed on a few joints by then but never a bong. After taking two or three hits from this thing, the weed toasted more than burned bread. The rest of the day, I was filled with paranoia, trying to hide from my mom. I hid from my mother because she'd most definitely have whipped my ass if she knew how fucken stoned I was.

I also didn't want to get the Austrian guy busted, either. I spent most of the time on the side pouch facing the mountains while secretly riding my high. How much I wanted my essence to intertwine with those fucken mountains and the surrounding stillness. They represented the complete opposite of my shitty urban life. They had no judgments. Also, that night, I made out with a cute French dude who worked the dining hall. I don't know or remember how we got to the playground and started making out. Let's just blame that on the weed, and I guess I didn't miss Author that much after all.

Since my mom and I were there the last week before Golden Acres was closing for the season, the last day was everyone's, guests, and staff's previous day on the property. On the second to last day, Roz, one of the Irish girls, another lifeguard, asked if a few of them could crash at our apartment until they got settled to wherever they were going the next day. Even though the house looked like its usual shit show, and my dad probably didn't bother changing the litter box, I was more than happy to have a bunch of strange foreign young adults crash in our apartment. I was even surprised my mom agreed to this. She knew how horrible the apartment looked—about seven of them, including the Australian with the bong squeezing into our apartment. The excitement did not settle my nerves. Whatever image they had about me was shattered as soon as they walked through our apartment door. They would see why I spend each summer trying to escape my embarrassment and disdain for our neighborhood. Allowing my place of escape to overlap with my crappy reality made the long seven-hour bus ride back to New York City not long enough. I also tried to warn our future European house guests that we lived deep in Brooklyn. We have to take two trains from Port Authority and a bus two. There was no hop, skip, or jump on this trip. The reality of this sheep didn't kick in until we were on the second train. Roz, the Irish girl who thought this was the best idea ever, quickly changed her mind halfway on the train ride into Brooklyn once her asthma kicked in. Not only did she have horrible asthma, but her backpack looked more extensive than she was. They were too exhausted to see our disgusting apartment when they finally got to our apartment. However, they were indeed eager to leave the following day.

# Pieces of MT:

I returned to Golden Acres the following summer and landed a full-time job as a camp counselor. They offered a small day camp to occupy children so adults could have time to do adult stuff. I was a counselor for the five to seven-year-old group, and a few other counselors, two other girls, and two boys from the Netherlands. The property owners and our boss believed the Dutch had the best skill set for entertaining small children. Not only was I the youngest of the counselors, but I also proved quickly that I could take charge. My semi-leadership role was clear because I was the only one who fully understood English. The two Dutch girls were fantastic, allowing the reins, but the Dutch boys were less appreciated. It wasn't because the Dutch counselors' English wasn't terrible. Most of the guests were New Yorkers, and I ultimately knew how to speak New Yorker. Most of the counselors were terrific at their jobs. My Arrogant American attitude didn't allow me to appreciate them as they truly deserved.

For these kids who traveled from across the pond, hills, or other vast bodies of land formations, working for Golden Acres wasn't as ideal as it seemed. The allure of travel was a manipulation to obtain cheap labor by various summer resorts and camps. Yes, Camp America covered their travel and living expenses. However, the owners of the property, the bosses, collected their return plane tickets, which the owners would return to the staff at the summer's end. Our living quarters, the bunk house, was a place I thought was so cool as a kid. The Bunk House was merely a shack with two Mobile homes-like features on each end for sleeping. The rooms were tiny, with just enough space for two bunk beds for four people. One side housed the girls, and the other contained the boys living quarters.

There were a few rooms in the center of the main shack. The center area was where my room was. The room was slightly more significant than the rooms on the side additions of the shack. My other three roommates were the two other camp counselors from Holland and another girl from Spain assigned to house cleaning. We all got along very well. I did feel bad for one of the Dutch girls who slept on the top bunk above. She was deathly afraid of spiders, and the occasional spider or two or teen would always camp out on our ceiling. It was a team effort to relocate them to the outside. Still, sometimes, we would often hear her scream "Spider" in her Dutch in the middle of the night. I didn't feel too bad because I never offered to swap out bunks. I wasn't dealing with any fucken spiders.

That summer, being my second summer on my own, I swore not to repeat my mistakes from three years ago in Camp Sussex. Being determined to keep my pants on as much as I could, which wasn't always that easy, was my summer goal. To be honest, this place would work us so hard that I was too tired to invent any bullshit, and so was everyone else. Plus, the same Irish girl from last year, who slept over at my house, was there again. Knowing she knew my mother, not like they were in any contact or anything, kept me in check. She was like my big sister with a severe drinking problem. However, the bar in the lounge never stopped the underage drinking that the owners disregarded. My eighteen-year-old ass ran my very own bar tap just like every other underage worker there. I would usually order a rum and coke or, if I was feeling extra fancy, sex on the beach. Our tabs would come out of our paychecks each week, which was a blessing and curse to some, considering the size of the weekly tabs.

Everyone tends to couple up like any other camp or summer location where they hire young adults to work. So instead of becoming the summer slut, I looked to couple with someone as well. When in Rome, right? MT was from the UK and was a year older than me. The Ranch hired Matt as a wrangler to work with the horses. Even though he had limited experience working with animals besides household cats, he cared for the horse well. The other wrangler didn't mind his limited horse experience because someone had to clean up all the horse shit. People would say we both looked like siblings, and maybe it was a narcissistic attraction that caused me to be the enormous pain in his ass. He clearly stated that he didn't want the trouble of a girlfriend, but I wanted to be part of the coupled club.

I wore this English boy's ass down. It was like he could go anywhere and hide. We became a cute couple. We were one of the many items on the property that shared beds. Being on a bottom bunk has many perks. One is that you can create an illusion of privacy by just tucking up a couple of sheets from the upper bunk mattress. Most rooms have the lower bunks covered by sheets—anything to have a slight sense of space. MT always slept in my twin bed bunk. Since we were both super skinny, it wasn't too much of a tight fit. Of course, I never asked if my roommates were okay with having a boy sleep in our shared room.

We were in love. We even had a theatrical mock wedding in the bunkhouse with a charming guy from China who worked in the kitchen as our Buddhist priest. The Irish girl who stayed over my house last year acted as my mom. This Australian guy, who she hooked up with, acted as my dad, who gave me away. It was fucken hilarious. My semi-fake summer family seemed much more functional than my family in Brooklyn. Even the slave driver owners of the property came to witness the hilarious nuptials. That night was the first night Matthew and I had sex, too. It was his first, and at least he could say he waited to get married. It was a mix of the Cure and Greek toga theme.

Even though MT wasn't my first sexual experience, I was his. He was the emotionally healthiest person I was ever with as a teen. Having enough in common to find a pure connection, we were willing to learn from each other's experiences to understand where we were coming from. It was nice to know someone who cared about me and wasn't in this relationship just to get laid. We were indeed the poster children for young summer love. These were the experiences that all those teen romance books are talking about. Except there was one hitch, one big fucken hiccup to our great romance. As soon as summer was over, MT eventually had to go back to England.

I refuse to have that reality devastate me. I was planning to visit "A" in the Netherlands even though it was short for "A who?" Having already purchased my plane ticket from the money I saved from working before the summer, the UK and the Netherlands were only a ferry away. I could make that happen. I could keep this superb torch lit. The romance doesn't have to die. I planned to stay with "A" for no more than a few days anyway. What difference was it if I went to the airport back to the States or a ferry to the United Kingdom? Yeah, Author and I stayed in touch a bit, but no one mentioned we were hooking up at any point. As far as I knew, Author was still keeping his dick for that older woman he was seeing back in his neck of the world. I didn't owe him anything.

I could stay overseas forever. Maybe I didn't have to live in my shitty apartment with my dysfunctional parents any longer. Perhaps I could put the memories of Starrett City behind me by hopping on a plane and never looking back. Although my mom seemed okay with her eighteen-year-old daughter traveling alone to the other side of the world, the idea of never coming home didn't settle well with her. Unfortunately, I could not care about anyone's happiness but myself. Leaving home and Brooklyn itself was for my survival.

One thing I didn't consider was immigration laws, and the United Kingdom had some tough ones. The only visa I could obtain was a six-month tourist visa, which wasn't enough time, but I took what I could get. I was hoping for the Happy Ever After Visa. That six-month visa gave my mother some hope that I'd have to return home. I planned to get MT to marry me so I'd obtain UK citizenship. They did not remember that I was eighteen and he was nineteen. MT was still living with his parents, meaning I would be living with his parents. Never considering what anyone else truly wanted, no one bothered to ask if they would mind a strange American girl living in their house. I'm sure that MT's parents jumped for joy when told, not asked, but said that an American girl they never meant would be living with them. Holy fuck, who did I think I was anyway to disturb another family's life because I didn't want to be part of mine anymore.

My heart broke into tiny pieces along the Belt Parkway the day my father took us to JFK. By then, Dad had embraced sobriety and respected most public urination laws. Even though I knew I'd see Matthew in about a month, saying goodbye to one true love is like repeatedly forcing a blunt ice pick through one's chest cavity. It felt that fucken bad. Oh, the tournaments of young, long-distance love. Sometimes, I wonder if the technology we have available now was available then, if I'd still feel devastated watching MT pass through the International Airport gates. Would the advancement of video conferencing lighten the blow?

Before falling head over heels for MT, the original summer plan was supposed to be to travel with the "A," who was working in different parts of the country through Camp America, and his best friend, whose name I can't even try to remember. He and his friend would stay with us for a day or two before we'd travel to the Netherlands together. "A" was a bit confused about the nature of our relationship. While I thought of him as a friend who I might have fallen in love with and would have been happy to fuck a year ago, I guess he still believed this was still the case. Maybe if I had been more transparent on my intentions of running away to England with a boy I just meant this summer, those few days with Author wouldn't have been so awkward.

While desperately missing MT and counting down the days we would be reunited, I didn't do the best job of maintaining boundaries with this Dutch boy now in my house. Having Author's friend around was a well-needed third wheel and a necessary buffer. Apparently, "A"'s so-called best friend didn't think too highly of "A." I got the impression that their bromance was a one-way street in "A"'s mind, and his so-called best friend was at the point of breaking up this illusion relationship. The way this so-called best friend spoke about Author gave me the impression that "A" was some sort of town idiot that no one actually liked but just put up with. "A" was oblivious to this information. However, being aware of this new information made me super grateful that my Holland stay would be brief.

Doing my best to maintain boundaries was not good enough once I had sex with Author on my parent's bed. Yeah, I know; what the fuck is wrong with me. All I remember is him being persistent about it and me agreeing to get it over with just to shut him up. I don't know if this was a pity fuck or if there is just something implanted in my brain where the 'no' switch is just stuck. My memory of that moment is very foggy. I remember being with him in my parent's bedroom. I remember both being on my parent's bed. I remember having him on top of me. I recall my body not cooperating and not granting him access to enter me. I think I remember his tip, barely scraping the surface of my entryway. I remember him ejaculating quickly even though the tip of his penis was hardly inside me. I remember him commenting on how beautiful making love was while I remember being relieved that it was over with. I also remember agreeing with his so-called best friend that "A" was an absolute fucken idiot. Strangely, the blinders can come off, and you see a person in a new light.

"A" also had a bit of change in our upcoming travel plans. "A"'s parents were divorced. Initially, we were to stay at his house, where he lived with his mother and young brother. However, his mom would be out of town when we were to land in the Netherlands. I don't remember where his younger brother was. "A" had no access to his own house. Now, you'd think that a parent who hadn't seen her kid for an entire summer wouldn't be out of town the same week her child returned home. At least she could have left the key to the front door with a neighbor. Maybe, just like Author's 'so-called best friend,' she didn't care for his company either. Instead, we were to stay with his father and stepmother until I embarked on the UK to be with my true love. "A" 's dad met us at the airport. Although a bit stiff in personality, he seemed like a nice enough person. A little bit late in the game, Author warned me that his stepmother was a bit of bitch.

How bad could this lady be? Europeans were supposed to be nicer than Americans in general. So maybe his version of "bitch" just meant she just wasn't the warmest and fuzziest. I didn't need his stepmom to bake cookies or tuck me in at night. Long and behold, this woman was an absolute fucken bitch. This woman, who I never met before, who knew shit about me, would talk and complain about me in Dutch. Even though I didn't speak one Dutch word, I knew by her tone, facial expressions, and pointing at me that she was talking trash about me with no concern at all if I understood or not. I hated every minute of being in that house. At night, instead of wandering through the house looking for the bathroom in the middle of it, I peed on some of her house plants.

I was to take a ferry from Holland to Dover, England. "A" and his father drove me to the ferry that would bring me to MT and my new life. "A" was pissed at me, and I honestly couldn't give a rat's ass what he thought. My life is about to begin as a step on the vessel that, in seven hours, life would restart itself. This ferry isn't like the Staten Island Ferry, but it's no Norwegian Cruise Line. There were maybe three or four flights with seating areas with chairs that looked like beaten-up coach bus chairs. There's a movie theater and places to eat. No assigned seats exist, so people can move about wherever they want. I'd mostly find a quiet corner on the floor to crash. The ride to Dover was exhausting, with the seven hours feeling like seventeen. The love of my life awaited me on the other side of this body of water. Every hour of the seven hours on this vessel is so worth it.

At around 10 pm, as the ferry was about to dock at Dover, passengers began to gather their luggage and other personal belongings. The readiness to start a new life, to be in a completely different country and away from shitty Brooklyn, helps me to summon enough strength to lift my heavy pack back and strap it onto my body. It was the most oversized backpack I could find in any store. I could stuff as much as possible. It was also heavy as fuck. Ignoring the weight now attached to my back, I waited for the docking procedure to end and for those doors to open. It takes a while to completely dock before they open the doors to my new life. My back is close to giving out while I'm fighting for air with this thing attached to my body. I refuse to take off until I'm out of the ferry. Jesus Christ, I hoped there were those luggage trolley things on the other side of those doors because I think I'm dying under the weight of the remnants of my life that I jammed in this heavy-ass backpack. What the fuck was I thinking?

Once they finally open the fucken doors and the first thing I see is a few luggage trolleys. With the last of my breath, I hurled my body in their direction and hurl this fucken backpack off my body. Holy fuck, air. Managing to catch my breath, I wheel my luggage trolley with my overstuffed backpack to immigration, my new home, and my new life. I did it. I escaped fucken Brooklyn, Starteet City, my shitty roach-infested apartment, and my past existence. I'm finally in the UK and will finally be in MT arms. Once It's my turn to be greeted by the person behind the immigration counter, he doesn't rush to stamp my passport with the stamp of the Queen's approval.

I had difficulties entering the UK because I didn't have a return ticket. I have nothing to prove that I have no intention to stay because I have every intention to stay. I'm just not going to tell this immigration agent that. I should have brought the return ticket I originally had for my arrival in the States from Holland in five days. Those plans changed. I didn't get it. I should have got it. If I brought the return ticket with me, even if I changed since I originally bought the tickets, I'd probably have a stamped passport within minutes. However, not being the brightest eighteen-year-old running away from home, this immigration officer is blocking my way to true love. I'm trying to explain that I'm staying with my boyfriend and will be living with him. Then the immigration officer asks if my boyfriend is waiting for me and I answer "yes"! So, while all the passengers from the ferry have left for their journeys, I'm being held up by immigration. I'm panicking.

What if they call the CIA and ship me back, and then my mother could say, "I told you so." Then I see him, MT, my literal knight in shiny armor. After we hugged as though our lives depended on physical contact, the immigration officer asked him if he claimed complete responsibility for me so that my existence would not burden the great people of the UK and the crown. Of course, MT agrees to take full responsibility as though he just adopted a new kitten from a shelter. There are no papers to sign or documents to fill out as my passport gets its six-month visitor visa. Hello UK! I'm home.

MT is with his friend Neil, who drove MT from Exeter to Dover, a three-hour drive. Neil seemed happy for his friend, who obviously will be getting laid often now but is also exhausted by the drive. MT and I sit back in the car, holding each other as Neil drives us to my new home in my new city, country, and life. Sitting in the car next to Matthew brings warmth to my body. It's about 2 am when we finally get to MT's house. MT lived with his parents, grandmother, and an evil, mentally deranged cat named Inky. Home sweet home, but everyone is sound asleep when we get there. Our new room is part of the attic they recently redid for his father as a man cave art room with its bathroom. Unfortunately, my immature selfishness and the desperate need to hold onto MT robbed his dad of this lovely sanctuary. I don't care about that. Our clothes fall onto the floor. We make love on a twin mattress on the floor. Being both extremely rail thin, it's big enough for us. To feel his warm, naked body next to mine is nothing short of peaceful. I am finally safe. I am finally home. I'm finally here. I'm finally with MT. Nothing else matters, and I slowly learn, with much resistance, that other things matter.

The next day, I finally met MT's parents and grandmother. I just invaded and claimed their home as mine with absolutely no consideration for how they might feel about having this strange American girl in their home. Also, their youngest child, although nineteen at the time, will be engaging in various sexual activities with such a peculiar American girl. His dad, an older gray-haired version of MT, is a driving instructor and runs his private one-man show business teaching. The man is also a talented artist who works with watercolors. A couple of hanging pieces of his work were landscapes on the seaside walls. His mother, maybe five years younger than his dad, works in an Art store. She tries to look happy to see me and welcomes me, but she's not thrilled by the American takeover of her son's life and her home. They would have preferred MT somewhere in the University than playing fake house with me. Then there's Nan, MT's grandmother, who has this tiny, wrinkled-up perfect image of what a grandmother should look like. She's adorable. She seems like god knitted a sweater, had some extra yarn, knitted her, and then gave her the shirt he originally knitted. There's no other way to describe MT's grandmother.

Exeter isn't a massive city at all. The beautiful cathedral in its center is the only thing that allows it to qualify as a city. This small city has a mix of ancient Roman ruins and historical structures mixed with modern structures. Outside the city's heart are suburban rows of houses running up and down its many hills. MT's family's suburban semi-attached house is about a thirty-minute walk to the center of Exeter. There is a bus system with small mini-buses on various routes that go in and out from the city center to the outskirts of the hills. Exeter also has a college and a huge University. There is a young adult population of eighteen to mid-twenties mixed with the general population of families and retirees. The steep hills surrounding the city sometimes make walking challenging for those not fit enough to walk the steep inclines. It may not be a vacation hotspot, but this is my home. Matthew's house and the surrounding area are homes of similar design on these hills. Walking five to ten minutes opposite the city center, you'll see sheep. A mountain and a glorious countryside of hills and farmland surround the outside rim of the city. Sometimes, the soil underneath the mountain is exposed. The soil is red. The red soil is because Devon, this region of the UK, coloration is due to iron chemicals only found in deserts. Due to some chemical reactions to oxygen, the overlying desert rocks passed down into the Devonian rocks beneath, staining them red.

MT's parents do their best to try to be gracious hosts, but as any parent should be, they are concerned with his current life choices. I'm not being his best one. Matthew is not working or going to University. All he seems to be doing is entertaining his American girlfriend. Although it wasn't much, I gave his parents money to help pay for the extra food I would consume. All they feel and see is their youngest child throwing his life away. MT's life choices were not their proudest parenting moment, and it's easy to point some of the blame on me. They might have been terrified that I would never leave and return home. Reflecting on them, they were highly patient but not completely tolerant of this bullshit of two barely adults making crappy life choices.

Eventually, MT got a job working in a pub kitchen at night. As an American with a six-month tourist visa, I could not work in the UK. I didn't have any marketable skills to offer the United Kingdom. However, I needed to find something somewhat productive besides hanging out with my boyfriend 24/7 when he wasn't working. Someone, maybe it's Matt's dad, suggested I look into volunteering. I wasn't supposed to volunteer on this six-month tourist visa, but who will report on an American girl volunteering to help the local English society? It wasn't hard to find a place where I could volunteer. I became one of many volunteers for a Cancer Association thrift shop. These types of charity thrift stores were prevalent.

These stores were run mainly by little old ladies and retirees who, like me, just wanted something to do. I worked as an assistant with a woman named Margo Wilson. Margo was a robust and feisty soul in her mid-seventies. Most women who worked there were between fifty and eighty years old. However, this is a bit of a ballpark guess on my part. The way our shop operated was that someone would sort through all the bags and boxes of donations and weed them. Our job was to inspect all the donated men's clothes and price them. I knew nothing about men's clothes or British fashion as an American teenage girl. Margo made it her mission to educate me on men's secondhand fashions. I learned which items and fashion labels to price high or low and which we could not sell.

As the only person under sixty-five working in the store, it didn't stop me from enjoying afternoon tea and listening to all these senior ladies' stories. Boy, did these ladies have stories of family, previous romantic relationships, and anything under a PG-13 rating. In Margo's earlier life, she was a nanny for a family for many years. She seldom would mention all the fun she would have with a gentleman friend. Although she never really described anything too romantic, it was clear that she, too, had a love of her life. Margo never married or had children of her own. Then there was Elli, who was a tiny ancient thing. She often mentioned a different man's name in each story she shared. Again, like Margo, Elli's stories were lightly romantic but not even close to being graphic. It was easy to love these old souls.

Although I was not making a cent working in the store, they gave me super cheap discounts on items I liked, like floral dresses. We're talking about two or three pounds for a dress, which would cost five dollars. My favorite item I bought for five pounds was an old black and white television set. If I wanted to watch TV, I'd typically share my television watching with Matt's parents. Watching TV was extremely uncomfortable and awkward when MT was working in the pub those nights. Those nights, I fought off the guilt of invading these people's space. However, looking back at it now, I don't know why I didn't just stick my head in books in the privacy of my room. Now, with this second-hand TV set, I can enjoy what I want to watch on Britain's four channels in the privacy of our room. There were BBC-1, BBC-2, and then two lesser channels, which worked out because this set only has four buttons for those stations. The thrift store ladies even allowed me to decorate the display window a few times. I did a couple of wedding displays in my creative heaven because someone donated a wedding dress and a couple of bride's maid's dresses. Without a doubt, I loved working there and being part of these warm-hearted older women's conversations.

Matt's cat, Inky, was not just evil but fucken deranged. Being a black cat comes with various demonic stereotypes, which are, of course, stupid and unfounded. However, this cat was a fucken four-legged psychopath who had access to the outside world. Now and then, Inky would go on a hunt into her mode when she was inside. You could tell when she was about to attack and in pre-pounce mode how her tail was flapping back and forth as well as her body posture. She had a habit of attacking legs and feet for no reason but just to shed blood. When I say attack, I mean literally out for a pound of flesh with her nails and teeth punctuating through the skin. If she weren't hunting passing limbs for sport, she would go into her rare cuddle mode, which meant pretending to nurse on sweaters and only sweaters. The cat was fucken nuts. She was regularly permitted to go outside, where she would torture every living thing that crossed her path, including other cats. I felt for every friendly cat that would follow me too close to the house if Inky were outside. She would kick their poor fluffy asses. If you didn't see the onslaught of the poor neighborhood cat, you most definitely heard it.

During my six months living with MT and his family, I had to call home at least once a week. The phone calls home were something nonnegotiable with my mom. Sometimes, not all the time, but occasionally, these phone calls would be guilt-ridden on her part. Not seeing my newly born nephew was one item on the list that made me feel guilty about it. At the tender age of only a few months, I doubted if this kid even cared if I existed. There was a series of phone calls with my mom that was nothing short of full of drama. It had to do with MT's mother. My mom told me that she got a letter from MT's mother complaining that I was being a burden and that I needed to go home for the love of God. She was shocked and completely disbelieving when she heard that MT's mom would write such a letter. She completely denied ever writing such letters when I soon confronted her. So, this meant my mother was lying. I would not put it past my mother to lie and emotionally manipulate everyone to have her baby daughter back in her arms. It was not going to work.

Eventually, my six-month visa was about to expire. At least my mom had UK immigration laws working for her. If I stay past the expiration date, I won't be able to return to the UK if I ever leave to visit home. Also, to my disappointment, MT didn't want to marry me. Getting married wouldn't have helped my immigration status anyway. Unlike the United States, a marriage certificate didn't hold as much water in the UK. My escape plan was unraveling, and being powerless to change immigration laws, I had to return home. The return home was only temporary as my funds were dramatically depleting. The need to earn some money quickly was my top priority. Even though I was determined to stay in the States only briefly, the fear of the possibility of never returning to MT was beyond devastating. I was returning, but MT and I would find a cheap apartment this time. The next time would be much better. Matt's dad and MT drove me to the airport, where we had a tearful goodbye.

There was no question or doubt that I was not happy to return home, much less to Starret City. The first thing that struck me as soon as I walked through my childhood front door was the apartment's intense smell of cat urine, which is why I left in the first place. My top priority was to find a job. That was easy. A brand-new Men's store was opening at the King Plaza mall. It was a trendy men's clothes store. I knew nothing about men's or anything trendy. However, adding working in a men's department for a thrift shop across the pond to the job application helped. It was a brand-new store called CODA, and most of the clothes they sold were, in my opinion, cheap, cheesy, and just horrible. The store was like a 90s fashion vomit for men. I was working as many hours as I pretended to care about cheap-looking suits made from rayon.

The store managers knew I was faking my enthusiasm but didn't care too much because I always showed up on time and was always happy to clean the staff bathrooms when needed. Getting back to Matthew in the United Kingdom was my inspiration to deal with working in sales. My natural talent was approaching and selling the most thuggy of costumes for those who needed to spend their drug money. Most of the staff, primarily skinny white boys, felt intimidated by these customers. These members had to issue a few G's on a hideous black leather jumpsuit. Therefore, I was usually resented by most of the staff because sometimes I made the highest commissions. Fuck them.

Most of my free time was outside the house; I would try to stay with my sister and her new little family or at a friend's Susan's home as much as possible. One day, my friend Susan had an extra ticket for a Metallica concert. This guy she was seeing on the side bought the Metallica concert tickets. Initially, she was going to take her best friend, Kathy. However, Kathy was not into heavy metal, so I went instead. Susan's romantic relationships were a bit complicated around this time. During this time, she was still with her boyfriend from high school but also saw this other guy, the guy who bought the tickets. What was super weird about these relationships with both guys was that boys would be at her house at separate times. Susan was still living with her parents and older brother. So, her family had to take notice of the revolving door of two boyfriends. These relationships were just the beginning of Susan's history of romantic revolving doors.

We had decent seats at the Metallica concert. Although I am not the biggest Metallica fan, I knew a handful of their songs were able to enjoy myself. However, when I looked towards my far right, I noticed Susan's man-friend would be staring at me.' Like, what the fuck, dude.' It was one of those stares that someone with another should not be doing. To this day, I am highly allergic to drama or into boyfriend stealing, so I kept my return stares to a bare minimum. As emotionally dysfunctional as I might have been back then, that was one line I would not cross. Plus, I was still with MT, who was a million miles away. That night, we all slept over at Susan's house when we returned late from the concert. Again, I thought it fucken bizarre that Susan felt it was perfectly ok to have her man friend sleep over when I knew her other boyfriend would sleep over too, and her parents were ok with this. I found this man's friend particularly annoying. We are all outside the front steps. Susan was sitting on the front steps, making her usual thoughtful poutine face while her male friend repeatedly nudged her with his knee. He was trying to get her attention while she was attempting to ignore him. My inner voice screamed, "dude fuck off already! She's ignoring your sorry ass for a reason!" That morning, her man-friend insisted that he walk me to the bus stop, which I also found bizarre. I've stood at that bus many times at different times of the day and never once felt I needed an escort. Years later, I found out that Susan banished me from her home and her life for trying to steal her man-friend. I did not find out about this banishing until over twelve years later when I reunited with a so-called man-friend, whom I eventually married. It either never dawned on me, or maybe I had little concern for not hearing from a close friend after that day. I was too focused on returning to England to pay attention to Susan's drama anyway.

You really should not purchase a one-way ticket upon entering any country. It is a lesson my now nineteen-year-old didn't learn from my eighteen-year-old self. Plus, having information about the college in Exeter with classes marked off was another red flag for immigration not to let one inside their boundaries. I don't blame the immigration officer at Heathrow Airport for doubting my intentions of just visiting with all the evidence in my luggage, suggesting I had no plans to return home. Once again, they had to locate Matthew at the airport to claim full responsibility for me and provide all his information just in case I wandered off into the country. Is trying to get into heaven this stressful? It's not like I'm ever going to heaven.

During this stay in England, MT found us our apartments, or 'flats' as they call them in the UK. There was no longer a concern about burdening his parents, and his mother wouldn't have to deny writing complaint letters to my mom. While I was back in the States, I found the letter his mom supposedly never wrote. MT and I had our place now with our rent and bills. His mom insisted that we come over, especially over the weekends, and insisted we bring our laundry. Maybe she felt guilty about writing and lying about those letters. I never brought the letters up to Matthew or her. At this point, it no longer mattered. We finally had our own space away from her and the psychopath cat.

Our Flat, located within the city of Exeter, was one decent-sized room with a tiny kitchen area in a corner. The flat was with an old, musty couch, dressers, and a nice bed. However, there was no bathroom in the flat. We had to share two bathrooms with at least five other tenants. The landlady was the only person with their bathroom. However, sharing a bathroom or two was considered normal in most of the flats on our block. These buildings were initially huge houses that eventually, with time, were created as apartment buildings. Since Exter had a college and university, most tenants were students and old retirees.

Living within city limits made traveling to stores very convenient, and I returned to the volunteer thrift, where I returned to volunteer. MT still worked as an assistant cook at the same pub, but he now had a much longer commute than when we lived with his parents. Although it was far from any dream job he might have wanted, MT enjoyed learning how to chop and prepare food. I was happy to reunite with the old lady at the thrift store. They were my surrogate grandmothers now. However, I'd often be alone in the apartment because I worked during the day and MT at night. Once in a while, I'd go to the movies by myself, but otherwise, I was very bored and even very lonely. I knew no one besides MT, his family, and the surrogate grandmothers. Most of Matthew's friends went off to University. MT didn't have too many friends left in the area anymore. Sometimes, a friend or two would visit from university, and we would hang out with them. I don't remember any of their names, but I do remember not liking one of them at all. One of MT's friends was extraordinarily arrogant and even a bit snotty. He would love to take jabs at me because I was American. Apparently, in his mind, all Americans were alike. I thought he was a fucken asshole, but his family did have loads of cats. Whenever we'd go to his house, I would socialize with the cats instead of the people. Finding a family pet to socialize with is something I still do when I'm somewhere I don't feel comfortable.

After two months, on my second UK visit, we moved to a new Flat outside the city. The new apartment was cheaper and slightly smaller, but we had our bathroom. However, I was still incredibly bored at night when Matthew was at work. All I had for entertainment was that small black and white TV from the thrift shop. I wished I was into reading, drawing, or anything besides a constant emptiness. Reflecting on my experiences with Matthew, I often wonder how things would be different if we had today's technology. My trip across the ocean probably would have still happened because all the technology wouldn't have erased everything I was trying to escape at the time, or would it? The boredom and the feeling of complete isolation might not have been as bad when Matthew was at work at night. I know I would have been on the computer all night and connected with my handful of friends back in the state. Well, probably not Susan because she would have blocked me as her form of banishing from attempting to steal her man friend. Well, fuck her.

My second tourist visa finally began to expire. It was time to go again. MT and I agreed that spending part of his life with me was time. Strangely, MT was issued a three-month visa to come to the United States. Living in our disgusting Brooklyn apartment would not be an issue. My family was set with plans to move to Staten Island upon my return. My sister became a new mom and moved to Staten Island a year ago. My mom would not allow the distance from Starrett City to Staten Island to rob her of being an available grandmother. There would be a new beginning for me after all.

If I had packed my life in an oversized pack back going to England, I would have left England with three times as much luggage. One piece of luggage I brought back was an old suitcase that Margo Wilson gave me. Margo was one of the old ladies from the thrift shop with whom I became the closest. She took me under her wing from day one and always looked after me as much as possible. Her name is on this suitcase, which has lived in my closet for eternity. Margo and the other old ladies from the thrift shop are long gone. They were all fantastic, and I have this particular piece of luggage to remind me that they were part of my life. Immigration or customs never bothered me when I returned to the States, even though I probably looked like a sight with so much luggage for one now twenty-year-old adult.

# Pieces of College

When I returned home, my family was ready to move to Staten Island in 1991. My mother wanted to be near my sister and, of course, her new grandchild. We lived in an apartment building across the street from Silver Lake Park. Our new home was a far cry from the shithole in Brooklyn. Everything around was new to me, and we had a clean slate, meaning the apartment was clean. No one knew us as the white trash Jewish family on the seventeenth floor. Unfortunately, we still had to contend with the fucken roaches, but that situation seemed a little more controllable. The intense urge to escape wasn't as present as when I tried to escape Brooklyn. Staten Island seemed like an oasis when we first moved. The feeling of being boxed and living on top and under so many people was gone. I loved living across from a park where I would paint when the weather was nice.

As mentioned, Matthew agreed that he would make his way to stay with me in the States once he saved up enough money for a plane ticket. Being twenty years old with no education above high school and barely any marketable skills, finding a job myself was daunting. Most of my employment back then was babysitting for some of my sisters' new mom's friends and house cleaning. Although my parents didn't seem too concerned with my lack of realistic prospects, my sister was not having it. She was married with a toddler and in the middle of a nursing program. I guess she felt since she was getting her shit together, I had to follow her lead. I knew I didn't want to be a nurse or anything to do with the medical profession. I had no idea what I wanted to do with myself. Having an undiagnosed learning disability hindered any hope I had of being successful in doing anything but babysitting and basic house cleaning. In fact, because of little understanding of my learning disabilities, I just thought I was just too stupid for college.

My lack of self-esteem didn't stop my sister from pushing me to apply to the College of Staten Island. Even Though I was quickly accepted, I still had to take three CUNY assessment tests. Since I never took an SAT and, let's face it, I haven't been in any classrooms in about two years. Standardized testing and I do not mix well. In high school, when I had to take the practice SAT in the eleventh grade, I made a smiley face on the bubble answer sheet. As I handed in my decorated bubble sheet to the teacher monitoring the class, I could see the complete shock, if not concern, on her face that I was making this terrible life choice. As I recall, she asked, "Are you sure?" I responded, "Yep," and walked out. My rebellious front for standardized testing was the perfect cover of how stupid I believed I was. I had to take a Reading Comprehension Test, a Math assessment, and a writing assessment test. The only test I passed was the reading comprehension test. Failing meant I had to take remedial math and writing before being allowed to take many college-level courses. The only other courses I registered for were Introduction to the Performing Arts and a gym class, which included Tumbling and Trembling. Neither required me to have any pre-requisite college classes or assessment testing.

Back then, the College of Staten Island had two very run-down-looking campuses. I took the Intro to the Performing Arts at one site in St. George. The other three classes were on the Sunny Side campus, now The Michael J. Petrides School. Due to Staten Island's laughable mass transit system, walking to the Sunnyside campus was the better option. However, going to the St. George campus wasn't too difficult since almost every bus on Staten Island goes in that direction because of the Staten Island ferry. If you didn't live near a main bus route or the Staten Island Rapid Rail, a.k.a. "The train," getting around Staten Island was a pain. Our first apartment on Staten Island was on Victory Blvd, across from Spring Lake Park. Traveling by bus wasn't too horrible.

The Introduction to Performing Art class was one of those bullshit classes people take just to fill out elective credits. A lovely African American man who thought highly about himself and his dancing skills taught the class. He performed with the Alvin Ailey American Dance Theater, which is impressive. The workload in this class was very light, with a couple of simple papers to hand in. It was an easy A. However, the gym class was a disaster. It was basic gymnastics, and I was maybe six or seven the last time I attempted to do anything close to gymnastics. Out of all the classes that gave me any anxiety, it was this particular gym class. I fucked hated it. Some requirements were to pass the ability to do cartwheels, handstands, and other basic flips. I could do a cartwheel to have my life. The thought of propelling myself to go side down and back again scared me for no reason. My body was never meant to be propelled or upside down. I could barely perform a front tumblesault, which they teach four-year-olds. After weeks of stressing over cartwheels, I discovered I could drop it, which I did in a heartbeat. I could let it go. Let it no longer be part of my life. The gym class was the only class I ever needed to drop in my college academic career. I have no regrets.

The disability made the writing class the absolute obstacle in my college career. Handwriting a five-paragraph essay correctly in a little blue book was in my way. I understood the structure of the required argument. However, the words in my brain could never fall into the lined page correctly. I would often misspell words with confusing vowel sounds. Letters frequently needed to be corrected in order. I would leave certain simple words like to, if, it, a, etc. No matter how much tutoring I had, my brain could not transfer the information correctly onto those blue booklets. When it came time to retake the writing assessment class, I failed.

Although I was devastated, I also was not surprised. That summer, I had to retake remedial college. No matter how hard I tried that summer, it wasn't enough. When it came to retake the test the third time, I failed again. Not passing this test meant I could not take the required College English classes, which also meant I could not accept any other class that required College Writing, which was the majority of the classes I needed to take. It was impossible not to feel stupid that I came close to dropping out of school. If I could pass this test, I could not take any Introduction to College Writing classes without any Intro to College Writing. I would be a complete and literal failure as an adult. Knowing you have nothing to offer society makes getting out of bed challenging.

During this first year in college, the Office of Special Services helps and assists all students with documented disabilities. They provide additional resources to disabled students so they can succeed in college and life. Even though I never had my disability documented in high school, the Office of Special Students service provided me with the support I needed, not to throw in the towel. To this day, I am very grateful for the service and support they provided. Just before I was ready to quit, my advisor from the Office of student disabilities advised me to get an appeal from a particular professor sympathetic to struggling students such as myself. This professor owned the power to keep me in the fight or send me packing. However, this professor was not easy to get hold of. I stalked his ass until I addressed the situation one way or another. After days of annoying the living shit out of the man, my appeal was approved, and I could finally move to college-level classes. Even Though I'm sure the professor approved the appeal just to make me go away, I was allowed to take college writing, which meant this fucken learning disability wasn't stopping me anymore. After that, I learned the power of word processing. I want to finally be able to type out words from my mind and quickly correct them with the aid of any capable proofreader. My disability could go fuck itself. After learning how to use a computer, I felt my mind take off during the four and half years in college. Most of my papers handed in received As. I graduated with a 3.75 grade point average. The stupid and useless feelings quickly died. However, to this day, I still struggle with the written word and have moments when the feelings creep in.

On May 25, 2012, I wrote a blog for work that summarized my college experience and my later professional journey, discovering that I wasn't stupid but determined.

*Dyslexia is a learning disability that, for me affects my writing and reading abilities. I don't write letters backward, but I spell words with the letters switched around. I refer to it as abstract spelling or surrealist writing. It affects my writing skills much more than my reading skills. I'd be lost and highly frustrated if it wasn't for Microsoft Word and spell-checking. You know the old advice that if you can't figure out how to spell a word, you should look it up in the dictionary? In my case, I couldn't even figure out how the word looked to locate it in the dictionary.*

*As a teenager and before the age of computers, I threw many dictionaries across my bedroom and sometimes cracked windows and dented walls. The typewriter was and is still my sworn enemy. If it wasn't for my Mom, who was more than happy to type up my homework assignments, I might not have graduated high school on time. As for college, I did not start college until I was 21 years old because I was so afraid of how my learning disability would affect my academic performance. I was scared and thought I was too stupid to get through college remotely. If it wasn't for my older sister emotionally blackmailing me to apply to the College of Staten Island, I might have never gone. I remember crying the night before my first day of college because I was that terrified.*

*The first week was terrifying, but after that first week, I began to feel more and more confident. The college had the Special Students Office, providing tutoring and support. I met so many other college students with so many physical and learning disabilities who were these academic soldiers. I still admire them. I also learned how to use the computer, which ultimately turned everything around. I was getting excellent grades in almost every class. I graduated with honors and could believe my journey from fear to achievement.*

*Somewhere along the recent line, I decided to become a librarian. I loved reading to help people and always had a thing for putting things in order. As a baby, I used to classify stuffed animals in my crib. Does my learning disability affect my job as a librarian? Yes, it does. It's easier to look up certain words in a database if you can't spell them. However, that fact has never stopped me at all. Many databases check spelling, and I know how to cut and paste from and into other not-so-helpful databases. In other words, being a dyslexic librarian does not mean I cannot do my job. I just adapted different ways to get it done. I love being a librarian and will not let dyslexia stop me from doing it. I've also taken advantage of the library's books on CD, where I can keep up with the collection with my colleagues.*

Remedial math class was a different experience. It might be a slight understatement when I say a completely different experience. My brain understood the basic logic of this math. When I say math, the class mostly covered the basics that one learned in high school. The math was rarely too complex to grasp, and I would help other students in the class when I could. The ability to sometimes multiply fractions and solve for X or Y in my head was fun. Math problems were simple problems, and once I understood the rules attached to each puzzle, I could solve any algebraic equation. My inability to write a proper paragraph was a nightmare, but simplifying algebraic expressions was like numerical poetry. I might have felt like a retard when it came to the written word, but in math, I felt confident. During the day of the midterm, I woke up with a 102-degree fever. It was the flu, and it wouldn't prevent me from taking the one mid-term I knew I would ace. Loading up on flu medication and Tylenol, I dragged my ragged ass into that classroom. I managed to get a 96 on the midterm.

I passed out for maybe forty-eight hours when I got home from taking the math term. Taking the double dose of Contact Flu medication was a significant factor for the near comma. The near overdose was probably the main factor in having this crazy dream that my math teacher was a vampire whom I had to seek out. This dream occurred approximately five years before one of my favorite TV shows, Buffy The Vampire Slayer, came out. The few details of this dream I recall is finally finding my math teacher in a gray-colored dead forest. There were no leaves on any trees because all the branches looked cut off, leaving only these stumps for branches. The pools and streams of blackness were like veins of death on the ground. My math teacher awaited me in this bleak forest and wanted me to be like him in the darkness. It was an invitation I wasn't going to refuse. Before his deadly fangs were about to puncture the surface of my neck, I woke from my self-medicated coma.

When it was time to return to math, I would look at this man in front of the classroom trying to teach us math in a slightly different light. Once the weather began to warm up, too, I could put away all my oversized, grumpy sweaters and start wearing shirts and dresses. One day, I remember wearing a short, hippy-looking dress with a cute denim vest. These were some of the garments I claimed from the thrift store in England. I remember walking towards the classroom where the math teacher stood in the hallway. His eyes scanned my body as I was in his full view. His eyes moved up and down my body. It was a look that could be felt on and passed my skin. 'Ummmm hello vampire?'. Soon after that brief moment, this mild flirting between us lingered between inappropriate and appropriate. No one else noticed the secret languages of our little glances or gestures. Some people are naturally talented in communicating in secret and hushed language. The only language spoken allowed was within numbers and equations. Simplifying mathematical equations and solving complex word equations were our only foreplay. I should also indicate I still had a boyfriend in England who was due to visit in a few months. I should not be thinking of mathematical vampires.

When it came to taking the CUNY Math placement test, unlike the Writing Placement test, which was bitch slapping me left and right, I aced the shit out of it. As soon as the test was over and I handed it to the appropriate offices for grading, remedial math was behind me. I could now register for the required college-level math. My now previous math teacher made his move, and I unfortunately welcomed it. His name was Bob, and Bob was fifty. Bob didn't look fifty, but I looked at him with rose-tinted mathematical glasses and thought he was attractive. Instead of making my way home like I should, I ended up in this man's car. The exact reason I thought getting in his car was a smart move is still to this day. Maybe he offered to drive me home, which he did. However, I didn't get home until much later in the day. I think I remember going to Brooklyn. Maybe it was Brooklyn College because I recall him saying he had to request an incomplete and talk to his graduate professor. He purchased some Chinese food. However, I clearly remember going to this man's apartment.

Bob was fifty, divorced, and had two kids. I was twenty-one at the time. His older son hated his guts while still having a decent relationship with his youngest. I never met his kids, but he often discussed his relationship with them. Bob lived alone in an apartment by the mall. There is always a series of events that led up to moments. We exchanged some words that I can't remember.

There's communication in body language. However, I don't fully remember the series of events that played out that led me to fuck Bob in his bed. While I had a boyfriend in England, my fifty-year-old math college teacher was between my legs. That was my very first semester of college. Go me. Although fucking someone you've fantasized about fucking for a couple of months is pretty hot at that moment. The energy that finally transfers thought to reality is phenomenal. However, that energy does quickly deplete itself once the actions complete themselves. All you have left is an underwhelming feeling in your gut. It was also highly underwhelming that Bob's cock was, and still to this day, the most petite cock I have ever encountered. It might well have been a large clit. How the hell that tiny thing was able to produce two children is still beyond me.

So here I was, screwing up my close to a three-year relationship with MT, which was pretty much packed and ready to travel to New York around this time. Now, I made the boyfriend situation clear to Bob. Once MT was on American soil, I needed to place Bob in the past. What happens in Math stays in math. Whatever Bob and I were doing, whatever the hell this was, it was finished. It needed to be locked away into the 'nothing happened vault.' My short infatuation with Bob was never love. I can say with a clear conscience that I did not love Bob. Our involvement was nothing but infatuation that started with a coma-induced dream and nothing more. If I had any feelings for this man came and went within seven days, we fooled around. However, Bob couldn't easily let go. He was into writing poetry and insisted I take an entire folder of his work. "Yeah, sure, I'll read your fucken poetry while my boyfriend is in the room', I thought to myself. However, it wasn't until MT finally arrived in NYC that I realized Bob had deep feelings for me. Shit!

Matthew could only get a three-month visitor visa, so our time together was much shorter than our time apart. He didn't know what to expect while staying with my parents and me. Although there was still some battle of roaches, our Staten Island apartment was still in decent shape for the most part. For some reason, Matthew assumed he was supposed to get a job, which was not the case. I was the one bringing some money from babysitting. He'd often tag along and help entertain the kids. He enjoyed being silly with them. Although we were apart for some time before Matthew arrived, he noticed something was wrong with me. I didn't write to him as much as I usually have in the past. Being busy with school was my excuse, but that was particularly true. The college itself did occupy most of my time before I was fucking or more like blowing Bob toes sized dick.

Bob didn't help the situation at all. He constantly called the house even though I repeatedly told him not to. The fifty-year-old man could not chill the fuck out. Every time the man called, I had to hide in the bathroom, which looked suspicious. Back then, there wasn't a way to block an unwanted phone number. The word 'ghosting' wasn't known back then. Bob would beg me to meet him, which I agreed to, but only outside and in public. There would be no risk of any mixed messages or signals. This man had to fucken chill!. When I finally agreed to meet Bob, he gave me a ring. A mother fucken ring! I just wanted this fifty-year-old mico-dick dude to stop with the bullshit.

Matthew was not stupid. He found the stashed poetry and, of course, hiding in the bathroom to take phone calls made it so fucken evident that something not right was going on. MT confronted me with all the bullshit, and I could not lie. I could have easily lied to him, but I didn't. I cheated on what was then the love of my life with a dino-micro dick fifty-year-old fascination. As hilarious as it may sound now, my actions ripped MT's heart apart. It would have been more humane if I took a knife and slid his throat in the middle of the night. Nothing in this world is as painful as seeing how my actions hurt MT. Without question, Matthew returned to the UK heartbroken, and we broke up. My actions were devastating and ugly. Being a damaged twenty-one-year-old with a history of sexually acting out was no excuse. I was a fucken monster. The truth is that I was a horrible and selfish brat. And if I were to be even more honest, I don't think I changed that much to this day. I've just learned to hide the monster better inside myself. I am a well-rehearsed horror story and will one day take full responsibility for all the damage I have caused and continue to cause.

**Fast Forward:**

Throughout the past year, MT, his mom, and I would touch base once in a blue moon. The last letter I received from Matthew was in 1996. All I remember from the letter was the mention that his dad left his mom and how upsetting seeing his mother devastated was for him. At some point, his parents got back together. The very last communication I had was from his mother before Covid. MT married an ex-girlfriend. She was someone he dated before we met. Matthew, his wife, and his daughter live in Canada. MT is a Language Arts teacher at a middle school. Their daughter is about my son's age.

**Nightmare**

I could hear his stumbling and grumbling from down the hall. If I lay still enough, maybe he won't come this way, but I can hear him moving closer. I wanted to turn over to face the approaching monster but couldn't. I can't make my body turn over. If I can turn over and face the door, the beast might not enter. "Don't come in. Don't come in," I think I'm trying to say, but it's too late. The monster is in my room. With all my strength, I summon my body to turn over to see the beast standing over my bed. A feeling of disgust bares down on my body. I wake in the blurriness of the darkness, screaming, "No!"

# PART III: Repetitive Patterns
# Pieces of an Illness

I always took off my wedding ring before meeting up with S. Removing it signified that I belonged to him in those moments of togetherness. That life existed outside our particular room did not exist once the door was closed tightly behind us. Once I removed the ring from my finger, it left as if stepping into a portal of a different existence, blocking out any reality that S and I did not belong together. Perhaps not wearing the wedding ring gave a moment of denial to become utterly lost. However, I could not get the ring off my finger the last time I saw S. My hands had become strangely swollen. Keeping the fucken thing in my hand while with S felt like a violation against that thin line of my two separate worlds. As days passed, my hands continued to swell up. The swelling became scary, and I was afraid of losing circulation in my ring finger. I rushed over to urgent care to have it removed. It was painful once they yanked the ring off my finger, but it was off.

Soon after, I was having trouble holding down food. Having a weak stomach was nothing new and something I inherited from my dad. My father had a particular talent for destroying the bathroom with his projectile vomiting. His vomit would be in the tub, the floor, the walls, and the door, but rarely in the toilet. Sometimes, he wouldn't bother to make it to the bathroom. This one time at my sister's house, she was hosting Passover or something similar. She had family and friends over. Instead of running to the bathroom, our father ran outside the front door to throw up over the front pouch, giving everybody a perfect view outside the window. Luckily, I always tried to keep my mess where it belonged: in privacy. In my mission to make it into the bathroom before my stomach felt it was too late. However, I failed to get to the bathroom promptly once. There was a meeting in the city I had to attend. Feeling my stomach beginning to fight the laws of gravity, I tried making it to the bathroom stall. Unfortunately, I didn't get to the toilet. The feeling of mortification on my face was recognizable when I located a custodian, apologizing for the mess I just created.

Then, my hands started to feel cold and stiff. Often, I would find myself being woken at night by sharp pains in my hands. My knees began to hurt as well. It becomes a struggle to stand from a sitting position with something to lean on or someone to help me up. Going up and down a set of stairs also became difficult. Going up or down, I take one step at a time. My regular doctor at the time diagnosed possible carpal tunnel syndrome in the hands and tendonitis in the knees. He recommended wearing a wrist brace. The wrist braces did help relieve the pain and discomfort at night. However, the new braces did very little except cause significant discomfort. Due to excess nausea, I was losing weight drastically. My energy was practically nothing, and I stopped seeing S. Although I felt horrible about that, I struggled to have enough energy to deal with everyday life.

Someone suggested I see a Rheumatoid arthritis specialist. Only one on Staten Island took my insurance, and I had to wait at least a month to get an appointment. By the time I made it to visit the doctor, my body felt stiff as a board with pain and nausea. This specialist of the medical profession had no clue what was wrong with me as if I was some sort of medical mystery he couldn't solve. By then, my hands were so stiff. I could not straighten my fingers. Even though this medical specialist had no clue why this was happening to my body, he prescribed something that, after some research, medicine that would have some shitty side effects. Not feeling confident about taking some crazy meds for something he had no clue about didn't seem like a wise choice. I never filled the prescription and made another appointment to see this doctor.

Then, someone else recommended a different Manhattan doctor specializing in rheumatoid arthritis and other autoimmune diseases. Traveling into the city and walking up and down the subway stairs was difficult. Taking a cab would only risk the chance of needing to get out and separately find a place to throw up. Even though this doctor required blood work to confirm, he felt confident enough to diagnose me with Scleroderma. According to Wikipedia, Scleroderma results from an overproduction and accumulation of collagen in body tissues. Collagen is a fibrous protein that makes up your body's connective tissues, including your skin. Doctors don't know what causes this process to begin, but the body's immune system appears to play a role.

Once the blood work returned, I had a diagnosis explaining everything. Scleroderma is still causing my body to slowly kill itself by making too much collagen. The new doctor recommended I also see a particular pulmonary specialist who was very familiar with this disease to see if it was attacking my heart and lungs. After several tests, Chest scans, and more tests, my heart and lungs were slightly affected. It is not enough to cause alarm, but it needs regular monitoring. The doctor finally put me on medication that represses my immune system enough that my body stops attacking itself. Once I got my diagnosis and the medicine, I was able to tell this disease to fuck off. 'I know what you are now and what you're trying to do, but you can go fuck of.' now. Forcing myself to go up and down the stairs like an average person, I was determined to place this disease in its place. My stomach still likes to talk back to remind me what is happening to my body. The vomiting hasn't gone away completely. There are days I can still eat food that isn't digesting properly. I can just feel the food sitting there. , Often, I purge the food before it can return. Unfortunately, I was able to put back on the lost weight and then some.

# Pieces of a Hole in My Tooth: 2021

According to most online dictionaries, 'Normal' is defined as conforming to a type, standard, or regular pattern characterized by what is considered usual, typical, or routine. Although the world is far from perfect, we all follow a regular pattern of work, school, and whatever time we can find for recreation. The job was celebrating 125 years of existence in New York City, and we were all expected to perform at the highest standards. Those who worked with teens and children now had quotas to fill and numbers to reach. I would easily reach the quota for my program/ school outreach numbers would be easily reached by June. I had various programs for the 125 celebrations craftily planned out. When these challenges pop up at work, my brain goes into solving problem mode, and I manage to make it work. I felt like my condition was well managed, and I felt better about performing at the maximum level at work.

January 2021:

News of a viral outbreak somewhere in China, not here, China, the other side of the globe. It sounds more like someone else's problem way over there. China had nothing to do with plans for a fire slime program or The Harry Potter wand-making program for which hat I was ready to purchase supplies. All I cared about was planning my programs in the spring and hoping I would have a decent turnout.

February 2021:

There are cases of this virus, now called the Coronavirus, spreading from China into part of Europe. People were dying from it, a lot of people, but none here. Watching the CDC map of its spread became a morbid daily ritual. A few random people came to where I work wearing surgical masks. "That's a bit of an overkill," I thought. It would be stupid to believe that a vast ocean could protect us. I hope viruses understand when to arrive conveniently and when not to come, and I expect it won't affect my son's 16th birthday next month. The kid wasn't much for big parties or big crowds. My son is content with a family gathering at one of our favorite restaurants. There was a class trip on the actual day of his birthday to some sort of indoor amusement park in New Jersey that he was looking forward to. I prayed that this virus would be patient in crossing the ocean and that my son could at least enjoy his sixteenth birthday.

Beginning of March 2021,

There were coronavirus cases in the country, but nothing is yet on our doorstep. We had to cancel most of our programs. If possible, any public programs had to be activities where patrons couldn't share equipment or supplies. I did have to be inventive to create activities where no one touched anything. More people who come to where I work wear surgical masks. The sense of anxiety slowly began to thicken. If the shit could wait until past the thirteenth of the month, I would be highly grateful.

March 13th:

My son's birthday, and not only was the class trip he was looking forward to canceled but there was talk of schools closing for a week or two. The lockdown was the same for the place where I work. They were too close for a few weeks, but we could continue soon after. The clouds of uncertainty joined the sense of anxiety and became thicker each day as one witnessed an approaching storm on the horizon.

On March 15th,

Only a few family members made it to my son's birthday dinner. He wasn't as disappointed as I expected. As he's gotten older, he's gotten more easygoing when life doesn't go his way. I've always sensed an old soul lingering within him with all the wisdom included. That week, schools closed. The world closed in one full sweep. People are scared. I'm scared. The dark cloud of death, fear, and uncertainty was beginning to down-pour on us all.

End of March:

We are still determining when we will return to work. It could be a month, or it could be more. No one knows. Schools are now learning how to be "remote." My son's classroom is currently in front of a computer as some of his teachers struggle to do their jobs and try to teach high school sophomores. No one goes outside. The outside was forbidden. The world has gone into a primitive survival mode. We don't go anywhere, but we need food and cat litter, and getting anything delivered is impossible. From various online vendors, I purchased some basic staples and several months of toilet paper, rubbing alcohol, and some antibacterial Windex. There was a small, tiny crevice on one of my molars. It doesn't hurt.

April 2021:

The word 'remote' was now part of regular vocabulary. Schools tried to navigate through this remote learning concept. Teachers are struggling through new technology to reach their students not just to learn but to get these kids some sort of connection with the outside world. My son managed to adapt to the changes in his life. The small aperture in my back molar was now a tiny hole my tongue could quickly feel. It still doesn't hurt. My job is struggling to reinvent itself, too. How do we engage the public without seeing them in person, a wheel we are all working to invent? Some staff figured out virtual programs launched by us and lightly attended, but at least it's something. At least we are doing something to make us feel like we are contributing towards something resembling normalcy.

My husband checks his blood pressure and takes his temperature almost every hour. He seemed nearly angry that his temperature was average, but his high blood pressure made up for his disappointment. He's confident that he's sick even though I knew perfectly well that most of his symptoms were in his head. All except for his high blood pressure, the only illness he suffered from was mental. It's dangerous to say that aloud to him because he knows how to rip me apart from the inside out. Being yelled at is something. I've grown used to it. However, it's difficult when there's nowhere to go to escape. I walked around eggshells, trying to keep it together in our two-bedroom apartment.

In the middle of the night, I was awakened again by my husband because he was confident that he was dying then and there. Although he had no fever, his blood pressure was extremely high. He was insisting that I call 911, which I did because he was losing his shit altogether. The city was in the middle of a pandemic. All hospitals were past capacity. All emergency first responders got stretched thin, leaving me in the house with a crazy person. However, God bless 911 dispatch. Instead of sending an ambulance with overworked EMS workers, they direct his call to a nurse. God bless this nurse who quickly recognized that she was dealing with a person with extreme anxiety and not sick or dying. The nurse on the phone asked about his symptoms. This angel on the phone did what I could not do: talk my husband down from his mental rooftop. I was hoping they would send a prescription for some Xanax. We all could use some Xanax at this point. During that time, I could fit the tip of my tongue in the hole in my molar. There's no pain, but it is concerning. I thought I might lose the tooth. It was as though some unseen force was eating it away.

Even after that night, my husband continued to check his blood pressure and temperature. He was sure he was sick and dying still. I'm a horrible human being because I'm doing nothing to help save his life. Repeatedly being yelled at and snapped at because I couldn't help him. I don't know what to do. I'm not a health provider. I could only suggest that he go to urgent care to get tested, which isn't good enough. Being treated daily like the enemy with nowhere to go, I began to chip away at any walls I had built up in the past years. The seams of the tapestry that held me together were starting to come apart. This man knows how to revert me into feeling like a helpless child, which he manages to do.

Sometimes, I wonder if it makes my husband feel better when he manages to break me into a heap of broken emotional rubble. Does it help make his internal pains feel less than him? My husband had to check in with his therapist. Thank fucken god! Going to urgent care or checking in with his therapist was being debated. The man has lost his shit and doesn't know what to do. Go to urgent care or therapy. Being the horrible person that I am for not knowing what he should do. Therapy? Urgent care? Why is it up to me? Everything I say is wrong. Thank god he picked therapy.

God bless his therapist for verbally kicking and bringing him down to our planet. Although she repeated stuff I was trying to say, she got yelled at for saying them. She made him apologize to me for being an abusive ass before insisting to talk to me as well to make sure I was ok. Because I'm terrified to rock this unstable boat any further, I tell her I'm fine. I was not okay. I was countries from the definition of fine. This situation had broken me into tiny pieces, but I accept the apology. God only knows how long we would become stuck together in this apartment. Survival was all that mattered. By then, half the tooth was gone entirely.

May 2021:

New normal? A recently invented term to make society feel better. According to online dictionaries, it means a current social custom different from what has been experienced or done before but is expected to become usual or typical. In other words, everything you know will differ from what you're used to if you don't like them, too bad. Nothing will be the same. You're lucky you or someone no one you know and love isn't in a body bag piled on top of other body bags in front of the hospital. So be grateful and embrace the "new - normal ." Otherwise, you must wait your turn to become exposed along with last week's trash and recyclables.

According to my job, we might return to working in person soon but in a minimal capacity. There's talk of vaccines in process. My husband is finally over his crazy shit from the month before and adventures out to get food. My only access to the outside is our second-floor terrace, which is through our son's bedroom. This tiny oasis is the only place where I have any privacy to read or work uninterrupted. The terrace became my mini sanctuary. I am trying to be productive virtually for work, but I only have an iPad. If lucky, my husband and son will let me use their computers. I attended as many Zoom or Google Meet meetings as possible to feel connected to the outside world. My molar was almost completely gone, but now I could feel another hole develop in the next tooth, my wisdom tooth. Maybe by the time this Covid nightmare has passed, I won't have any teeth. There's still no pain.

Joining a group project to create several virtual choose-your-own-adventure stories with colleagues from different locations on Staten Island made me feel very productive. I offered to try to draw illustrations for the stories they were writing. When I was in my mid-twenties, I drew in pencil a lot. I drew the faces from magazine covers at a location I worked at in midtown. I'd like to think it was half decent with charcoal and a paper pad. It was over twenty years since I drew anything, but I desperately wanted to be part of something that would fill my time.

June 2021:

We were returning to work but again had limited capacity. Only a few centrally located units were opening with limited service. No doubt, my location is selected to be one of the first locations to reopen. Returning to work meant seeing people I hadn't seen outside a device's screen. Many people, including myself, were nervous. Many people didn't want to come back. It wasn't safe. We could all die! As much as I missed any in-person connection, I was terrified. What if someone sneezed near me? What if someone wanted to lick all the books on the shelves? Like everything, I held my breath and did what my job expected us to do—nothing more and nothing less. Now, there was a hole in my wisdom tooth. I could just stick my tongue inside. Some of the drawings for the virtual project came out pretty good, and some were horrible.

July 2021

We opened. I was utterly terrified, but I managed to pull through. Wearing a mask all day sucks! It was hard to breathe correctly with these fucken things attached to my face all day. Wearing latex gloves most of the day made my hands sweat. The staff of our location merged, joined by other staff from a different location that did not open. Staff broke into several groups or teams; my team was Team A. Unfortunately, all my friends, whom I missed terribly and enjoyed working with, were on Team B. Each day of each week, we would rotate from working on-site to working from home.

I was not a fan of the people on the A team. My friends and people I used to chill with were on team B. Although the routine was weird, eventually, I got used to it. This new way of thinking was part of the 'new normal," So sink or swim. What choice do I have? Except for the new normal or get off the train! Even though I was finally out of the house and working three days a week, I struggled with feeling isolated and disconnected from people. The wisdom tooth was nearly gone by then, and no other teeth were affected by the mystery decay monster. My drawings were improving, although I needed a picture to draw from. If I'm drawing hands, I need to see hands. If I'm drawing a person sitting on a train, I need to see a picture of a person sitting on a train. My mind gets easily lost at sea without a good reference to copy.

August/Sept 2021

We have expanded our services at work, and more locations have opened. Our organization broke staff into two teams that rotated from working on-site to working from home. Many staff members complained about how unsafe it was to work with the public again. Since I've already been busting my ass on site for nearly a couple months, I find the complaining somewhat annoying. Being one of those people who are a bit more at risk due to my immune disease, I should have been one of those people fighting tooth and nail to work from home. With The virtual Choose Your Adventure project completed, I was incredibly proud of some of the drawings I could create for it. The experience reignited my love for drawing and expressing myself through lines and shading. Even more astonishing was that the team on this virtual project and I hosted three live performances where we read and acted out the characters in each story. This experience allowed me to find another creative element to come alive in. Voice acting, and I loved it. One of the characters I took on was a Greek god named Hermes, whom the others involved in this live performance didn't want to take on. My interpretation of Hermes was a mix of James Lynch, Gilbert Godfry, and almost every New York Taxi driver. Everyone loved my Hermes. If I had to list all my professional highlights, being part of this project would easily be one of them. It reconnected me to drawing, one of the few ways I can honestly communicate my innermost thoughts and feelings that words are difficult to say or write.

All left of my wisdom tooth were stubs I could feel with my tongue. It feels like a jagged edge of the roots that are still left. The rest of the teeth felt fine and survived the bizarre decay transition. However, my deep disconnectedness from the people around me still felt strong. The feeling of nearly being invisible to the people around me is something I'm used to. I felt cut off at home and sometimes at work when I tried to speak. It makes one believe what they think or feel isn't critical. However, this deep drawing of disconnectedness feels much more potent than my usual feeling of invisibility. The only thing anyone noticed was the drawing. A simple pencil and sheet of paper feel like my only lifeline to the rest of the world. I keep drawing. I drew portraits of famous people at least thrice a day as practice. My actual voice comes out through the abstract drawings. They are my new voice. The sound of the tip of the pencil scratching on paper becomes very soothing.

While on a computer one night, I put the term: "Feeling Disconnected" in a Google search. It was as if Google was programmed with any magic powers to make unpleasant feelings disappear. A grown woman pushing fifty should know better, which is no excuse for what I will find. Some search results are online dating sites as if those were the answer to my drowning. Again, a grown woman pushing fifty should know better. I clicked on one of the links as though I was about to find a rope to keep me from floating away from the world. A grown woman pushing fifty should know better. Without much thought, I started filling in the personal information about myself. The 'What are you looking for?' question stumped me. Was I looking to fill a void? Not remembering what I wrote, I should have written: "A grown woman pushing fifty should know better."

**Nightmare:**

His stumbling and grumbling could be heard from down the hall. If I lay still enough, maybe he won't come this way, but I can hear him moving closer. I wanted to turn over to face the approaching monster but couldn't. I can't make my body turn over. If I can turn over and face the door, the beast might not enter. "Don't come in. Don't come in," I think I'm trying to say, but it's too late. The monster is in my room. With all my strength, I summon my body to turn over to see the beast standing over my bed. A feeling of disgust bares down on my body. I wake in the blurriness of the natural world, screaming something that resembles "No!"

# Pieces of Autumn 2021

The site was called Badoo. It's your primary dating site that I should've been on, but there I was, a grown woman pushing fifty and, yes, I should know better. Logging into a dating website site was a stupid choice, but there I was on some random dating site—many message requests filled up my inbox on this site quickly. The high influx of women on this or any dating site is typical. All of these sites have a higher percentage of men than women on these sites. Also, an average of ten percent of the women on any dating website are fake or scammed. Men, naive men, are ongoing victims of various scams on dating sites. Sometimes, desperation and loneliness make them believe that the woman who resembles their high school crush is finally into them.

All the fish come running to all the new and shiny things in the water. Being on this Badoo quickly brings me back to the fifteen years I was on Fling and how instincts to the hunt come rushing back. The age range I was interested in (22-33). I might as well play up the cougar MILF card and see what fish I'd catch. At my age and my low self-esteem back then, I was an easy target for the shovel of shit virtually handed to me. These new and shiny men knew how to flatter me to flash pictures of my tits and other private body zones. Like a kid forced into a diet in a candy store, I began responding to many of these men. My first response to a few men was, "I shouldn't be here." which was completely honest. "I shouldn't be here" ended up being a decent icebreaker conversationally. It opened a few revealing doors. Let the games begin, even if a grown woman pushing fifty should know better.

My memory for every conversation I had online is beyond limited. We would move many of these conversations to different modes of communication and apps. Snapchat and Kik were apps that gave me new virtual access to communicate with strangers online. Kik was an app I tried before back in the day, but I got bored with it quickly. However, Snapchat was a different ballgame altogether. Being completely clueless about how to use this app, I was more than happy to have Sean's aid from Bayonne, NJ. He was glad to help me privately share pics, videos, and images required in the bathroom. My favorite part of the app was I didn't have to risk storing any of these private images on my phone. Pictures and videos of me touching myself stayed nicely hidden in the Snapchat app itself. Oh, this virtual world had changed since I last played in it.

A handful of young men got to know me intermittently on the virtual level. There was Sean, an adorable twenty-two-year-old chemist from Bayonne. Then there was Matthew, a gorgeous hockey player and electrician in his mid-20s from Long Island. J was also in his early twenties. Then, there was Dario in California. Almost every night after work was playtime with the exchange of erotic messages and some dick pics.

I would only try to run to the bathroom to reciprocate with awkward pictures of myself when possible. I was playing an addictive game of show and told between myself and the strangers I found on Badoo. The collection of men grew—Sean from Wiscon, Mikey from Connecticut, and others whose names I can't remember.

Around the same time, I discovered Delta-8-THC gummies or simply pot gummies. Autumn nights at home were edible pot gummies and a glass of Pinot Noir time. These minor substances added and somewhat enhanced my fancy-free virtual fucking. During the day, I would sometimes share a picture of myself, exposing just a hint of cleavage on Snapchat, and I'd have my playmates lined up for the day. It was like dropping a hint of blood in the ocean to attract the neighboring sharks. I used my cleavage as a bat signal. Even a ghost from the forgotten past named Tim W.

smelled the droplets of blood in the universe. Tim W looked like a member of ZZ-top, had a tiny cock, and was into daddy-daughter virtual role-play.

These onlookers were my audience, and I was their main attraction for now. Once again, and I know I'm repeating myself, I learned a grown woman pushing fifty should know better but fuck it. I was having fun. My renowned feelings of desire became my new muse in abstract form in my drawings. My art became my secret language with a forest of trees with hands holding out apples of temptation. Taking my art further, I would ask some strangers if I could attempt to draw them. A couple of the young men were into the idea. J, the lifeguard on Staten Island, sent me a semi-nude picture of himself, which he took just for this strange purpose. I was flattered that he would send an original photo for me to draw. It could be pretty good for a novice attempting to capture the original human form. Matthew, from Long Island, also contributed a few pictures of himself he kept stored on his phone to draw. One of the pictures he shared was of him playing hockey. Even though the view is of him from behind, and no one could tell it was him, it also became a pretty decent drawing.

Now, getting back to Badoo, there were still a couple of men I was communicating with on that platform only. Remembering any names is impossible but not even necessary. Some names are easy to forget. However, I recall Frank, a divorced New Jersey man who wanted to meet me in person. It has been years since I rode the horse of in-person hookups. Now, I was a fish on Frank's hook. Being divorced, besides having a couple of kids who were around sometimes but not all the time, meant he lived alone. I needed to plan these arrangements well by picking a day and time and getting directions. Once we picked, both parties selected and agreed on the day and time. However, when that day began to approach, I heard less and less from him, and when that day arrived, I was 'ghosted.'

According to online definitions, "Ghosting is when someone cuts off all communication without explanation. Most of us think about it in the context of digital departure: a friend not responding to a text, or worse, a lover, but it happens across all social circumstances. Ghosting may be tied to the way we view the world." Being ghosted was something I had to learn to get used to if I were to play in the adult reindeer games. However, when it happens, it completely sucks. I was, of course, pissed off. Who the fuck did he think he was anyway? Yet, in the broader perspective of things, who the fuck did I guess I was to begin with too. The 'ghosting' also happened with Sean, the Chemist as well. I was not a fan of rejection, but I had to learn to accept it if I wanted to stay in the game.

Rejection, combined with sexual frustration, made me feel like I was existing with a violent storm harvesting deep within me. This storm desperately needed an outlet, and soon. I texted my audience on Snapchat: "Put up or shut up." My short plea for human contact was the equivalent of cutting my hand open and emerging the bloody mess into the shark-infested waters to, you know, see what happens. Matthew from Long Island took the bait. In the very far reaches of the back of my mind, I had a feeling I was going getting played yet again, but this mother fucker kept dishing out some smooth operator shit, and, like a dumb ass, I ate it up.

Like the fucken dumb ass I was, I agreed to make plans to hook up with Mathew from LI. As the days approached, those familiar ghosting signs were emerging. Unfortunately, so was my denial. At the time, I was also chatting a lot with ZZ-top look-alike Tim W. There were moments when his daddy role-playing fetish wasn't always at the top of our conversations. We'd sometimes just talk like ordinary people would. I told him that, once again, I was about to be ghosted, and I was getting completely tired of the head games these mother fuckers kept dishing out. Then Tim W offered to meet for coffee somewhere in Greenpoint Brooklyn instead of thinking about Matthew from Long Island. We would be just two innocent lost souls meeting for coffee at a public park. Tim W. said I would hear from him before our morning coffee arrangement.

That morning, there was not one word for Tim W.. Well, like the dumb ass I was, I drove to Green Point, Brooklyn, to find this stupid park. It was not an easy drive, and I knew I was wasting gas and time by the time I started my car. Nothing is more annoying and painful than being played by someone who claims to be a friend. Tim W. knew Matthew had already played me and pissed me off. Like, what the fuck! Even though a grown woman pushing fifty should know fucken better, I cried as I strolled through this park. Deciding to find the nearest dog run in this park in Green Point, I wanted to sit among the four-legged creatures. Animals have always been a calming force in my life. I needed the dog's unconditional love on this day of disappointment. I also found a store next to the park that sold a mini drawing kit. Sitting on a bench in the dog run, I drew out my feeling of rejection. Trying to draw the disappointment in myself, I attempted to capture the frustration of the situations I was putting myself in onto the small drawing pad. A grown woman pushing fifty should know better than this but didn't.

On my return to Staten Island that afternoon, I randomly made plans to practically stalk J, the lifeguard. One would say I might have lost my shit a bit, too, literally intruding on someone I barely knew. One figure in Snapchat allows you to see the exact location of friends on a map. On the map, I could see where J was on Staten Island. He was at Midland Beach working. However, I was not dressed for the beach at all. So, like a degraded lunatic, I drove to the closest 5 Below store to find cheap and quick-beaching supplies and outfits. Finding a cute summer dress, pink Crocs, and a small beach blanket, I felt ready for some beach stalking. Messaging J, I not so innocently asked if places were available for people to change clothes in the area he was working at that day. One thing I always enjoyed about J, the lifeguard, was his lighthearted and easygoing demeanor. He seemed rather amused by my random question. There were bathrooms nearby that people used to change in if needed. I just changed my clothes in my car. In broad daylight, in my car, I changed out of the clothes I left the house into my 5-Below beach attire. I do not give any fucks who saw me or not.

Having limited expectations or a sense of sanity, I stepped onto the beach, trying to fit in with the other beachgoers. I wasn't planning to get J into any trouble. I wasn't planning anything, but I planned to play it cool. Just a sad woman pushing fifty who should know better about visiting a friendly neighborhood lifeguard. Perfectly normal, right? First of all, let's just agree that the beaches on Staten Island are fucken disgusting. The beach is dirt and not even sand. All these people were lying on dirt, letting their children play in it, and god only knows what they were swimming in. The beach on Staten Island reminded me of the sandboxes in Starrett City. These sandboxes must have seemed like a cute idea at the time before residents began to fill up the apartment buildings. However, the sandboxes quickly allowed the neighborhood children to play in centralized litter boxes with broken glass and used syringes. 'Have fun, kids". This Staten Island beach was a much larger version of my childhood memories.

Unfortunately, J, the lifeguard, was on break when I got there to complete my staking mission. Sitting on my small beach blanket was not enough to separate me from grains of shit all around me. All empty of tears, I sat reflecting on how shitty this day turned out. How sad, pathetic, and deranged I must seem to the random observer. As I waited for J to return from his break, I tried to take my mind off my sad existence and attempted to draw the people around me. Eventually, J, the lifeguard, returned from his break and reclaimed his lifeguarding post. That afternoon was the first time we were meeting, and here I was, giving off this sad unhinged MILF impression.

After waiting and contemplating how to approach this situation, I texted J, "I hate the beach." J smiled after reading my message and waved me over. Even though we just talked for a good twenty minutes, J, the lifeguard, was sweet and even a bit sympathetic toward the crazy MILF lady. J didn't hit on me, and I didn't have the energy to hit him. I wondered if I looked like the train wreck I knew I was that day. We talked until I had to head home. Returning to my car, I changed into the clothes I left the house in. Again, not giving a fuck if anyone saw me or not change in the middle of the parking lot. I was tired and drained from the day. I took my pathetic ass home, got stoned and drunk, and blocked Mathew from Long Island and Tim Snapchat.

# Pieces of Baby Wolverine and Other Matters

I should have thrown in the towel after the multiple disasters that kicked off the Autumn of 2021. I should have given myself time to reflect on my most current devastations. I should have cut my losses and deleted my Badoo account. However, I didn't learn my lesson from this downward spiral, and I don't think this downward spiral was done with me either. The downward spiral wanted to chew and spit me out, and I gave it full permission. Maybe I could make insanity look endearing if I was creative enough. God knew I had the potential. This online social thing became my new drug dealer, and I wanted to drown deep into it as it slowly unraveled me. The rush and the thrill of flirtation would increase the intensity of the desire actually to feel real flesh. I was famished. The ongoing chase for that thrill felt like an endless series of soon-to-be regrets. Once a Mrs. Robinson, always a Mrs. Robinson.

Still lurking on the Badoo dating site, I stumbled upon another Mathew from New Jersey. Matthew was also in his mid-twenties and lived independently in New Jersey. The thought of Mrs. Robinson coming over to get screwed was appealing enough to him. Not only did I get an invite, I got his address as well. Getting an address felt like an insurance policy of not getting 'ghosted' again. I never got an address from someone before, and the parent in me wanted to teach him about the dangers of giving out personal information online to a stranger. The only mistake was that I planned 'meeting' him a bit far in advance. Not having my secret self-affect the self that everyone is more familiar with felt vital to me. So, I picked a day I knew would not affect my life or anyone else's. He looked like a miniature wolverine in a few pictures he shared with me. Being with him would be like being with a miniature Hugh Jackson. So, I would refer to him as 'baby wolverine.'

I was getting ridiculously antsy while waiting for the scheduled 'meet' with baby Wolverine to arrive. Matthew's communication skills or lack of communication skills did not help with numerous ants in my pants. Even though I had his address, the PTS of getting repeatedly ghosted was setting in. Now enter Derek from Badoo, who I think was in his late twenties or early thirties, to add to some bad life choices I was about to make. Derek worked for the Department of Sanitation on Staten Island. Before interacting with baby Wolverine, I almost met Derek for a quick lunchtime car 'meet.' The problem was, probably from the excitement of trying to get laid by online strangers, our wires got poorly crossed. Derek assumed I meant that exact day we were communicating, and when I meant it was the next day. This bit of hiccup in poor communication quickly presented itself ten minutes past the hour when I received a text to see if I was on my way or what. I was pretty sure that I was referring to the next day. Derek was super bummed and doubled but because he wasn't available to meet the next day. What they say about the blood rushing out of one head and into another is true; so much for Derek of NYC sanitation.

The sad desperation to have this intense itch scratched became maddening. I was a junkie who couldn't find a quick fix. At this point, cutting my losses and moving on with my life would have been a far better option. Soon after the Derek debacle, I meant Richie from Northern New Jersey. He had an intense energy that drew me in. Richie was in his mid-thirties and smoked a lot of weed. Automatically attracted to his unhinged vibe, I was willing to call out sick the next day to get laid and stoned off my ass. Fuck pre-cautions! This bitch was going to get her freak on. That night, leaving work, I got caught in a horrible downpour. This massive thunderstorm fueled my need to be as dangerous as possible instead of forcing myself to slow down. I got soaked before getting into my car. My self-destructive self had the wheel and couldn't give two fucks. It was terrifying, and I loved it. The horror of the sheets of rain and the brutality of the wind was as though my rage and desires matched the storm's force. I blasted music on my way home. The weather was insane. I was insane. What I was doing was insane. By some miracle, I made it home safely, but I had no umbrella. As I pulled up to my building, I began to feel a chill from driving in soaking wet clothes. By the time I walked into the house, I was drenched. Like a plane ready to take off, but one of the engines was malfunctioning, my body crashed when I walked into the house. All I wanted was to feel warm and dry. Chills started to kick in, and they weren't the fun type of chills either. I was still calling out sick the next day because, I honestly, felt like dog shit. Any plans to meet Richie went in a hamper with my wet clothes. Soon after canceling on Richie, he seemed super pushy, and some of his texts made little sense. He was sending the weirdest and most nonsensical videos on Snapchat. There was a little alarm inside my gut that I often ignored that was going off with the volume way up. Rarely do I make these sorts of judgments about people. My gut told me Richie might have been nuts and even dangerous. Eventually, I blocked him from Snapchat and removed myself from the Badoo. So, I guess I have some sense in judgment. Trust me, I was just as surprised as you are.

Soon after the hot mess involving Richie, I needed a break from Badoo. Baby Wolverine was giving me mixed signals. The familiar smell of ghosting was in the air. The bullshit to the point that it didn't upset me, but it differently annoyed the shit out of me. At this point, you'd think that closing up shop or packing it all in would have been the better option after the load of disappointment. We tried. We failed. Move on. No, I did not. Instead, I went ahead and created an Ashly Maison account. If you're not familiar with Ashely Maison, it's another dating site for married people who want to fuck around. Everyone on this site is mainly in the same shitty boat. If that downward spiral wasn't hitting bottom enough before, I was ready to hit below sea level now. My profile read something to the effect: Just looking at a quick detached drive-through fucking. Like any new female profile on these sites, the number of responses is overwhelming. Instead of just placing some fresh blood into the shark-infested waters, I emerged my whole bloody self to be devoured by any predator. There were a lot of bites. However, this time, I was willing to play with my age group or at least try to welcome the forty-plus crowd to the show.

Ashley Madison is how I met Stan the Man or Mega Man. Those were his profile handles. Mega Man for Ashely Madison and Stan the Man on KIK. This guy had a big ego or something, but I wasn't interested in being fucked by his ego. At this time, I forgot all about Baby Wolverine. Stan was close to my age and was all for the quick lunchtime fuck. After so many disappointments, I was finally getting laid. We didn't need much conversation before setting the wheels in motion the same day we meant online. Stan was decent looking and had an available cock. We only started talking that morning and quickly setting plans. The spontaneity of how quickly this was developing was extremely exciting. We meant He selected the location somewhere off Travis and Victory Blvd. just after 1:00 pm. It was off a dead-end street near a locked-up vacant lot with abandoned trailers and rusty vehicles. It seemed like a perfect location to hide bodies or even cook meth. As soon as I parked my car behind him, we slipped into the back seat of my truck. It was not like it would have made much of a difference, but I was lucky the inside of the car was clean enough to welcome company. Stan was average looking for a man in my age group. He looked as though he probably worked out often.

Under the assumption that men in my age category don't cum as quickly as their younger counterparts, It was quick. How fucked up it was to enjoy being pounded by someone I just meant online literally five hours ago. I even moaned thank you during the deed in his ear. Even though the area wasn't completely dead, we did it twice in the backseat of my car in broad daylight. There were probably one or two individuals in the area, and I could give a fuck if they were aware that casual sex was occurring in their proximity. Not only was Stan Man's flair for zero hour fucking exciting. He was a huge Star Trek fan. We had an excellent discussion of story development within the Enterprise between the two rounds of sex. I went back to work feeling difunctionally satisfied.

The very next day, Baby Wolverine finally reached out. Whatever tentative plans we made a couple of weeks ago were still on. Due to the advancement of electronic toll collecting, driving over a bridge was something I was cautious of. There was no more cash, only toll, and both options were getting off Staten Island. Because we did not have an Ez-pass, all tolls were billed and mailed to the house. Already waiting for the bill that recorded my journey to Brooklyn the past month, I had been vigilant over that mail for this New Jersey journey I was about to embark on. The toll bills reminded me of waiting to catch those school-cutting cards in the day. Now, I had to worry about toll booth bills in the mailbox. Although Baby Wolverine did provide the address a few weeks back, he didn't give an apartment number. If I ever showed up uninvited, I wouldn't be able to find him: slick Baby Wolverine, Slick. Before getting there, he texted me where to park near the dumpsters that weren't very close to his building. I guess he felt trash goes where trash goes. Meeting me outside, I didn't realize how short and skinny he was. The couple of pictures he shared of him didn't do him justice to the fact I probably could have kicked his ass if I wanted to. He was cute, but I could have thrown him around if I had wanted to.

When Baby Wolverine brought me into his tiny apartment, I first noticed that monster-sized couch in the middle of the living room. This monster piece of furniture could have been a full-sized bed, which would have made sense if there hadn't been an actual bed in the tiny bedroom. Seinfeld was on. It's not my choice of viewing for this scenario, but whatever rocks your boat, kid. When Baby Wolverine's hands were on me, his thin, long fingers felt neurotic; his fingers felt too pointing and chaotic, as though the kid had drunk down five Red Bulls. It was like he was trying to make his way around a brisket he wanted to eat and not handling a person he was about to fuck. He was bursting with nervous erotic energy that made this sexual experience slightly awkward. If there was anything to gain from this uncomfortable experience with Baby Wolverine, he introduced me to the Netflix show Squid Games. Besides having a new TV show to watch, this wasn't my best experience by far, and I got lost on the way home. He would be the last Badoo hookup I would get involved with. Ashley Madison was my new playground. Maybe the fucked games will continue.

# Pieces from The Backseat of My Car

Autumn is the perfect weather for car sex. The AC is rarely needed. Autumn rainy days help ensure privacy. One can easily forget one's self-destructive behavior when you're neither freezing nor sweating your ass off. If it ever dawned on me that my actions could get me hurt or even killed, I never showed it. Sex with random strangers online is a soul-murdering process. There's always excitement before a 'meet". It is an addictive electric energy I kept chasing. However, the numbness soon after was my actual drug. Passing me once need to feel connected, to shut off every emotional nerve running through my body, was my true addiction. It was the required insurance not to touch the microaggressions at home. To feel nothing was my goal, and fucking these men helped to achieve it. At this time, I was drawing my fingers to the bone. No one noticed the subtle hints of pain in some of my pieces. This downward spiral was my mid-Autumn in 2021. Fuck Covid. Fuck mental health. Fuck you. Fuck me. Just fuck it.

Using the location where I met up with Mega Man a couple of weeks ago, I also met up with a couple of men from Ashley Madison. First, there was the Ferry Captain. Unfortunately, I can't remember his name, which isn't essential. Managing to hook up with an averagely attractive Staten Island Ferry Captain was a notable feather in my cap. The Captain might have been in his late thirties. This time, we used his larger backseat instead of mine. Our sexual interaction started great. Everyone's parts were functioning and performing as expected at first. Round one was, as always, quick. However, round two was, for not for the lack of words, a whole different boat. His dick bent while engaging in what dicks are supposed to engage in, and apparently, it hurt like a mother fucker when a guy's dick gets bent. Now I didn't know that dicks ever had this bending issue. It was never mentioned in health class, not in any porn videos, or in any erotic fantasies I've read. No one warned me about the dangers of dick-bending. I guess the captain felt he needed to keep his dick safe, so I never heard from him again. Plus, I might add, it's a bit uncomfortable when your legs are open in the back seat of someone's car, and there's evidence of small children in their lives. Toddler seats are not a turn-on in my book.

Then there was Mike, another AM hookup, a locksmith from New Jersey who was also in his mid-thirties. This time, we used my backseat. There was no evidence of small life to make me feel even more like a sack of shit. Although I once had to remove a booster seat from the backseat of my car, so who am I really to judge? Mike was another quick draw in action. In other words, he came faster than my ability to enjoy him. I wasn't getting much out of the causal drive-thru sex scene, and wasn't cutting the mustard. While we were amid passionate quickness, some old guy parked his car near mine. Like, what the fuck, old dude! Having some old guy stand approximately four feet from our sexual encounter made Mike sort of freak out. I doubt the old dude noticed us or even cared that I was naked in the backseat of my car with some man I just met and fucked. As I acted as though nothing was wrong with this situation, Mike was concerned that the old guy would call the cops on us. The old dude seemed more concerned about accessing the locked vacant lot than what we were doing. Maybe he had a body to dump and was more concerned about our presence than he was concerned with ours. At this moment, Mike openly judged my life choices. Like, who the fuck was he to judge my actions. Fuck him! If this old man was amid a body drop, I wondered how much he'd charge to add one more. It was perfectly ok for a dude to 'get some,' but for a woman, it's criminating. I never spoke to him after he left my car.

Hooking up with Mega Man again on the spot just resulted in more sexual disappointment. He should have been named Mega

Lazy Fuck. My backseat situation, in general, was pretty much a bust regarding these 'meets.' All these men I was 'meeting' were quick quickdraws with little concern for my satisfaction. Not to mention this particular activity was beyond the most fucked up thing I could be doing. There was way too much Russian roulette with my safety. I was lucky no one attempted to murder or left for dead by anyone. It was time to move on to less dangerous avenues and give my Ashely Madison account a break. There were also a handful of men that I also chatted with still on Kik and Snapchat. Men who wanted to meet but could never really strike up enough balls to follow through or who were just in the business of causal mind-fucking. My patience for any of these people grew thin. Nothing like getting a random message that some virtual guy's cock was hard at any given time of the day. Was I supposed to stop everything I was doing then and there to help him jerk off? "Oh wait, let me find a place to pull over." I think not. Farewell, Ashely Madison, until we meet again. Maybe I should have rethought my life choices.

**Rituals**

There are plenty of band aides at work. Although the incision is still limited to the size of the white padding, I take comfort in knowing that they are available when needed. So, is the cutting device in my desk drawer originally meant to help reduce lip hair? The point of the blade pushed hard as it crossed over my skin to release the elements of today. To blame the cats, I need to make no more than four cuts in one area before moving on. One more incision at the left shoulder before moving to the ankles and the area hidden under socks. The weather is beginning to cool, and I must wear socks daily.

# Pieces of Texas and Anthony

As the saying goes, "One door closes while another one opens. 'My take on that saying is "One door slams on your face while another sucks you out of the cockpit." As I closed shop on Ashely Madison, I relocated back onto Fling. It had been over ten years since I even looked at Fling.com for that special individual, and the website was just as revolting as I remember. The only noticeable difference is that users could comment on a person's profile. It was like its own bizarre version of Yelp, where you could openly criticize someone's profile and nude photos. Once again, the scent of my blood was back in these murky waters. Of course, the new girl gets flooded with messages the first twenty-four hours after posting a new profile. I could see a seventy-five-year-old female with a humpback and a missing limp, probably still overloaded with messages. There is a process and a standard I have when going through these message requests. First, I have to be somewhat attracted to them. Second, they can write complete sentences. Dumbasses or anyone who doesn't have a High School diploma is just not my cup of tea. The third is logistics. Where are both parties traveling from? For example, hooking up with a person in South Jersey is unrealistic. No one in their right mind wants to drive more than 45 minutes for casual sex. I know I don't. Part of logistics is also general availability. My availability was strictly on weekdays only. Nights and weekends are not an option. But My 'drive-thru' hooks up to rest and upgrade to the classier use of motels. I would also try to stick closer to my age group this time.

First, let's talk about Texas. I have no idea what this person's name was, so I will refer to him as Texas since that was where he was originally from. He lived in New Jersey. I think he worked with architectural design, I believe, and was in his mid-forties, I guess. He might have even told me his real name, I think. About this time, I discovered a couple of sites that allowed one to book a room at a decent hotel during the day for this particular purpose at a discount. Users of this site paid at the location during arrival, but there was free cancellation if things went a bit south. To Be fair, all parties involved should pay half. We're all in it together, right? Once our logistics settled, it was game time for Texas and me to 'meet.' There was no 'Let's meet for coffee and see if we have any connection".

This way, I needed to assert control in this meet-up. Taking care of the room, I expected to get paid my half before our final departure. Getting there earlier to feel comfortable in that space helped get my head together. My nerves also required an airport bottle of berry-flavored vodka to help calm them. The room was small, with a queen-sized bed. Unlike the Motor Inn from over ten years ago, everything looked clean and well-kept. My stomach was an absolute mess, and I needed thirty minutes to get a head start in the bathroom alone. My digestive lower track was in protest by trying to communicate the insanity of this situation.

I was doing my best to tend to it with a shit load of toilet paper before Texas would come knocking. It was a miracle I was able to get my shit together, literally, before Texas arrived. Besides a couple of pictures of Texas and some texting back and forth, I needed more information to go on or what I was getting myself into. Texas was on time as he knocked on the door. He was tall and in decent shape. It may be a little awkward looking, but not too bad to cause my legs not to open. We got straight to business with minutes of greeting each other. There's no reason for small talk or introductions. We both knew what we were here for, so we might as well get straight to it. Fucking Texas didn't blow my mind, but I got what I ordered. Nothing was quick about it, and I was able to sink into the moment. My mind could turn itself off enough to experience the various sensations. During those in-between times, we talked about books, work, and what two strangers talk about between cranial rounds. It wasn't fantastic or mind-blowing, but it wasn't horrible either. It wasn't a complete shit show. He paid up his half as we parted ways.

Now let's discuss Anthony, a retired firefighter working part-time with legitimate hustles. We were either the same age or maybe just a year off. Since I was attempting to improve the quality of my game, I requested we meet for coffee first. We met one morning at a local Tim Hortons. I think I come off as even more awkward during these public 'meets.' Sex is an easy costume to slip on, and without it, I have tiny places to hide. Anthony wasn't too bad looking for a man in my age group. I'm just of no use for vintage models. Besides the normal beer gut some men develop as they enter their forties, he seemed to be in decent enough shape. We proceeded to the next step, which included the basic logistics of time and place. We had our wheels in full motion and the logistics perfectly laid out. We had a day, a time, and a place in the exact location I met in Texas. One thing that I didn't plan on was getting my period that week. Since I've been on an IUD for almost ten years, I don't have a regular menstrual cycle. After being period free for months only to get hit with aunt flow out of the fucken blue. Since I had the IUD, when Auntie Flow did make her presence known, it was on the light side. Light or not, my plans with Anthony, who described himself as very oral, were a no-go. He was cool with rescheduling, which we did for the following week.

The day I finally 'met' with Anthony was the week before Thanksgiving. Like with the 'meet' with Texas, I got there early to deal with the same stomach issues. Once again, my lower digestive tract often yells, "Bitch, why can't you get the message!". Of course, I do my best to ignore it. This time, I took a weed gummy bear with the airport vodka to calm my ass down. After many similar experiences, you would think I would be cool as a cucumber before each 'meet.' To this day, that has never been the case where I'm not an internal mess. When Anthony knocked on the door on time, I was only wearing a thin red V-neck top and underwear, figuring out why I should wait to start the engines promptly. By the look at me, you could not tell there was or is an inner chaos within me. As if about to dive into deep waters, I take a long breath and plunge into the moment. The chaos switches in me and turns off as something more primal takes control of the moment. Anthony was not disappointed at all with his performance. Finally, I was getting adequately laid to the point of pure euphoria. Although the pot might have played a bit in my sensitivity to his busy tongue, the awaited feeling of pure release was exquisite. After round one, Anthony shared his concerns about his heart condition, which was information he should have shared prior. He had a heart attack a few months back. Internally I was yelling, "Now you're sharing this information!!" "Are you fucking kidding" All I needed was to be in a hotel with some guy dying. Like, what the fuck, man! If you remove the critical health issues from the equations, I have to say that I enjoyed my few hours with Anthony. Due to his upcoming work schedule, he wouldn't be available until after the holidays. He was never available at all after. Was it me or his heart?

Now, back to Texas. He wanted to arrange another meeting, which I agreed to. As before, I took on the responsibility of booking the room online. About a couple hours before our arranged fucking, Texas texted that he arranged for the room somewhere in Amboy, New Jersey, even though I thought I was clear about I preferred taking care of the arrangements. When it comes to a poor breakdown of communication, these things tend to get screwed. Annoyed that he decided to change the venue on short notice without consulting me, I reluctantly played along. He was changing the location, which required going over a bridge and risking a toll bill getting mailed to my house. As I'm about half a mile to this new venue, Texas texts me again that he got a flu shot earlier that morning and wasn't feeling up to it. 'Are you fucken serious, dude?' I thought to myself. Another text with a picture of him with a broken arm followed that text, attached to the text, "I broke my arm the other day." Not knowing what to do with the added information, I drove back to Staten Island extremely pissed. First, what did he think he'd accomplish with one arm? I'm sorry, but I consider myself a two-arm-needing woman. Talk about a complete waste of time. Plus, to add insult to injury, later in the afternoon, Texas texts that he is feeling much better and I should drag my ass back to New Jersey. I passed on the invite and deleted his phone number. One thing I will never tolerate is flaky ass people.

# Pieces of J (Late Spring 2022)

Some monkeys are hard to eliminate. The same monkey was again attached to the back, telling me it was time to hunt. Once again, I found myself on Ashley Madison, but I would try up my game and standards this time. There would be no fast food fucking requests to anyone. There would be no more cock takeout in the backseat. That proved disastrous, and after too many soul-sucking experiences, I needed more. No, this time, I would have "standards '—no one under 35 or single. Age-appropriate vocabulary proving they had at least graduated high school was necessary. The men must be respectable at all times unless prompted not to. They would also have agreed to meet for coffee and leave their dicks in the car before we made any other arrangements would be created.

After the previous autumn of absolute failures, I didn't need any more disappointments in seeking a friend with benefits. Due to the various devastations of deplorable choices, I fine-tuned my. I needed to develop a particular process and set standards in my search: first, fundamental attraction, basic communication skills, and some, they needed to have some sense of class. Returning to Ashley Madison, the men selected must fill these particular shoes. Jason seemed to be a good shoe fit. Jason was a married lawyer from New Jersey in his late thirties. He was attractive, and his writing was far from the two-dimensional basic nonsense of show me your tits. He followed a different script than the rest of the pack, which intrigued him enough to investigate. The texting between us was, of course, hot and even rather creative on both ends. We finally agreed to meet for coffee at a Panera Bread near the Outer bridge.

Jason arrived only a few minutes after I had just finished ordering a basic coffee. He was a bit taller than me and adorable. While awaiting my order, I hear a seductive whisper, "I'm not disappointed." My toes curled in my boots as the worker behind the counter handed me my drink. Did I hit liquid gold? While he was waiting for his order, I found an excellent table in a far corner way in the back so we could begin the game of seduction with little attention from anyone else. We sat across from each other while the flirting continued and intensified. Feeling his hand on my leg, he whispered all the creative things he wanted to do with my body. Although his tone and mannerisms were utterly a turn-on, I could barely determine what he was saying. Maybe I should have included that I'm slightly hard of hearing in my online profile. Trying my best to react to what I thought he was saying, I didn't respond verbally. Instead, I just nodded in agreement with whatever he was saying. Jason could have been whispering that he was going chop me up and eat my dismembered body, and I would shake my head in agreement. Biting my lower lip, I looked immensely turned on to indicate that we were on the same topic, but he could be whispering his love for rabbit stew and gangster movies. These are moments when using my dad's 'pretending to hear you' skills might not benefit me. However, he suggested we sit in his car for a bit. That was clear.

Even though the parking lot was far from private, Jason and I agreed it was private enough to make out in the front seat. His hand revisited my leg and traveled upward to that dangerous area where his intensity became apparent. As my hand returned the similar gestures between his legs, he continued to whisper all the nasty things he wanted to do., Although we were sitting incredibly close, I still could not discern what he was saying. I was pretty sure it was sexual and had nothing to do with cannibalism. Moaning and kissing him as seductively as I could muster was my best response to indicate that we were on the same page. However, he asked if we could move to the car's back seat. The back seat was two separate seats and not entirely conducive for sex. There were signs that a small child might have occupied the chair I was sitting in if I went down that emotional road as my legs opened, my welcoming fingers on and in me. With little resistance on his part, I was able to take out his average-sized cock and proceeded to give him head. I was performing this task well or to his liking because Jason came quickly. Soon after his ejaculation, Jason had to 'get going.' The change in his mannerisms indicated his completion for the day. The texting barely existed after, and I knew the writing on the wall that he was not the shoes I was looking for.

He didn't try to talk up any game or try to bullshit me. The definition of a beautiful, raw truth of a person was sharing a giant-sized cookie with me. I think we talked for a good thirty minutes. I like this person, and I also wanted him to like me. One thing he did mention is that he wasn't into sleeping with multiple partners. It wasn't 'he's a thing'. I just nodded and wondered if blow jobs in parking lots counted but kept my questioning to myself. We left Panera Bread, and he walked me to my car. He kissed me on the cheek and said he'd text me shortly.

To his word, he texted within a couple of hours, "Finally a moment to digest the wonderful experience meeting you. As you probably sensed, I'm looking for more than just action. It's the feeling of being loved and appreciated if that's not weird". In that short time, we were together, I felt a connection between us. We must respect our other lives and still have those moments between us. "I wanted to take you back to my apartment," the text continued. You got me with the (Moments in Time). And I'm capitalizing on it". He was referring to a previous text I wrote 'So I guess we're, for now, just waiting for the cracks of time to give us further opportunities to let us in". For some reason, J brought out some cliché version of Emily Dickinson in me.

The word "love" was used in J's text. This word was a word I've been avoiding since S. And "feelings"??!! Could I allow myself to feel and take that chance to express them? This word was a bit terrifying because I knew from experience that "love" is connected to "pain" in these arrangements. I understood it would eventually hurt if I went down that emotional road. I've been avoiding "hurt" at this level like a motha-fucker. My response was, "When I started this AM process, I expected it to be like having to try on a shit load of shoes (Shoes as a metaphor) before finding a pair that fit." Putting that thought out there sort of made me feel cheap and even a bit gross about myself. "I can't say yet if you're the shoes (sorry. I think I need a better metaphor); however, I think it's safe to say I'm going to explore this one pair alone and leave the others at the store." I terminated my Ashley Madison account after sending a message stating, "I apologize, but I think I found a particular path I wish to explore" to the tiny number of men I was still in contact with. Allowing this person to know me, I would slowly reveal what I kept under the curtain to someone, which terrified me. Could I allow myself to show love and be vulnerable?

The following Tuesday, I set out to steal a moment in those allusive cracks in time. On my lunch break, we met at the park near work. Finding it impressive that he discovered the 'make out' portion of the park on his own, we stood by his car talking. However, J refused to kiss me because he treated himself to something containing onion and peppers for passing his physical for work. He kept saying he wished he had time to brush and floss. His reasoning was adorable but yet a bit annoying. I was wearing a long black skirt and a black tank top that made the view of my cleavage a challenge to a man who consumed onions and peppers. We leaned on his car, and I leaned into him, making his rationality on his breath unimportant. I honestly didn't smell anything offensive.

Finally, J read my body language and asked if I'd like to sit in his car. He eventually kissed me with some hesitation because he was so nervous about his breath. There was no taste of any onion or peppers, just him. Car kissing in these arrangements, I usually feel slutty because that's what I ordered in the past, just sex. However, kissing J was passionate. I didn't feel dirty like I'd normally expect to feel. I felt like this was what I wanted to be doing: being with him. There was such a need beyond the physical in our kiss. There was a communication between two people who wished for each other more than just sex. What the hell??!! Unfortunately, having to return to work, it was evident at this point we wanted and how we felt. Well, I had a lovely assumption of what we both wanted.

After that, J did something very unexpected. He granted me access to his Instagram. Knowing this sounds a bit stupid, but it's a big deal in my head. He lowered his curtain to reveal his life, or at least the part he wanted to share with everyone else in his circle. It's like saying, 'This is me. I'm real. What you see is what you get". How could I not develop feelings for a person who does that? I can just shrug at this gesture. Here is what I learned after reviewing his Instagram. Jon adores his children. He loves music and is probably very close to his sister. There are videos of him playing and even singing. How the hell can I not be completely blown away? There are a couple of clips of him singing Leonard Cohen's Hallelujah. The Katie Lang version she sang in the 2010 Olympics opening ceremony in Vancouver is my favorite version of Hallelujah. It is still my favorite. J also has access to my Instagram and sees my art, cats, and son. The only two people I ever shared that level of reality and trust with were Joe and, of course, S, but although I loved them both, they were so far away from the present, and I am not who I was then.

To go to someone's home is a big deal for me. Not only do I save 50.00 bucks on my half of the hotel room, but it's unsleazy. Also, it shows the level of trust of the person giving their home address to someone they met only a week ago. My only minor request was a place to park and music playing when I arrived. We texted back and forth prior. The text's tone had a romantic level I was not accustomed to. Usually, these texts between men and myself are purely sexual. However, these are between everyday conversations and romantic prose. J's creative energy somehow summoned the Emily Dickerson in me. I was feeling aroused by him and, at the same time, terrified that I would feel feelings I typically avoid feeling. Feelings on this level are not my best quality. This situation would only end in some or many levels of pain because pain is permanently attached to love. There is no discontinuing the two.

Calling out sick from work, I arrived at J's apartment around 12:45 pm. As requested, he left the driveway available for me. Entering the front door, I heard the faint sound of music from the bedroom. Without much hesitation, allowing sexual aggression to emerge from deep within me, I kissed him hungrily. We both needed this moment to turn the world off and roam within this created bubble for ourselves. However, I did gulp down a small bottle of vodka and a pot of gummy to enhance the experience and calm my nerves before entering his tiny one-bedroom apartment. I found it easy to let go and be with him. My mind was able to focus on the singular sensations. J led me to his tiny bedroom. His music was soft and romantic, but I didn't recognize it. I find that music sets the pace of the moment. Having him select the music placed him in charge of the pace I was to follow.

I was allowing my heart to guide my body in this naked connection. It was like revisiting a foreign land and not permitting my heart to explore anything since Stephen was the center of my world. It was like riding a bike, but you know you'll fall and crash into a wall. I usually leave my heart in the car during these moments. This time, it came attached to my body. Permitting myself to feel passion instead the simple act of fucking, I was able to maintain eye contact. At least I could carry out the illusion of togetherness while we were together. Some costumes are just easier to put on than others. J came good three times. The first one made it pretty clear that, due to the excitement that was building up and the fact it was a bit of time since he got laid, his orgasm would come hard and fast. He did not disappoint. Plus, I summoned my seduction skills to go on full force. The poor man didn't stand a chance, and neither did I.

I completed J's needs once he found his last release. He offered me the use of his shower, which I accepted. Before leaving his place, he wanted to show off his musical skills and played three songs for me. Two of them, he wrote and composed himself. Trying desperately not to melt on his couch, I watched him sing and play. Not being a good judge of what can be called musically talented, his music came from his soul. There's no denying having someone share this part of themselves completely took my breath away. I wasn't concerned if my breath would never return. It was just after 2 pm. I confessed that I had not eaten anything. Feeling horrible over my malnutrition, he wanted to go to Panera Bread. We sat. We ate. Looking at him as though I wanted to devour him with my Lobster mac and cheese, we talked like two normal human beings would sit and talk. We said goodbye.

J simply just wants someone to fuck without any drama but with a catch attached to it. He desires to feel connected to someone, which confuses me. How do you know when and where to draw the connecting lines? Wanting to feel loved with a hidden notion, this would be pretend. The limit on the give and take when emotions are concerned is not my wheelhouse. Seeing and understanding the limits of 'feelings,' I didn't know if my heart would close my eyes to the nature of the reality of the situation. What can two people expect to gain when they have found each other on Ashley Madison?

I didn't understand why J limited himself to a dating site for married people because he's separated and has his place. There's no need for him to seek around. He could easily find someone on a single dating website if he wanted to. It is as though he has not permitted himself to be happy. He is denying himself a normal relationship. Maybe that's why I've been brought into his life, even though it's pretty clear he will never find that happiness with me. However, having a knack for playing pretend, I could give him this required illusion. Either way, this relationship, arrangement, affair, or whatever you want to call it has a sad ending. Through my weird way of expressing myself metaphorically via text and art, I wondered if he had any idea how I felt. For some reason, but no fault of his, feeling a high level of insecurity made this 'pretend' thing challenging. Our pretend play brought out the layers of the various layers of myself I was initially trying to escape from. Or maybe it was proof that I'm incapable of handling monogamous relationships. By juggling more than one relationship at a time, I would find it much easier to detach from just one person. Plus, I'd feel balanced. My emotions wouldn't be stuck on one person, and the hurt wouldn't be an issue. Each relationship would be an emotional buffer from the others.

With only thirty-five minutes to spare, we met again for a lunchtime quickie a few days later. From all the sexually explicit texting between us beforehand, my blood was overboiling as I walked through J's front door. There is no time for pleasantries or conversation. I stepped up to J without saying hello and allowed my lips and tongue to communicate everything. Quickly, our bodies found his bed, and our clothes found the floor. J's choice of music seemed a bit emotional, making me feel a little uneasy. Whatever this was, emotions had no place. Strange how thirty-five minutes felt like an eternity yet offered no time to catch a breath. Before getting dressed, J offered me his shower, which I declined. He was afraid I'd turn to work smelling like sex. Not wanting to wash him and the moment away, I needed to feel him on my skin a bit longer.

Wanting the moment to sink into my pores and bloodstream, I needed every last bit of the memory still attached to me as long as possible. As I was leaving, J thanked me for coming over like I had some sort of community.

Sometimes, my mind has a moment of clarity where I may not see a start and finish but the breadcrumbs in between. However, most of the time, I feed myself a load of horseshit to justify my actions. One load of horse shit I tried to sell myself was thinking I was J's segue to the meaningful direction life destined for him. I knew I wasn't any destination in his life but a bridge or a series of bridges in his life. I was deluding myself to believe that he would taste a preview of that happiness. As painful as that might sound, these thoughts keep any emotions at bay. By over-rationalizing, I pretended not to have any feelings whatsoever for J.

Again, I am leaving J's place, as these moments we have together aren't long but long enough to begin to sink deep into my core. It's been a while since being with someone in which it didn't just feel like fucking. One of J's issues is that if he's super excited, he tends to cum a bit fast. I overexcited him on purpose, and I think I get off watching him struggle to control himself. Having this sort of control over him is somewhat of a turn-on. One day, I didn't make it easy by arriving with a short dress and no underwear. As a last-minute decision, he told Alexis to play the doors my body moved to as we stood against his bedroom doorway. My hips moved against him to the music. I have to say that he brings out the evil, seductive side of me. Once that evil is allowed out, it's hard to bottle back up. He managed to last longer than he had previously, which I appreciated. I could only stay for a bit because I had to get to work, but J always seemed to have pieces of the world on his shoulders. J's life doesn't allow him much time with work and family. His mom expected him to power-wash her house on top of him, working long, crazy shifts. So, for him to find those cracks in time for himself was a challenge. It was easy to tell that he wanted to be an excellent father to his kids. I will never even try to compete with that.

Sometimes, over the weekend, J would go silent. Compared to the weekdays, there's little to no texting on weekends. He's usually with his kids and shouldn't be focusing much time on the married librarian that's been coming over some mornings for a good fuck. Not being good with silence, I quickly become restless like an unsupervised puppy. I hunt for new noises or summon old ones to keep the silence at bay. If I'm lucky, little ghosts from the not-so-different past emerge from months of their silence. Because there's something a bit broken inside me, I end up welcoming these tiny distractions to fill the emptiness within the deafening silence. Literally at once, as if I had the power to bring back the dead, three ghosts appeared in a Snapchat message: Sean, Jay, and Tony. The bizarre comfort I felt from chatting with them would lead down another broken path or paths I should not venture. The silence at least stopped or at least muted for the time being.

Jay was perhaps the simplest to deal with out of the three ghosts. We knew we would never meet. He was exclusively into 100% virtual fucking. Some people just love sharing virtual masturbation, which is perhaps the safest option. The only problem is that it does require a good level of privacy, and, on my part, that's not happening at home. Jay and I tried to jerk off together on camera, but it ended up being far more stressful than actually meeting someone in real life. Preferring to keep my fuck up behaviors outside the house, my interest in Jay didn't last long.

Then there's fucken Tony. He was a guy in his late twenties whom I met on Ashely Madison over a year ago. After months and months of sexting with empty plans to hook up, it was easy to get bored with Tony. However, hearing from him after a few days was refreshing. We finally agreed to meet, but I controlled the situation completely. In the back of my mind, I knew he would come with a big fucken warning label. Plus, I've always sensed that he was just fucking with me. Knowing this would be a complete bust, I wouldn't invest much time or energy in this meeting. We would meet in a public park on Monday morning and take it from there. Even though I knew he was probably full of shit, I was my usual nervous self with a messed up digestive system. Adding a peach-flavored vodka to my peach-flavored iced tea helped settle the crazy butterflies. I waited on one of the picnic tables, avoiding feeling foolish. I didn't hear from Tony in the morning, and that provided enough information that I was wasting my time. After waiting for fifteen minutes, all I got out of it was the nice buzz from the shot of vodka in the iced peach ice tea. After waiting a full fifteen minutes, I blocked Tony. Having no time for bullshit, I'm tired of these mean men thinking they have any control over me. I was only slightly bummed, but as I said, he only got fifteen minutes of my time.

Sean is another ghost that lingers on and off Snapchat. Although we've tried to meet, it always falls through. Normally, Sean would ghost me the day of the planned meeting, only to say 'hi' again a month later. It was like he had some bizarre memory loss or something. I am not sure if he falls in the same category as Tony. I think the kid was just completely clueless. We have tentative plans to meet near him at a hotel in NJ, but we've had these plans before. Either one of us will bow out with some sort of excuse. It's a weird flirting ping pong game that's been going on since last August with a series of these tentative plans. Our plans to hook up on Saturday will fall through, too, but the random texting on Snapchat will probably continue.

These were merely distractions needed to stay somewhat centered and not romantically disillusioned by fucking J once a week. Wanting to believe my actions were working and the restless emotions I was fighting had faded. The things we do to feel detached and numb and to kill the illusions of romance. Soon enough, J will probably get tired of me or him. I just didn't want to feel anything in the process. A forward motion toward nothingness is a more straightforward way to exist. There will be more distractions that will pop up. The forgotten ghosts of Chat's past will probably never remember that strange woman they chatted with. Maybe they need the same distractions as well. The need to forget our lives leads moments to part from our familiar skin. Whatever pain that harbored under the surface slightly dulled into a minor tweak of my heart.

After a weekend of near silence, J and I meant to meet again at his place on my day off. However, the cycle of my female body didn't like that plan. My cycle has been a bit more frequent these past months, with no rhyme or reason for when it wants to present itself and for how long. Talk about an unwanted visitor showing whenever it damn well pleases. Although it was an extremely light flow, the parts required to meet with J were out of service.

Expecting him to say, "Oh well. Maybe next week then," or something along those lines, but instead, he stated, "No problem, there's still coffee and breakfast." I needed to clarify that this meant being in a public establishment, having coffee, and just hanging out like ordinary people. This type of arrangement was untested water for me. To be in a man's company like regular friends without any sexual encounter was simply unheard of. When was just enjoying someone's company ever an option due to sex being currently unavailable? Apparently, to J, it was. That just doesn't happen. It took me a while to allow this new information to sink in. To feel like a human being and just have holes of availability to fill.

We agreed on an old hangout, Panera Bread, around 10 am. J was just coming off his twenty-four-hour shift, and I was off from work that day. Our regular booth was available. That was the booth we sat in during our first meeting and again after our first meeting at his place. It's a smaller booth than the rest there, but it was ours. We talked for nearly an hour and a half. Well, he did most of the rambling. However, I did ask questions about why he joined the fire department and what he did before he made the choices he made professionally. We discussed our creative process and how music and the written word are connected. Talking like ordinary people would speak in a public establishment made me feel normal. This 'normal' feeling scared me because I simply never learned or had the proper tools to understand it entirely, but I did appreciate it.

J's interpretation of what "we" are, or how I understand his interpretation, is that we have a 'nice thing going. This 'nice thing going 'doesn't have to be rushed or forced to fill our voids. For the most part, I see and understand his point of view. The voids could also mean a certain emptiness. I think I understand the emptiness in his current life. Sympathizing and relating with that emptiness, my 'void' is far more complex to his understanding of these terms. My voids are cannons scared and pox marked by various memories. If you look closely enough, you can see the claw marks on the walls of these voids where the various demons keeping residences have attempted to claw themselves to the surface. J cannot understand such voids. Throughout the years, I have built walls to keep such voids safe from the world and the world safe from them. These structures have been my safe place where I can't be hurt or touched. Or at least that's the bullshit I try to sell myself every so often. I might be too much of a broke person for J to comprehend. I struggle to understand sometimes. Still chatting with other men online to fill these caverns of voids imprinted in me is only silliness. J has no clue how broken of a person he is dealing with and the depth I am capable of trying to fill the empty spaces only to hollow them back out again. He has no fucken clue. However, I doubt I do anyway.

As for little ghosts popping up from the online world, there's Alan. I met Alan in the same place as Jason and J at about the same time. We have been chatting on and off for some time now. Alan was either my age or a bit older. Like J, he's musically inclined with the guitar. He also wrote and composed some original works. Maybe I have typed these days. These musically inclined men with tunes wondering with their souls. As a result, I removed Alan from my hook-up equations because J swept me away at the time, too. However, Alan also ruled me out of his equation. He was uncomfortable with the multi-partner setup he deemed a "Deal breaker." Ok, I respected that and let him go about his business. Certain situations are just not meant for all.

Alan reached out again when I needed to find a distraction from J. Reminding him about his "deal breaker," he said he would stretch his horizons. Interesting. That probably meant he was striking out left and right with other options in his view of how dispersion makes us lower our standards just to feel human touch. Unfortunately, I understood that logic way too well. Between the legs, I'm probably the only option he has to explore close to an actual human. In this lifestyle, yes, I'm calling it a lifestyle; things can often change on a dime. People of interest disappear without a virtual trace while ghosts of texting past knock on your device's screen. Attempting to be as honest with Alan about this J situation, I told him my need for balance. The emotional rollercoaster caused by focusing on one person seemed too much like drowning in an unwanted void. Alan had my attention since I hadn't heard from J in almost 48 hrs. and because I'm like a child who requires entertainment. He was just another shiny new thing, and in words that would be too insulting, I made clear to him.

Creating a day of escape became second nature by then. Calling out of work and just going missing for the day wasn't something I did too often. If I had nothing pending at work and it looked as though my absence would not affect the flow of the day for any of my co-workers, I would sometimes monopolize the opportunity to just fall off the radar. In these missing hours, I hoped to have a chance to meet Alan for a drink. I would determine whether it would be more than a drink within meeting Alan for the first ten minutes or less. I'm sure he hoped for a good car session. If we could locate a decent parking spot near the place, I'd choose to meet him, and if I found him somewhat attractive, car play could be on the table. The hotel thing was something I knew I wasn't ready for. However, as I said, things can change on a dime. Not hearing from J makes specific changes become fact without much hesitation.

Just as I typed that above paragraph, I got a text from J. Yeah, like, holy fuck. J apologizes that his schedule has been busy. Saying I understood. I sympathized. The adult part of my brain empathizes and understands how our adult lives can easily overpower us. He hoped to have some free time very soon. Does that mean he'll have free time for me, his dental health, nuclear science, what? In my response, I mentioned great escape plans soon. J either didn't get the hint or missed the concept of free time. Either way, the plans to meet Alan would still be in effect. Even if J somehow sneaks in on my escape day with his "free time," canceling on Alan was not happening.

I planned to meet Alan at 1 pm at Applebee's. If I'm going to do this, I'm going to need a bar at finger reach. As of now, the 'meet' would just be drinks. Seduction and maybe some car foreplay could happen if things worked out and if we could find a private parking spot. Since J has been up in the air about having me come over anytime soon, Alan would be a welcoming distraction. J had been working multiple shifts. I should get that he's exhausted while still trying to be a good dad to his kids. It's not J's fault that I'm a bit fucked up. That I'm planning to fuck someone else in the Applebee's parking lot. He didn't do anything wrong. It's me. It's always been me and how I deal.

The night before I met Alan, J said he was available that morning. I've never met up with two people back to back in one day. I thought about it and had some close calls of being that fucked up. That morning, J had just gotten off the 24-hour day shift, so my expectations of what to expect were rationally limited. It would be quick and hopefully lack any emotions. What can be called an adorable version of lingerie, J comes to his door wearing Cookie Monster pj pants. That was maybe his third time wearing them after I commented on how fucken adorable they were. Without hesitation, the energy in the room eloquently becomes electrical. Sensuality becomes our central language, which our inner predators hear and obey. In the smallest of details, I experience things new to me. No one ever lifted, so my legs could straddle around someone as they carried me to their bedroom. They were always concerned that some might throw their back out. J lifted me with ease. Even though I hit my head on the light overhead, it felt nice to feel that level of passion. My head wasn't the worst for wear, as I giggled while he carried me onto his bed. 'I'm meeting Alan at 1 pm' echoes in my mind. Our bodies respond to each movement with ease. 'I'm meeting Alan at 1 pm', the echo repeats. Instead of listening to an echo, I focused on all my sensual resources on J's weak zones of his body. These are the zones that cause various moans from his throat. For someone awake for 36 hours straight, even he is surprised by his capabilities to satisfy me as I come apart underneath. 'I'm meeting Alan at 1 pm'. The echo returned to bury any emotions trying to surface.

Still having some time to kill after leaving J's apartment, I ended up at the same Panera Bread where I met Jason a couple of months ago. Sitting at the exact table, too, I said, "Hello, Jason" to the empty seat before me. Having too much time to kill forces me to reflect on this day more than I want to. I just left J's apartment and will meet Alan in about an hour. The knowledge of my actions keeps my veins slightly frozen. This layer of ice keeps my inner heart locked and hidden. I'm not permitting myself to feel anything. However, it didn't help that J used the term 'Love Making' while I was there. Is that what we're still calling it? I'm not sure what "this' actually is. The word 'love' cannot be digested at this time as I force it out of my epiglottis. Sometimes, J says words like he has randomly plucked them off the verbal tree.

My actual test of character was to take place in an hour. To sit at a bar with a man whose intentions are based solely on what was between my legs. 'Can I do this?' I thought to myself. How hollowed out from within can I be without my inner voice whispering pleading,' Please, no"? Will this layer thicken just enough so I don't hear that whisper? Will the rest of my body absorb the numbness in my veins? How fucked up have I genuinely become at this very moment and this particular hour? Even before I got to the bar, my body began its protest. Not eating anything all day, I felt the burning sensation build up in my chest. The only thing lingering in my body is some iced Peach white tea. Why didn't I get a bite to eat at Panera Bread?

I am just getting to Applebee's before 1 pm. The bar's location is throwing me off since it's outside the restaurant's center. All the Applebee bars are located in the center of the establishment. Instead, the bar is off to the right and front of the establishment. Not having the bar wear, I'd imagine it to be thrown off and cause the burning in my chest to rise into my throat. Taking the seat at the end where there's some sort of a corner because corners give me a sense of security. However, sitting in this corner, my back is to the door, which cancels out any sense of security the corner seat offers. It doesn't help that the automatic hand sanitizer is attached to the wall directly behind this corner seat. My stomach protest continued in full force as Alan arrived.

At first glance, I can tell this isn't going to work. There was no attraction to Alan at all. There was not even a tiny spark. It's not like he was terrible-looking. This person was just not for me at all. He's older than I thought, closer to 60 than 50. I was ordering a White Peach Sangria and nachos, wondering if the spark would make its way into me after a decent drink. Instead, the drink is making me feel even worse. As I tried to engage in as much small talk as possible, my humor kept going to dark and morbid topics. Telling someone you just met that you're probably e coli resistant because your dad never washed his hands after he took a shit is probably not the best go-to topic.

Feeling the nausea take hold of my inner body is probably my conscience trying to protect me from doing anything fucked up. "Listen to your body, listen to your body', I echo in the back of my head. Pushing the sangria away, I order a club soda, hoping it will prevent me from puking all over Alan's pants. " My stomach often acts up," I say apologetically. Of course, he saw that as a tactic in communication that I'm not interested in, which is entirely accurate. Yet the stomach thing is for real. Not even a symphony blow-job in the back of the car isn't going to happen. The thought of someone's cock testing my gag reflexes would be the worst idea ever. After an hour and a half, I threw in the towel. Any ability to pretend now became drained up. The show was over. All I wanted to do then was lay down for a few minutes. My head was beginning to pound, which usually indicated whatever was in my stomach had a good chance of coming back up. Alan walked me to the car. We hugged. I drove home to crash on the couch and reassess the entire fucked situation as well as my life choices for the week. If I didn't hear from Alan again, I would be perfectly ok with that.

I received a text from Alan to check how I was feeling; he asked what the possibilities were for moving forward. As I hugged a bottle of ginger ale, he asked, "Moving forward or moving on." Now I should have been a fucken grown-up and responded "moving on " with no hesitation. That would be the correct answer. "No' was the answer my body wanted me to text back, so why do I get stuck in these moments of hesitation? The situation was not that complicated. Why is the word 'No' a challenge to say? There was no attraction to him. The plan of drowning out my feelings for J by fucking someone else has completely backfired. My body had stepped up and made the decision I shouldn't be struggling to make. Trying to act some sort of resemblance to my age, instead of typing "Moving on ", I just typed "on." "Good luck" was his last response.

J and I saw each other again a week after almost vomiting on Alan. We both seem to possess what feels like an enormous sexual energy when we're together. There is rarely any need for verbal communication because our bodies have mastered the required communication. Often, I don't have a chance to put down my phone and car keys when I walk into his apartment. It's like a magnetic force that pulls us together. How easy it is to let yourself float the euphoric present. J always has his Cookie Monster PJ pants on for me as well. Who said romance is dead?

Joe and S were born nearly a decade ago. They were both, in each of them, whirl-wind romances. The level of trust between each of them came naturally over time. There were moments of experimentalism. J and I discussed experimentalism in our texts as we began to trust each other. Luckily, I still had my strap-on and required accessories hidden in an old beat-up suitcase in the closet. J wanted to be fucked in the ass. Getting pegged is a much more considerable male fetish than most of them will openly omit. Many men have this bi-curiosity but refuse to explore it on any level because they are afraid of being labeled 'fags". Unfortunately, there will always be this clash between socially instilled machismo and the beautiful spectrum of sexuality. In some form and spectrum of 'love,' there was a level of trust between Joe and Stephen to share various inner desires that we don't usually share developed between them. I did love Joe and Stephen, and in their ways, they loved me and trusted me to share something they had kept secret. Now, J was developing that level of trust and wouldn't deny him. He wanted to become 'My Little Bitch".

Nothing ensures a significant connection between souls like well-plotted plans. To provide some quality time with J, I called out of work. The strap-on was packed and hidden in the car. I prepared and packed all needed tools and dress attire throughout the weekend. He wanted me to dominate, control, and even a bit humiliates him. Although I have always been at home in a submissive role in these games, I planned to dominate him how I wanted to dominate. My actions would mirror my desires. His ass will be red and sore on the inside as well as the outside. I won't be able to bind him the way I wanted to be tied. Instead, it will command stillness. I planned to punish J for every unrequited movement or unasked word.

Giving him what he'd asked for while sharing this moment made me feel so close to him. Yes, this was some kinky shit, but it's also trusts. J trusted me with the knowledge of an inner dark desire. This kink is something he'd never shared with anyone due to the typical fear of judgment. Making it clear that he had no reason to feel ashamed or embarrassed, J lowered his guard as I entered his apartment wearing a fishnet bodysuit and heels. As I attempted to remain in a dominant persona, with little hesitation, J went on his knees as ordered to be collared. The collar signified my ownership.

I then ordered him to attach the strap-on and the purple plastic dildo to my body. "I'm going to fuck you with this'. Adding the leash, I led him to his bedroom on his hands and knees. With a leather riding crop, I smacked ass as J crawled towards the bed. Although not the strongest person in the world, I wanted to ensure he felt each blow. "Lips Sealed," I commanded as I was making each ass cheek a little pink. I ordered him onto the bed, still on his hands and knees. With his ass up and out, I continued my aggressive punishment. As soon as I saw the delightful shade of red, I began switching from tender caress to hard smacks. With my pointing finger, I started slowly and lightly foundling his tight asshole before penetrating the opening with lubrication.

Hopefully, J was feeling like a little bitch' as I teased the lubricated tip of the dildo around his virgin hole. It was either now or never as the tip attempted to open him. J screamed as soon as I began to penetrate him and turned over as though he was having second thoughts. From my own experience receiving anal, it does hurt like a bitch if your body is too tense. Also, certain positions allow better entrance with less pain. Ordering him on his back with his legs spread upward, I made a second attempt. This position worked for S and Joe. So, I hoped it would work for J. He took a deep breath as I slowly slid the tip of the purple dildo inside him. 'My brave boy,' I thought. Deeper and deeper with each thrust, he moaned loader and loader. By the intense look of ecstasy, I knew I wasn't hurting him. His body was drowning in a new experience. The shock first embedded entry might have assumed the entering of a violent interaction. Was it the walls of convention-breaking that he felt? The rebel of the expected or just a dare he had within himself? Maybe it was patience or trust; what once felt like a penetrating rage became an invited sensation. An opening of delight discovered as a new understanding of textures and shiny new things are new ventures to revisit between the mixture of all other new possibilities. As I struggled to keep my rhythm in tune with his groans, the thrusting began to become exhausting. Except for giving him a pleasurable experience, I wasn't getting much out of fucking his ass. My thighs were starting to burn from using unused muscles. Pretending to dominate someone was also draining. It's like walking in a pair of shoes that don't fit. Eventually, your feet will protest before needing removal. J would comment a few days later that he could still feel the impact I made in his ass.

The need to find some sort of emotional balance had decreased. Unfortunately, my emotional attachment had increased. As a result, I began the slow spiral of insecurity when J wasn't as available as I'd like. He apologizes for becoming swamped working for over 24 hours. Plus, he always wants to be there for his kids whenever possible. I need to respect. The man also has a very close life with music. He's often rehearsing or going to a concert. All of that needs respect on my part and not allowing the abandoned feeling to take control. Having to get over myself by filling my time with things I'm passionate about, like drawing, writing, and spending more time with friends instead of trying to cause more internal damage to myself. The withdrawal of him kicked in. I hate feeling like I'm un-tethered balloons left afloat, waiting for his fingers to reach and hold me in a quiet moment of silence. Until then, I drift. The only temporary relief I found was writing. I would write out all the complex feelings hovering inside as letters I'd never send.

*Dear J,*

*Suddenly, I feel electrified and renewed as my hand opens the screen door, and I hear a voice. My body doesn't flinch in defense as my guard goes down. A feeling not felt in over a decade finds itself in the present. My mind doesn't try to escape into the several narratives. The pieces of myself not felt in over a decade come rushing through my bloodstream and out of my pores. The primitive creature hiding within is now in control, hungry, and willing to please and be pleased. If bodies could have an open discussion, we'd hear their agreement.*

*Until next time.*

My emotional well-being has taught me to accept balance on its own without seeking out any distractions. Those moments of feeling abandoned when I don't hear from J aren't as frequent. The storms that have caused so much restlessness inside me in the past have quieted. They are only to be awakened when there are well-planned plans, as there is almost every week. If I was in love with J, it doesn't feel like I was clawing at the walls out of desperation. Instead, I learned to appreciate the moment as one would understand the beauty of clean, newly fallen snow that will eventually melt and never fall again.

*Dear J,*

*Knowing you will never read these chapters and the words that fill them as they were never originally written with you in mind. This project of writing my experiences down began before we met. Once started as a simple outlet to try to understand myself and my actions, it has mutated into chapters. Why does a married female of my age seek comfort from random strangers and manage to go about it like a fucked-up heroin addict? If you or anyone knew of all the various unsafe situations I have put myself in before I met you, you would probably walk away shaking your head in bewilderment. Writing down as many pieces of myself as I can remember them is daunting. Most traumatic events were more accessible to revisit than the happier ones. Most people have the luxury of suppressing their trauma like a dog covers its bones. I can recall various horrors on the surface at the snap of a finger. I know there is nothing ordinary about how my mind works. Even with a safe detachment between us, your presence keeps me safe from myself without any emotional investment. However strange as it may seem, you evoked the emotions I've tried to stay dormant, and those feelings have inspired me to delve into this so-called project. You accomplished this by just being yourself from day one. Not once did I ever manipulated, mind fucked, or discredited as a human being by you. I hope you will at least read this part and feel grateful. I also wish to know you in some capacity for a long time.*

*Best-*

I can leave work early on a Friday and cherish these moments when I can fall off the radar. To zip out of my existence to become something else became as easy as one zipping off a jacket. This time, J was given the reins of dominance in our ongoing roleplay game. How he liked to handle me in our previous encounters, I already knew he carried the gene of dominance. J can be sexually aggressive on a dime's notice once he's given the green light to do so. As I walked through his door at 1 pm, I offered him the green light to let loose his darker appetite. Give him complete creative freedom to express his darkest side, and I wondered if I would be tied up, blindfolded, or restrained by other means.

As I entered his apartment, I locked the door behind me. It would be punishable if I didn't. J is standing in the middle of the kitchen naked but covering his cock, which is a bit odd since I've already met all his man parts. "You better get your fucken clothes off now!" he orders. 'Yay,' I think to myself. J is character. I obey as requested, but with a smart-ass smirk, I make him see. "Get that smile off your face, you slut!" J orders. He's enjoying himself, so I refrain from showing any resistance, and it feels wonderful to let myself go and become his slut, whore, plaything.

Getting smacked in the ass a bit, but it's barely hard, and I know I'll have to the point that out after. My ass can take a spanking, but J holds back. Respecting him for that, not wanting to cause any pain, I could discuss our limits later. Being restrained by his hand, J ordered me always to keep my hands above my head. J was very verbal in this dominant role. He mocks, slapping me by slapping his hand that's near my face. It's almost like erotic theatre, and J is the playwright setting a brutal scene. He was super conscious about not hurting me. However, that quickly changes as he bites my toes. For some reason, my toes became fair game in the welcoming brutality of J's teeth. As painful as it was, it's almost adorable. Allowing him to explore this dominance assisted him in having better control over his orgasm. J is usually a quick shooter in the sac. He owned the situation entirely and ensured I organized, which I did more than once. It's was awhile since I felt so completely fucked. After an excellent twenty-thirty minutes of being bitten, restrained, mock slaps, flipped on my back, flipped on all fours, flipped sideways, and beautifully verbally insulted, J finally permitted himself to cum. We were both completely done with no regrets.

As we shower together, J seems to want to wash me, which, again, is adorable. Making a bad judgment call, I allow my hair to get soaked. Shit, I knew he didn't have a blow-dry because of the lack of hair on his head. Luckily, neither of us was in any rush to leave. I'm about to have a free show as J starts to play his guitar. Struggling with his voice because he skipped the required vocal warming up, he tried to loosen those vocal cords the best he could. I loved watching him in his musical element. Music is a natural language to him. Deciding to take several pictures of him, his hands on the guitar, his feet perfectly perched on the stool, and his fingers on the cords. I captured these beautiful elements to draw later.

It had been a good month since I drew anything, and I feared I might have gotten rusty over the past few weeks. Messing up the first attempt, I began drawing the photos I took of J. I ensured I hit each angle perfectly and allowed the space between shapes to guide my pencil along the paper. It felt so sensual to draw him. It's feeling like I'm fucking him all over again with the tips of a sharpened pencil. Completing four drawings using color and charcoal. I rarely use color in any drawing, but my experience with J demands colors in these drawings. I am posting them on my social media pages, titling the series of them as "Pieces of a Musician," and I wonder if anyone could fully comprehend the emotion behind them.

I thought I was cool with this arrangement because that's what it is, an arrangement that's lasted four months. I find myself not emotionally cool with it. One day, we were to meet up, but he canceled. His responsible life wore him out before I could. I should be cool with it. I should understand that's just the reality of the 'arrangement. J's priority was and should be his kids. The same holds true with my kid. It is the silence that seemed to increase little by little each week that gnawed at me. This abandoned inner kid in me wasn't cool with it. Knowing what I'm capable of when these overwhelmed me, I tried so hard to stay away from the websites where I could attempt to take the edge off these irrational feelings. Even knowing how unsafe those actions are, I thought about every escape hatch out there to help me become a little numb. I hate this. I hate feeling. I hate wanting. Fuck I need to grow up. Sometimes, I redownload my Kik and Snapchat apps to see who might have contacted me and who I can distract myself from. The few messages on the app aren't exciting or even distractible. I delete the apps quickly.

J canceled again. The last time, he canceled because of general exhaustion. This time, J will be out of town for a good week. He went to the Adirondack Mountains with a handful of his co-workers. Not only did I miss him, I was jealous that he was going to the mountains as well. It sucked. From his texts that I seldom got by then, he still seemed interested, so I knew I should rule out that he was trying to blow me off. At the beginning of this arrangement, we agreed there would be a decent conversation if things weren't working for us. I was wondering if and when that conversation would happen, as promised, but I didn't want that conversation any time soon. If I'm lucky, J will send me pictures of the mountains to draw. I needed him to send images to draw so I could hold on to any bit of a connection left. The photographs and drawings were the closest things I would have as a lifeline. I'm not sure he understands me. Sometimes, I think J got me; occasionally, our brain waves felt so far apart.

J canceled again. He received a call to work at the last minute. I should take a hint from this guy because he keeps canceling. However, his texts, although fewer and fewer, were from a man with a tremendous sexual need. He repeatedly said he missed me, so perhaps there are no hints to take. In one of his last texts, he wrote he was afraid of losing me because of these back-to-back cancellations. What sort of human being was I to take comfort in another person's insecurities? We both had professions and family obligations that often can't be pushed away. Once again, I had to stomach the disappointment while putting on my big girl pants and chalking it all up as life. 'We will try again' was a whisper I would randomly pretend to hear.

When J and I finally managed to meet up, it felt like we hadn't seen each other in forever, and at the same time, it felt like no time had passed. J always had his Cookie Monster pj pants on as I entered his apartment door. I sometimes wondered if the man owned any other PJ pants. He had extra candles lit, but I wasn't sure if it was for romantic reasons or because he hadn't had an opportunity to clean his apartment.

I have a hard time not instantly getting turned on when I'm with him, which helps me quickly forget about my two awful days at work. Before going into his bedroom, he put on. Because J recently attended a My Chemical Romance concert, he had them blasting from his bedroom. A piece of rope on J's bed was exciting to see. Loving how playful he was and willing to spice things up, he spanked my ass a bit. This time I felt the sting of his hands on my ass cheeks. Still, his slaps weren't too painful but just enough to make my blood boil. He used the rope to restrain my hands before entering in various directions. The sexual chemistry we had together made it difficult not to want more and more of him. It is impossible not to enjoy every second and every inch of him. Then J did something a bit unexpected for me. He gave me an excellent massage. Having massages before but also knowing was only something that led up to sex. J was something special for me, and I wasn't required to pay him back. It was impossible not to melt even more than I already had. Afterward, we held each other and talked. Well, he mostly talked. I listened. My lack of communication is not due to any fault of his. From years of conditioning myself to stay silent, I forgot how to ramble in these situations. My voice just never felt welcomed in this world. J didn't try to push or force my words out. He would give me a moment to talk, but I would give him a look as though my words were stuck inside. There was no pressure and no expectations. He held me until it was time to go. However, while attempting to get dressed, I allowed my eyes and body to speak for me. J could pick up on my body language, and neither of us managed to get dressed for another fifteen minutes.

The first day of autumn arrived, and it was difficult to comprehend that I'd known J since late spring. If I had any expectations, I was not expecting to feel connected to someone as I did. It was strange to be in each other's lives without actually being in each other's. Randomly, but not frequently, I would check up on the old apps Kik and Snapchat. The apps didn't provide anything to strike my curiosity. The feeling of needing distractions from the distraction just wasn't there. J had given me a sense of inner balance that was missing for such a long time. I found I could exist in my reality better. For once, I had a sense of calm. Trying not to ponder what was to come was still a struggle. Things do end as quickly as they start. The moments of neediness would still go on, but I hope those moments would have less of an impact than they did many times before. Our essential life obligations will always be a property. Getting lost in abandonment was something I felt I could escape.

Five months ago, I first met J at Panera. Since then, we've met maybe once every other week if I'm lucky. Every time I leave his apartment, I wonder if that will be the last time I will ever see him. These feelings were coming from a place of extreme insecurity within me. The digestion of the experiences in my life has always made me feel like I was walking on shaky ground with people. Moving forward, I should wear a warning label for my inability to have 'normal' and 'healthy relations in any capacity. J and I had our routine down pat. We'd fucked as usual as soon as I walked through his door. If time allowed, I had an opportunity to hear him sing and play his guitar. He sometimes improvised with the lyrics he wrote and the chords that fit them best—mentioning that I have written a few songs myself here and there. When I write, the words often become summoned by music I never knew how to play. It's like being half-heard. Anyone could read or listen to the words I've written, but they will never hear the music behind the lines. J said he'd happily check them out and emailed me to send a few things. Maybe after he'd read them, you would know what chords would best fit. Someone could finally add music to my words. I always hear faint melodies pushing out the words from within me, and onto paper could become a reality. Although we both felt perfectly cool with the idea, he warned me that he might change a few things to turn my words into something musical.

Not only did writing express my various insecurities about him, myself, and this arrangement, but other brief arrangements in the past. I sent him something called "Play me one more time," which I had written over a month before I met J. That night, I allowed myself to tap into those adolescent insecurities and wrote: "It Hurts

Like Hell." It undoubtedly expressed my feelings about the current 'arrangement.' The only feedback I received was a thumbs-up emoji two days later when I asked if he got them. For the time being, it was the last communication from each other. Refusing to reach out after sharing my inner soul with someone when all I get is a thumbs-up emoji made me silently put my foot down.

It hurts like hell
Walking out your door
It hurts like hell
Walking to my car
I think I knew from day one
This would hurt like hell
But baby, I'll take these lonely nights
If I can hold you for a second
Baby, I'll hold my breath
Take what I can get
And bury it deep in my heart
I know I keep my cool. Still, it hurts like hell
I know I my thoughts to myself
But it hurts like hell
I know I should keep this feeling to myself. Still, it hurts like hell
I think I knew from day one
It would hurt like hell
But baby, I'll keep up my tough act
If I could feel you one more time
Baby, I'll keep playing it cool
If I could hold you in my arms one more time
I promise not to let it show

Those insecurities made me doubt not just writing it but also sharing it with J. If he rethought our whole situation after reading that 'it hurts like hell,' I wouldn't blame him. Knowing I should have just chalked it up as one of those many learning opportunities instead of taking it as an excuse to wear my pain on my sleeve. Instead of hoping for some artist collaboration, I began the painful process of checking my phone for a text or another thumbs-up emoji.

The devastation settled in. After sinking even deeper into insecurity, the destruction settled in. Logic and all rational thought had escaped me. If I could rip out my heart right now from my body and squeeze every bit of emotion out of my body, I might have felt some sense of relief. I was fighting to urge not to sink into my destructive patterns of lurking in shadows to hunt for distractions because I know precisely the brutal damage to create to feel dead inside. Desperately trying not to fall into that pattern of fucking away my pain because I know what gun to use and where to aim it. When J and I first met in Panera Bread, he said we were both adults and would have that 'conversation.' However, I was beginning to question if I was an actual adult or still a little girl waiting for a grown-up to rescue me from the kitchen of roaches and the kids who took delight in torturing me. Are these events at all connected? I'd rather have that 'conversation' and just move on. Maybe the 'conversation' is approaching soon. Will he put on big-boy pants and attempt to break the news? Will I pretend to have my adult-size pants on and pretend not to be affected by the 'conversation'? Maybe I'll just get another thumbs up.

Does stripping emotions take the same effort as stripping paint off a wall? Does it take as much time to return to the original wall color before you apply the first layers of colors? Trying to strip J from the interior walls inside me feels like repeatedly removing a scab off an unhealed wound. It was stupid and careless of me to let him pass the first layers. Another life lesson learned. Returning to AM one night, I hoped this letting process would move quickly. If anything, AM was there to shut off the emotions. I wanted to achieve that blissful numbness soon through a series of behaviors and actions. However, it didn't help when J started texting again. This time, I will use this current communication as an exercise in detachment. The walls will be up, secured, and unpreventable.

J's text said, "We should have grilled cheese and tomato soup after a live session." The detached devastation was now replaced by confusion. After not hearing from him in almost a week, thinking the song I sent was over the top, and there was an offering to confront foods and a 'love' session. Was that what we were referring to sex now? When asked if he would be available in a few days, he responded, 'For you, of course,' which I find confusing. "Of course," feels like an empty promise along the lines of 'For you, anything' and 'For you, anything'. Those statements are pretty much lying because there's no such thing as 'anything ', especially in these arrangements. 'Anything' belongs in fairytales and Nicholas Sparks novels, not in this arrangement. "Anything" makes the emotions I've tried to scrape off the walls sweep through to the surface. I need to eliminate them. I don't want them. Returning to AM, hoping to find an adequate drug to help crave out these nerve ends.

One thing that is hysterical or extremely sad about being back on AM is that there's always the same handful of men that were there over a year ago. These men are always the first to jump to any "new" female profile within the first 72 hours. I called them the welcoming committee, which was my private joke. However, knowing who is reposting, even if there isn't a picture to go with the profile, makes weeding through the first series of a billion messages more manageable and efficient. Being super careful about not posting any photos or personal information about myself, you'd still think they pick up on my sarcastic writing style, which I am consistent with.

Here is what I wrote to reintroduce myself to the AM world:
*Done Playing*

*I'm just over 50, just under 145 and 5 ft, looking for something between connections and distractions without any games. I don't have time for nonsense or pretend romantic gestures. I think my personality is a mix of goth, gunge, nerdy, and maybe a touch ghetto. I'm not much of a beauty, but I believe I look decent for my age. I'd like to consider myself creative and sarcastic. I'm not interested in changing anyone's situation or changing mine. I think life would be a lot simpler if poly relationships were acceptable in our society, but then those concepts would cause this site to be obsolete. I am often stoned and not too sober in the evening, and the sun is going down as I write this.*

*I'm looking for like-minded souls that I can feel connected with without some dumb fairytale notion attached to it. If I could be a bit more specific, I'd say I'm looking for a human version of Muppet Animal but with more advanced verbal skills. Please be real. But someone who doesn't have the intention of just being a sexual one ride per person. Unfortunately, convenience is also vital, even if there's a visual attraction. My general availability is typically one or two weekday mornings. No evenings, no weekends.*

*Attraction is crucial and must work both ways; otherwise, what's the point? Discretion is also important but should be apparent; otherwise, we'd all be on eHarmony.*

Out of the blue, I asked J if he had any musical ideas or thoughts on the lyrical nonsense sent weeks ago. Wondering if there would be any response, I didn't bother to hold my breath. He responded, "I came up with a melody for the first one." Since I sent three, I'm unsure which one he considered the 'first.' However, he did not discard them like I believe he did. There was an actual attempt to put music to my words. Immediately, I felt like a fucken child whose fucken emotional insecurity is always in the driver's seat, steering me into destructive patterns. As soon as emotions begin to swell, I'm on shaky ground. Then, I was only talking to a couple of men on AM. These conversations were only occupying the space I recently dug out. They were only simple distractions to the rampant emotions flooding my interior. I knew 1 was in some way in love with J, which is not much different than dancing on thin ice. I was never a good dancer.

Exactly a year ago, as I write this paragraph, there was a shooting in front of the high school J's children attended. His daughter was a bit extra sensitive to these sorts of things, which was why I would not see J for some time—expecting that his life did not allow any space for me to occupy—instead of seeing him once a week had turned into once a month. Even the regular texting that used to occur every day dwindled to a couple of times a week to nothing. In reality, it wasn't me or him, just the complexity of life that affected that arrangement. There was nothing overly complicated to understand or analyze.

None of the men on AM seemed to be keepers, either. There were no sparks to investigate. The lack of contenders was because I was being super picky and trying to hold to higher standards than before. Plus, I thought the majority of them looked like serial killers. Although talking to them did help dull the pain a little, I deleted the AM account. After a while, it just felt like we were all collecting Pokémon cards of people we might consider to fuck. There were one or two men I felt were worthy to keep in touch with some slight possibility that I might 'meet' them. One of them was a large tattooed man named Matt, who works somewhere in security. There was a chill aspect of him that I liked. Matt, the guard, asked what my ideal scenario was from 'meeting' some time off in the morning. I felt he was worth an honest response:

*'Ok, so let's be clear, I'm too old to have my head up my ass to believe in fairytales and ideals. This quest isn't my first rodeo, either. My actions are partly a mix of rebellion, balance, and distraction from previous rodeos and life. It would be nice to find an individual who gets me enough where I feel seen and heard when I'm in front*

*of them. I think my busy schedule next week is forcing me to take it slow before jumping into bed with whomever. I want that person to feel comfortable enough to take it to a physical level. Otherwise, it's like jumping into a pool of freezing water with full warning. I have to feel a little safe with that person. For a guy, I know sex is the main goal, and I get it. This rant is probably a long and confusing answer to a simple question. As for the scenario, meet for coffee or something and see if we vibe. If we do, the scenario includes basic logistics issues, such as where and when. If we don't, we try to be respectful and honest to say, "Sorry, I don't think this will work for me" or something to that degree.'*

Although he fully agreed, agreeing could mean anything or absolutely at this point. I got a brief text from J just saying 'hi.' Even though I have not 'met' anyone in the morning, I feel somewhat calm. The emotional turmoil I felt slipping into seemed to evaporate from the previous Pokémon AM experience. It was like being satisfied with a six-pack of beer after craving heroin. Strangely, simple actions can lead us to a sense of, if not peace, a somewhat quiet stillness. Maybe I wasn't as fully damaged from within as I initially believed.

Holding my breath with any plans with J was something I learned not to do. No matter how solid any plans seemed, they were always up in the air until I walked through his door. The emotions holding my rationality hostage appeared to perch over the past weeks. If I felt anything, it would be annoyance from his repeated cancellations. I don't think he or anyone fully appreciated or even understood the work needed to 'meet' on the down low. I have to lie to my husband about my whereabouts. If I said I was working, I needed to be out of the house for that time. Escaping would have been followed by having to call out of work. When J canceled on me, I would have to wander around Staten Island until the appropriate time to come home. These cancellations were highly fucken annoying. Sometimes, I'd kill time at the movies or find a place to hide in the mall.

One day, J wanted to meet for coffee instead of in his apartment. His son is staying there due to the kid's asthma, but he still wanted to see me. Since his son was sixteen, J felt it would be ok to slip out for a coffee and a conversation. The word 'conversation' brought me an expected dread. All my insecurities came knocking on my back door. As J and I sat and drank our beverages, I waited for the final shoe to drop, but it never did. The conversation was a typical round-of-a-mill conversation. We talked about our previous selves and also about art. J seemed to understand the nature of my art. It felt like the first time anybody took a moment to understand the stores behind the shaded lines on paper. Desperately trying to keep my emotions in full check was nothing short of a challenge after spending the past three weeks attempting to drown them out. Although my ability to find and hold onto anything positive was non-existent, J could find little cracks in my walls. It was impossible not allowing those mother fucken emotions to sneak back in due to J's humble sincerity. Maybe one day, we will have that 'conversation,' but it won't be that day.

It is as though I'm still that little girl from apartment 17G, and the dark shadows of that childhood seem to dictate how I think and feel in most of my relationships. My expectations of neglect, abandonment, pain, and disappointment seem to be the driving force in my inability to function like a grown adult. I'm waiting for the spitballs flying toward the back of my head. I lack the tools to grow the fuck up. Before getting into our cars, J challenged me to draw a person standing before nothing. "How would you draw nothing?" he asked. I think I might have drawn something sort of similar about a year ago. It is a drawing of a naked woman standing in a lane of decay. The road becomes cracked, and there are skulls scattered on the road ahead. I think to draw nothing; you need to have something next to it. There must be 'something' to create the contrast of 'nothing.' I sketched a naked female standing before a black empty 'nothing' which appears in the middle 'something.' In this case, the 'something' was a blue sky with green ground. It wasn't the best drawing anyway.

He wanted to meet again on my lunch break at Willowbrook Park, but of course, he canceled because life happened to happen once again. It feels like a miracle when we finally meet at his apartment. The word 'miracle' is an overstatement, of course. J was fighting a sinus infection. On top of that, one of his cousins was in hospice, dying of lung cancer. Like I said, life happened, and we could barely find a crack in time to share any intimate moments. The sex itself, although reaching the moment of intensity, is over quickly, like a short-lived rollercoaster ride. We had brief moments of silence in each other's arms. Usually, J would doze off. Otherwise, he rambles about 'how life happens' while I listen. Due to my inability to ramble, I mostly stay silent. I was still trying to keep an emotional distance. Before leaving, J insisted on making me tea with honey. He set me on my way with this hot beverage in an old travel mug, which I'm unsure if it's a loner or I can keep. Although, from reason, I felt a couple of tears escape, I managed to keep myself partly detached. Distance was my key to survival.

It was three weeks since I saw J and left with a cup of tea. My emotional levels for J had finally quieted to a more painless level. It was as though I better understood what we are to each other. If anything, we are two souls in need of connecting on a sexual level that doesn't interfere with our regular lives. We were respectful friends who fuck well together. He was part of my outlet of ongoing rebellion and was perfectly aware and okay with having that role. He needed the illusion of a 'real' connection with someone I provided. Unfortunately, the rationality to these situations either comes late in the game or is challenging to hold onto.

After a month passed, I finally saw J on a Monday morning. As I walked into his apartment, it was easy to notice that most of his furniture was missing. There were no Cookie Monster Pjs either. Instead, he was wearing just a towel around his waist. J was moving back with his family. As I tried not to show this news that just completely punched me deep into my gut on my face, I maintained a black face. J said we could still see each other, but I knew he told me this news was less of a blow. I'm not fucken stupid to release the end of a road when it stared me in the face.

J stood in his towel while I took a minute to let the whole reality of the situation sink in. It was clear whatever time we were to have then, there would be our last. In our goodbye fuck. J even lasted much longer than he normally does. Usually, he couldn't stop himself from cumming after minutes of entering me. It was as though his cock wanted to make a lasting impression. Trying to keep my emotions in check and establish my walls, I felt the tears slide down my cheek when he wasn't looking. J was just another piece of myself that I allowed to linger, and now he'll fade into the realm of memories like those before him. Before leaving his apartment for the last time, J gave me a Mr. Clean Magic Eraser sponge. He was so impressed by how well it cleaned the toughest stains he thought it was an appropriate parting gift.

I might have been sad for a few days but I wasn't as heartbroken as I thought. The feeling that I was falling apart came and went like a bad thunderstorm. Whatever deep emotions I once felt were already felt months ago before our final goodbye. Moving on seemed logical and not even too difficult to comprehend. I had no one to replace J or even feel the instant need to do so as if I was slowly but surely aging out of this bizarre need to find these distractions from my reality. Let's see when spring hits. Something about the warmth in the air triggers that dark, lingering shadow inside me. Time will just have to fucken tell.

# Pieces of My Sister

While typing these words on my phone, I sat by my sister's bedside in the ICU. Sometime in the afternoon, she had a severe stroke at work. Because of her work, her office door was closed for an extended period. As her place of employment was closing for the night, her co-workers noticed that she was not leaving with the rest of them. Finally, at about 7:15 pm, someone opened her office door to find her lying on the floor. They called 911 and contacted her son, who was on a family trip to Disney World. He soon reached out to me that they found her passed out at work. He had a recognizable undertone as he said, "We know what that's about." In previous issues, he referred to her drinking. He pretty much assumed she drank herself to a state of oblivion. Unfortunately, she hit the bottom of a bottle and could not return. Later that night, her son called again after speaking with someone in the ER. It was a stroke.

She's lying in the hospital bed with tubes and wires attached to her body. In and out of conscience, she has a temporary awareness mixed with a look of disbelief and confusion. She could not communicate. Whatever wires in her brain that connect speech got served along with the right side of the body. If devastation had a face and body, it lay in that bed with tubes and wires attached to it beside me. Seeing her lying in the hospital was no different than seeing the coastal damage from a hurricane. Yet we were well aware this storm was approaching land. It is only the time until it fully hits land, leaving pure carnage. We all failed to tether her down while the tidal waves rose and the Gail winds became apparent. I failed her.

She texted me about two or three weeks ago while I was at work. She said she felt as though she might be having a stroke. Based on what I understand about strokes, stroke victims usually can't text about it and are debating about going to the ER. Being torn between running to her then and there or taking other modes of action, I called 911. Considering I have absolutely no medical background, I still believe I made the correct choice in getting her immediate help instead of any immediate intervention I was incapable of conducting. She texted me not soon after the EMS cleared her. It wasn't a stroke. She was fine. It was just anxiety. They suggested she should follow up immediately with her doctor, but of course, she never did.

My sister was supposed to find a therapist because her inner demons wouldn't release their ongoing chokehold on her. She told me that she had finally found a therapist, but of course, I didn't believe her. I heard most of her excuses for not finding the "correct" therapist, and it was hard to believe she settled on one. Maybe she found a few phone numbers to call, and like her physical health, she never followed through. These fucken demons had won. Stopping by her apartment to feed her cats, the place looked nothing short of a crime scene. Those demons were partying hard in the empty wine bottles, small bottles of Titos, and the empty bottle of cranberry juice. A section of her counter looked dedicated to an endless supply of prescription drugs. There was one questionable packet that looked like it contained some sort of powder. I looked up the name on the packet. It is a drug meant for extreme withdrawal. Withdrawal from precisely what, I couldn't say, but she digested the powder recently with applesauce.

The rest of the kitchen proved that those demons do not desire to do dishes. My sister and I have had similar demons rampaging through our lives. Since I began writing these words, pages, and chapters, I have recognized some lingering demons I know, always watching and waiting for those opportunities to surprise me. While I was sleeping, one demon liked to make their presence known at night. As I lay in bed in panic, the shadowy figure stumbled through the hallway closer to my bedroom doorway. I lay silently, hoping the demon wouldn't enter my room. Yet it creeps into my bedroom towards my bed. An inner scream becomes stuck within me as he hovers over my face. As conscience finally breaks free from the nightmare, either the helpless sobbing or a scream emerges through the night, awakening the person next to me. Never discussed, my sister and I have shared this demon from childhood. Although I can't make myself write it or even say it, we both know his name.

Being in and out of rehab a couple of times, my sister has had a long history of drug and alcohol abuse. Being a licensed therapist gives her super ability to bullshit herself and others about her addictions. People with an addiction are just notorious for lying and manipulating, and she's no different. The only hidden blessing about this stroke is that she won't be able to access any drugs or alcohol ever again. She can't try to hurt herself again. All the late-night suicidal texts I had to read will stop. The ongoing need to constantly rescue her from herself will hopefully end as well, but I doubt it. She is a good master of my buttons of response. Even when I try to detach from her downward spiral, I begin to run and save her as though I am rescuing myself. Who else does she have?

As I visited her the following day, she was still in the ICU. The horror on my sister's face when she had a brief moment of awareness was heartbreaking. Those perfect moments of awareness were like watching the world realize it had ended. It was a year and a month ago that we were in the same hospital. She was in a horrible car accident, leaving her with a shattered ankle. Never fully covered by the accident, as well as other losses in her life, she has a stroke to add to the list of misfortunes. Before the car accident was her rehab trip #2 or 3 after her partner D had passed from lung cancer. It seems like every time she finally manages to get up, life fucks her over and knocks her ass back down. I saw her pleading face in her slightly aware face, "Why!!!?". "Why!!??". 'WHY!!!???" Why the fuck has this goddamn mother fucken universe smacked her down. Unfortunately, I had a heartbreaking answer to give, but I wouldn't say it then. We can't even blame the demons. She'll never fully recover from this enough to live alone. Maybe, in all respects, that's a good thing.

She squeezed my hand lightly with her left hand during the third day. As sisters, we'll always be close. We communicated in the language of hand-holding and sorrowful facial gestures. Reading her face and eyes, I could see her struggle to make her mouth work. Attempts to make word sounds only resulted in the silence of moving her lips. These moments of full awareness came and went like a broken TV signal. Her nurses might not receive her signals, but they don't have our connection.

The apparent disbelief written on her face of 'How?' and 'Why?' was evident. I am doing my best to hold my tongue because I unfortunately know the particle answer to 'why?'. There's no great mystery. The answer or answers were crystal clear. What lay in this ICU bed was partially self-inflicted. She would complain to me, as well as her son, repeatedly of various symptoms she was experiencing and our repetitive responses telling her to see a doctor. It quickly reminded me of my mother, who refused to see any doctors in her adult life before having her heart completely give out long ago. My sister was not much different. Although she did see doctors occasionally, her follow-up was highly lacking. If I wasn't by her side at the hospital, I was cleaning up what I called the 'crime scene.' Not one empty bottle of wine, vodka bottles, and other signs of alcoholism were left for her son to find. I even hid the dirty ashtray and vape pen left on the floor. Her son and the rest of the family didn't need to see the carnage left behind. While in her apartment, I noticed a small framed photograph sitting on her windowsill of our demon holding her when she was about three or four.

Later that week, I spoke to S, a well-seasoned paramedic. Although S was a critical chapter of the past, we still stayed in touch. I told him about when I was at work, and she texted me about those symptoms. I informed him I called 911 from work because I could not trust her to call herself. It's better to be safe than sorry. They came. They checked her. She said she seemed fine, and the EMTs went their merry way. According to S, they should have strapped them to the stretcher and shipped her to the ER immediately, no matter what. I sent him the screenshots of my and my sister's text that late afternoon, mostly to prove my guilt of my lack of action. S offered to investigate EMS logs to see if he could help shed extra light on that past event. In my years of knowing my sister, I've learned that sometimes, it may not be entirely accurate when she says what others have said. S wanted to see if EMS fucked up the call as well. He would bring me a couple of heads to point the blame. There was a list of names of heads who I'd like included, including mine.

Nearly a week had passed since my sister became a patient in the ICU. The hospital removed the feeding tube, but she had a new demon living inside her. She refused to acknowledge me. She saw me as her enemy, as though I'd summoned a clot to form inside her brain to cause her world to crumble. She demoted me because after so much glare of "why," I mistakenly blurted out the answer. By her immediate reaction, so much for me being the "best sister," the keeper of secrets, and the best friend. My answer was pure betrayal. "You weren't taking care of yourself." I knew I shouldn't take any of her hatred toward me personally. After crying as much as possible, I had to find strength in my new role. I was no longer a beloved sister, but I still ensured I received the correct level of care. Each day I visited, the look of hate stabbed me as brutally as though I had become her new demon. After each visit, I'd run to find the hospital chapel to cry. On the side table of the entrance chapel was a journal for loved ones to write their secret prayers to their chosen high power. It became my ritual to visit the chapel and write in that journal before and after I visited her.

Feeling so fucken lost, hurt, and hopeless, each visit was acid on an open wound. My sister needed to hold someone accountable, and my card came up. To look themselves straight in the soul and say, "Yeah, I fucked up," Not everyone can take responsibility for their actions. Sometimes, she even refused to look at me, but when she did, it felt as though she was trying to stab me in the heart. "I fucked up." "This is my fault". "I did this". Did I? It's better why it was beyond unbearable. "I am guilty".

However, whatever guilt I felt, I knew I should not be bearing in alone when you add the day before the event. A few days before the stroke, on her Facebook feed were newly posted pictures of her son and his family at Disney World. Typically, this would not have been an issue, considering her first ex and her son's father were coughing up loads of money to take them on these expensive family trips. From being the sole recipient of both his parents' lofty inheritances, the man began the 'sugar granddaddy.' Not being included in any of these trips did upset my sister often. She would always ask me why they excluded her. However, these current pictures include her 2nd ex-husband and his new wife. That was the final nail in her coffin. Lately, her son had included the second ex-husband in every family event, disregarding how my sister felt. These ex-husbands seemed to be placed on Petal while she was constantly villainized as the 'fuck up parent.' Even before those Disney World pictures got posted on social media, my sister's heart was already breaking. The pictures were like cleaver chopping tiny, unrecognizable pieces. Therefore, she did the only thing she knew how to do to help relieve the pain. Hence, the crime scene. Her son didn't return from Disney until after the stroke. However, I was fully available to be at her bedside to feel her hatred every day.

On Christmas Eve, I dreaded going back to the hospital. Everyone dreads having to see their loved ones lying in hospital beds. My loved one doesn't want me there. I was the last person she wanted to visit. Obligated to go, I was the battery acid to her pupils. My sister's friends, whom I'd contacted, require daily updates. Leaving out the fragments of horror that were ripping my heart out, I did my best to keep them informed. Today I'm supposed to tell her, "I'm here to support you fully, but having her treated me like shit" is something I fight so hard not to scream at her. By then, I filled several pages in the hospital chapel's book but the entranceway, hoping that god might listen. Maybe the hospital chaplain takes time to read those pages and say daily prayers on our behalf.

It's only been four days short of a month since my sister's stroke. Now, in a regular room, she is still rioting away. Only the nurses would elevate her body, and she could move in various degrees of lying depending on whether she ate or slept. She required help to eat. The bottom of her feet has not touched the floor. Sometimes, she attempted to feed herself but failed to spill food all over herself. The concept of language appeared trapped within her. She will move her mouth as though she believes she is talking, only for absolute silence to emerge from her lips. She looks at me with frustration as though I'm not trying hard enough to listen. I will take frustration and annoyance over the look of disdain, which seemed to taper off. It's perfectly normal for stroke victims to go through a vase of pure hatred and not take any of it personally. Knowing that fact made seeing her a little easier. If I'm lucky, there is a slight laugh when I mention her cats. With every crack of a smile and sound of slight laughter, I grasped with dear life into my heart. Mostly, her face carried a veil of sorrow and tears. Visiting her was still like an ongoing punch in the gut but less brutal. Due to work, I don't go to the hospital as often, but I am at her apartment nearly daily, feeding and spending time with her two cats, Gracie and Bowie.

The pit in the middle of my stomach tripled every time I was about to see her. The visits are primarily silent since I'm the only one who can speak, with very little to say. All I have is her facial expressions to guide the conversation until we are both left in the silence and despair of the situation. I am learning not to take her mood swings personally, but they still break my heart nonetheless. We are desperately waiting for her to get placed in a rehab facility. There's little the hospital could do for her besides keep her fed, medicated, and thankfully safe. All I could do was attempt to put on a brave face and keep her cats fed daily.

The hope was when she went to rehab, pieces of her spirit would slowly return to us. Even though her feet might not reunite with the ground soon, they will get her out of bed, out of hospital gowns, and into real clothes. She might have to sit in a wheelchair for the longest time, but wheelchairs can move. She might have to rely on others to move her around but will have an opportunity to look out of various windows and see life outside of a hospital bed. The physical therapy will be aggressive, and she might even be able to walk with some assistance. She's been in the hospital way too long because the process of getting onto various forms of Medicare to get into a rehab facility is nothing short of cruel, with often nasty social workers who stopped seeing humans but lumps of flesh to transport out of their hands and into another.

Once a facility specializing in stroke victims took her, a spark of hope lifted my spirits. She would finally get the required treatment to regain her feet. The facility was in Northern Jersey, and reaching there took nearly an hour. Because I have no sense of direction, I went with her son the night she was first transferred. I had a bag packed for her as though she was going on a vacation to Stroke Camp with everything I thought she would need to make her stay as comfortable as possible. Compared to the cramped hospital rooms at RUMC, these rooms were huge. My sister looked upset and very disoriented when we finally got there. She probably wasn't told from the original hospital where she was going or the information wasn't made clear. All she knew was she got packed in a transport ambulance and to be bounced around until it got to, for her, an unknown destination.

In this case, it was called an acute rehabilitation facility. Acute rehab is for approximately four to six weeks and for those patients who could and would be, in some aspect, back on their feet During their recovery. Unfortunately, my sister needed subacute rehabilitation. Subacute is obviously for those stroke victims who need a far longer transition to some form of recovery. Her insurance only allowed the Acute rehab. Getting her on subacute required some sort of Medicare magic voodoo. There was a private sink and dress in which I unpacked her belongings. Her son and I tried to reassure her that all was well and she was in a good place that would not only take care of her but help her get back on her feet.

So began my weekly routine of driving to New Jersey to see her. Even with the GPS, I would still get lost, either coming or going. I'd either exit or make that wrong turn without fail. At first, I would receive the same death stares from her as though it was I, alone, who put her in this predicament. During those visits, I tried hard to remember what I heard about stroke victims. The extreme shift from personality to personality was standard. The look of absolute hatred was something I had to learn not to take personally quickly. No matter how loud my logical voice reminded me of all the rational aspects of the situation, most of these visits ripped through my soul with verity. There was no chapel to cry and try to get myself together. Sitting in my car for at least twenty minutes, I'd sit and try to calm myself down before tackling the New Jersey Turnpike.

A couple of weeks later, I got a phone call from my sister's son. Her oxygen levels were terrible. The rehab hospital needed to transfer my sister to a neighboring hospital for clots that had developed in her lungs. Although reassured that this was common for most bedridden patients who couldn't move and walk, I still feared the very worst. Doctors performed the surgery to remove the clots and add some sort of filter to prevent the clots from reforming again. However, for a moment, it felt like she was beginning to slip away from us, as though she was choosing to throw the towel. If I were to be bluntly honest, it would have been an act of mercy from god for her to die. That's a horrible thing to say or even think. If given a choice and the power to do so, my sister might have thrown in the towel on existing in the fashion she currently exists in. Death would be a sweet gift from what awaited. The only good thing about having her in the hospital again was access to a chapel. Once my tears tired out, I was ready for the return trip to feed her cats.

Each visit was an emotional kick in the gut every time. My sister still tried to communicate with me, but no audible words came out of my mouth. Shaking her head as though she believed she had made whatever point my sister thought she was making crystal clear. Standing or sitting nearby, I desperately tried to capture anything that might sound like a word in the hope of understanding her. Rarely would I know a fraction of what she was attempting to say, but most times, I couldn't. She got super frustrated, as though my lack of understanding was on purpose. Most of the time, she would just cry. My words and gestures brought little comfort. Again, I'm failing her. Whatever relationship we had before this life-changing event had died on her office floor. All that was left to do was grieve who she once was and our relationship. The person lying in the hospital bed was a stranger. Learning to understand and accept that we might never be as close as we were was something I wasn't ready to process.

Soon after, I was able to hear actual random words. Although I didn't fully understand my sister's word choice, hearing her voice's uniqueness felt like a tiny miracle to hold on to. Often, she would be stuck on one word, which, to her, had multiple meanings. At first, she would repeat "The thing," "The thing," "The thing", "The thing" meant everything and sometimes nothing. Trying to figure out what "The thing" was just another failed mission on my part. Then the "The thing" was changed to a short, complete sentence, "I don't Know'. "I don't Know', "I don't Know,' "I Don't Know.' During the "I don't Know' there was a sense of pure heartbreaking helplessness in her voice. "I don't Know', "I don't Know,' "I don't Know'.

What seems like weeks, even months, from one hospital bed to another in Paterson, NJ, hospital before finally getting her place at another acute rehab facility. In West Orange, NJ, my sister's hospital eventually relocated to a decent rehab facility. Still, only being able to visit her once a week because of the distance and work added to the feeling that I wasn't doing enough. Unlike the hospital and even the first acute rehab facility, she never left in bed like rotting fruit. She finally looked like an actual human being as she was dressed, groomed, and out of bed. If she weren't in a rehab session, she would have the nurses parked in front of her tiny TV set. The transformation and small moments of progress were remarkable during her few years at this facility. Although her speech is limited to only a few repetitive sentences, she can easily sing most familiar songs. The first time I heard her singing voice, I wanted to cry from the welcomed amazement of finally hearing not her voice but her soul within. Her soul was singing.

Her sarcastic yet silly personality also managed to sip out of her half-paralyzed body. During These brief moments, I felt like I had my old sister back. This part of her didn't die on her office floor but was slowly making a beautiful comeback. Although there were still moments of understandable depression that came and went like waves, she managed to make her jokes through facial expressions and random sounds. The positive energy that radiated from her was probably also due to the forced sobriety of being in the hospital for three months. In one horrible way, this stroke was a slight blessing in disguise. She will never be able to access any substances to assist in dulling any emotional pain life throws at her. Honestly, I believe that these nightmarish months have given her a small gift of not just fully feeling her emotions but also learning to rationalize them. The mad dash to run inside a bottle has ended. She had to remember to feel and attempt to rationalize her thoughts fully. Hiding from her demons like before was now a distant past.

Unfortunately, her stay at the West Orange rehab came to an end. We had no idea where the insurance system would send her next. Returning to her tiny apartment with its stairs and tight hallways was not an option. Having her alone to fend for herself was not fucken happening anytime soon. We hoped a place on Staten Island would take her so we could visit her more than once a week, as well as other friends and family. I believed most of her current heartbreak then was due to the isolation from familiar faces. If I was, to be honest, I didn't think she should ever return to her apartment. If possible, I'd have liked to see her in an apartment closer to me with elevator access to the outside world. Besides traveling in several transit ambulances during the various relocations from one facility to another, I don't think she has felt the sun on her face since December 12th. At least where she was in West Orange, she could see the outside world through a window.

My hope was when and where she ended up next, she would still be able to feel the outside.

Although only a ten-minute drive from my front door, transitioning into a new place wasn't easy; the first couple weeks in the new rehab facility took adjusting time. What could be considered the Hilton of rehab facilities of West Orange, she was at a Comfort Inn quality type of facility. The place is a nursing home that offers a more extended rehab plan. She could stay there for a few months until she was ready to go home. Unfortunately, the level of care she received in the last facility in West Orange was lacking in the new place. There were days when the conditions the facility left her in were utterly unacceptable.

My sister has been in four facilities before coming to this one and avoided COVID-19. However, she caught Covid within the first two weeks in this new one. They had to quarantine for ten days, and the nurses neglected her during the first couple of days. It was a Friday early afternoon when I visited her Covid be damned. Just give me an N95 mask and some extra protective gear. From the look of it, no one changed her diaper all that day. My sister was left soaked in urine all night as well as all morning. God be damned, I was going to allow her to leave like that any longer. Yet getting a fucken aide to help was more complicated than finding a person to jump your car at 3 am in the middle of a fucken highway. The aide assigned to her was on her break, so we waited. After an hour, her aide was still unavailable to tend to my sister's basic human needs. After only getting an attitude from the nurse and other staff, I was left with a front-row seat to my sister crying while being forced to sit in her urine. It is nothing short of a living nightmare. The situation forced my hand. Taking my complaint to the next level, I demanded to speak to someone in charge. It was either this or spending a few years in jail for beating the living crap out of someone. Fighting the primal urge to go completely psycho on these fucken aides was a miracle of its own. Going downstairs to the front desk lobby, separately fighting emotionally, losing it in front of reception, I asked whom I should complain about the current situation. Within a minute or two, I was speaking to the physical therapy supervisor. After that day, she was usually out of bed or at least changed whenever I visited her. The aides assigned to her seemed more on top of their game. They always peek into her room nearly every thirty minutes to ensure all is good. At Least they did when I was there. I could tell the conditions had greatly improved by looking at her. Even Though she cannot say all the words she wants to speak, she nods that things are good. She was always in her wheelchair in clean clothes.

In defense of nursing homes and the aides who work there, many of these facilities usually need to be staffed more to care for all their patients as they want to. All it takes is for one or two aides and nurses to call out of a floor for all shit to hit the fan. They are usually overworked, underpaid, and disrespected by their superiors. Often, there is little to no communication between aids and those who manage them. To me, it is a near thankless job, so I came to understand if she's not having the best day. There were days when I visited her; I could see these aides running and rushing from room to room but still faced the impossible task of satisfying everyone completely. Sometimes they have to deal with patients who yell at them through things and just treat them like shit. Luckily, my sister learned that being as patient and pleasant as possible resulted in receiving friendlier service.

The rehab facility's goal was to get her to walk with some assistance with a cane or even a walker. Because her right side is nearly dead, she has to learn to do everything with the left side of her body. Her right arm and legs were dead limbs of a tree that someone forgot to trim off. The left side of her body was performing the tasks we all take for granted. Her ability to adapt was remarkable. She began showing off how she can get around in her chair. If she has a wall or a piece of furniture to grab with her left hand, she will use it to propel herself forward quickly. She left the room and down the short hall to peek around the corner. However, on the return trip, she had limited access to the wall since her room was now on her right. With the encouragement of an older patient cheering on, she tried her best to get back into her room by herself. Unfortunately, the process of simple forward movement tired her out. Tapping out, I can wheel her back in. Still, her efforts were commendable.

When people ask about my sister, there's a fine line between what I want to say and what I do say. "She will never regain her full independence or the ability to walk. Whatever life she had prior is finished", and "Her prior mental health deteriorated bad enough to self-medicate to a degree of no return." is what I want to say. That I might be as guilty as her son and that side of the family for the years of emotional neglect and abandonment." I want to say, "I remain in my front seat as the ongoing witness as this tragic story unfolds before me. Instead, I just say she still has a long road ahead but still made excellent progress.

Visiting my sister on Sunday afternoon can be difficult because the Nursing Home often has to operate on limited staff, and my sister has no choice but to be forced to lay in bed with a piss-filled diaper longer than average days. Some Sundays were also good days too. When she's dressed, groomed, and in a wheelchair, It's usually a decent day. Since it was finally a beautiful day outside, I was able to take her out of the facility for a brief walk. Pushing the wheelchair on unsteady ground jwas difficult, so I cut our walk short. Some chairs and benches are on the side of the rehab facility so that we can sit outside for a bit. It had been a long time since she felt the sun on her and the cool, calm breeze in her hair playing with her hair; how we take the essential elements of nature for granted when they are sometimes little rare gems to hold tightly to. Seeing her slowly come back to some sense of who she once was gradually brought us back together. During the days when she was sometimes left in bed or occasionally chose to stay in bed, I would crawl into the bed on her left side.

Along with our souls, our hands would intertwine. It was impossible not to hold back tears. During those moments, I felt as if I had my sister back, and at the same time, I didn't. Strange as that might seem, these small moments summarize our relationship's history.

During my childhood, she was just sometimes one of my many tormentors, but often she ignored me. Occasionally, it was the mix of the two, like when our parents would leave me in her care for a weekend. If she were sixteen or seventeen, I would have been between nine and ten. My sister would throw these insane parties, which include the essential drugs and alcohol. Amid a couple of these parties, I don't know if they were her friends or just other teens who just showed up at these things and liked to play the game of getting the little kids drunk. Sometimes, they would hold me down while crying and beg them to stop; they would force the liquid of various substances down my throat. No one, including my sister, made them stop. Come to think of it, I don't believe she even realized what was going on because she was always drunk and high.

Our relationship finally changed when she invited me to a painting class with her. By this time, I was seventeen or close to turning seventeen. She had gotten engaged to her ex-husband number one. She brought me into painting, and we began taking a painting class together almost every Saturday morning in Coney Island. I was happy to hop on two buses because they took me far away from Starrett City. Because of our six and a half-year apart in age, we never really took the time to understand each other. I always felt worlds apart from her until we sat next to each other in this painting class; it felt like the first time we ever spoke, we connected like two adults instead of unrelatable strangers. While learning how to blend greens, blues, and white to create the illusion of water, I understood that her existence was not that much different from my own. We were both just trying to survive the disgust and embarrassment embedded in us from growing up in a home where no one told us that changing our underwear and brushing our teeth was a daily necessity. Part of me believed she always regretted not protecting me enough or teaching me how to take better care of myself. We both shared similar demons. How could she look after me while struggling to survive her childhood?

One day, my nephew shared a video of my sister walking or attempting to walk with assistance. They have fitted her right leg with some sort of brace to keep it straight so she could have a sense of balance on two legs. With the guidance of a PT aide holding her for support and a cane on her left, we could see her take her first steps forward. Her right arm, which still appears useless, is kept in a sling. I was worried that she wouldn't be able to catch herself if she fell. Would she be able to get herself up as well? Tears were impossible not to shred when I watched the video repeatedly. I noticed the mix of fear, determination, and amazement on her face. I could tell she was terrified that she could easily fall but allowed a fierce determination. "Oh baby girl, you hold on tight."

Her language skills were still an issue. Most of the time, she would repeat, "same," "same," or 'same thing," 'same thing," 'same thing" instead of being able to say the words stuck inside her. However, she could sing the lyrics to most songs as long as she knew them. Music was a trigger that released language from within her. Soon, a complete sentence would appear as though the planets had become perfectly lined in those fleeting moments. Although rare, these moments of clarity were precious beyond comparison. Soon after, she would get in the habit of repeating what was said to her with a glow in her eyes that she perfectly understood every word.

Another thing I've failed at was maintaining the cleanliness of my sister's apartment. Trying to keep up with all the cat vomit and piss was just something I found impossible to do in the forty minutes I had on my lunch break. Although the cat vomit was one battle, the cat piss that soaked threw some of the furniture was a battle I could not win. Already an existing problem, the smell of piss attracted more and more roaches. For a few weeks, I was reliving my childhood horror as I struggled to handle cat food dishes and water dishes. Eventually, I reached my breaking point in complete hysteria.

*"I can't". The roaches are everywhere in the kitchen today. "I can't. I can't." There are two. I have to find the cats. They are crawling all the cat food. They are on the walls. "I can't, I can't, I can't". I use the claw stick to grab the cat bowl to bring it to the sink. They are also in the sink. I turn the tab on high, as hot as possible, and squeeze out the dishwashing soap. I open a cat food can and fill the now clean bowl. I need to claw the reaching thing to put it back down. My hand grabs the closet bottle of roach spray. I spray the area as I am spraying for my life. "I can't, I can't, I can't". My body was shaking, so I went to sit on the couch. They're never on the couch. Not yet. But there's cat vomit on the floor. There's always a cat vomit on the floor. There is cat vomit on the couch. There's vomit all over the chairs. There's one chair, my sister's favorite chair, that they have been pissing on. I return to the kitchen to retrieve the broom, but they are there too. "I can't, I can't, can't, I can't, I CAN'T! My hands are shaking as I grab another bottle of spray. Tears and hysteria crumble out of me. I didn't even look at what I was spraying, but I was spraying as though I was in a war zone. I am in a warzone. "I can't, I can't, can't, I can't, I CAN'T, I CAN'T! 'This is not my fault! I didn't destroy your life! "I didn't do this to you!" "I can't keep doing this! "I CAN'T; I CAN'T! I CAN'T, I CAN'T! I*

*CAN'T, I CAN'T DO THIS ANYMORE! Trying but failing to get myself back together as leave. "I can't, I can't, can't, I can't, I CAN'T! I try to control my breathing, the shaking, and the tears as I open the car door. When I return to work, I create a social media post to find the cats a new home. I can't do this anymore.*

Soon after that tantrum, I called an exterminator and hired someone to help me clean the living room and kitchen. One of the chairs was so soaked in cat piss I had disposed of it. It was a large and heavy chair that my sister loved to sit in. Being next to the window, she could sit and gaze outside. Out of breath and single-handedly, I managed to drag the disgusting thing out of the apartment and onto the curb for sanitation to put the thing entirely out of its misery. Under the chair were boxes and boxes of old family photos. They, too, were soaked in pissed and could not be saved. After several attempts to get the cats adopted, I banished them to the bedroom, and that's where they remain until my sister can return or if we can find other arrangements. Although the war between the roaches and myself continued, I've won each battle. Although the bedroom is cat vomit central with all its odors, the rest of the apartment didn't cause me to shake and cry anymore.

About a year ago, my family, including my sister, went to the Kreischer Mansion for their Halloween event. For thirty-five dollars, you get a spooky hayride and a walk into the mansion as members of their actors attempt to freak you out.

Except for the typical reaction to a jump scare, I love seeing each room's creepy art and layout. By the way, jump scares are not actual moments of terror. If an adorable kitten jumped out of nowhere unexpectedly, it would probably have the same reaction as someone dressed as a cannibal zombie jumping out of the bushes. Being a full-year fan of all things creepy and morbid, I usually have fun attending these events. Last, I got placed in a coffin and some sort of sacrificial box.

Once we walked through all the offered attractions, it was time to head home. Because I didn't want to inconvenience the rest of the family, we took two cars so I could drive my sister back to her apartment. Within ten minutes after leaving the parking lot, my sister started crying about her son and her relationship. Her tears were nothing new. Their relationship had been up and down since he got married. It was more down than it was up. No matter how often I tried to console her, she always returned to this point. "Why is he so horrible to me?" would be repeated repeatedly. He was a bit of a shit to her, but, in my opinion, she repeatedly placed herself in the line of fire when it came to him. She was tired through the majority of the thirty-minute car ride. Her tears removed any feeling of fun and enjoyment I had from the haunted house.

On the way to her home, my sister had me stop by a liquor store, which, in my gut, I knew was the last place she needed to go. For some reason, she had this manipulative hold on me that if I didn't help her access alcohol, her despair would quickly turn to hostility. 'How dare I even suggest she still had an on-and-off issue with drugs and alcohol?' Besides my husband, my sister has access to my inner buttons. They knew what button to press to comply with their needs, no matter what my gut was screaming within.

There is hope that my sister may finally return to her apartment. Her son had hired a lawyer to arrange a unique Medicare for her. When it comes to Medicare or any medical insurance, my understanding of the underbelly of this system is limited. She will have twenty-four-hour care at her apartment with a rotating shift of aides. Hopefully, I will notify at least two weeks' notice before her return to de-cat vomit-piss her bedroom. At least there are no roaches in there, so I should be able to handle it. One thing I am weary of is that I will probably be on twenty-four calls if things go wrong at the apartment with an aide calling out sick, not showing up, or just being unable to handle the task. Although

I love my sister with all my heart, having her life take over my existence is something I don't want. The expectations of my involvement will be attractive as I know I will fail each of them as a house of cards.

# PART IV: WE NEVER LEARN OR DO WE?

## Pieces of Spring 2023:

I am beginning to feel that hungry animal within me start to scratch me from the marrow; it is dangerous to me. The scent of spring begins the descent of restarting the hunt. Something dark inside me begins to thaw out from the ice. I have often felt like a great storm was forming from within me. All thundershowers are waiting to reach the surface. With all these previous experiences, I felt like a well-tuned animal ready to hide and wait. Unfortunately, the grass plains and rivers held nothing worth my attention. I would have liked to believe that I've built an immunity to various types of bullshit. On whatever site I choose to hunt, there's a lot of bullshit. Being older at this game doesn't help much, either. The 'boys' looking for cougars spark no interest in me. They usually have little to no tactics and little knowledge of properly handling me. The older gentleman reminds me too much of my dad, and that's a road I will never travel.

This carnivorous feeling is no stranger to me. It was like an old friend and a demon following me while I waited. The storm within begins to collect wind, and the need to surge outward gets more challenging to fight. The creature I carry has ended its brief dormancy and moment of self-reflection. It is hungry. At first, an old site is like visiting your favorite drug dealer you reimagined as your best friend. Let's see what lessons I have mastered and what skills I learned from my last dip in this septic tank. Unknown to me, the Kik app seems to provide its version of a feeding ground. Kik isn't like Ashely Madison, where specimens require attention before the net is retrieved. It's like sticking your toe in the sludge to see what's there. Kik has public groups of various interests, including some that appear to match mine. The app just offers a new way to approach the hunt. It's not as overwhelming as previous sites of a similar nature, where I felt like I was drowning in applicants the first week. I have one small fish on my virtual hook, but not for long.

Damian Darko was one of the Kik users I began to converse with. Darko was a short, overweight Puerto Rican in his early thirties. Living with an ex-wife, his mother-in-law, and two small children, he was miserable looking for a recuse. Darko's soul seemed to be slowly dying from a history of child abuse and neglect. The trauma appeared compounded by the emotional and mental abuse in his current living situation. Like some of us, his demons were eating him alive. Uber eats deliveries at night was his only outlet and sense of freedom from his tortured existence. I'm unsure of his educational background, which I assume was not a GED. Darko's previous employment before COVID was cleaning in a nursing home until a domestic situation between his mother-in-law and himself caused employment working with the senior population to become unavailable. When asked what he dreamt about being when he was young, Darko responded that he never dreamed of being; therefore, his goals appear limited. The guy was depressing as fuck.

Luckily, I never met Darko in person. Our schedules conflicted too much to make many chances of meeting realistic. Attaching myself to such an unhealthy person would be beyond ill-advised. Before discontinuing any contact with him, I tried to be supportive by discussing the importance of self-care and how it means mental, emotional as well and physical. If he didn't begin to face these demons, he probably won't have much time here on earth. The man was the poster child for heart disease. Going to the gym was hopefully doable, but he'll never follow through. He will probably be eating his emotions to death. Healing is a long bitch of road that I even choose to avoid like the plague. Just like my captures, his abusers will feel threatened whenever he begins to show any signs of personal growth. They will do their very best to knock him down. Learning positive detachment is something I'm still trying to find in the dark. Although something compelled me not to abandon this individual, I wasn't interested in becoming anyone's social worker. Being in constant battles with my demons, who am I to throw anyone on a life raft? Then, just like a switch that gets turned on, my concerns for this stranger rock overnight. Becoming a dumping ground for another person's life choices and depression is not one of my goal options or part of the hunt.

At first, I thought of Kik groups as the virtual bottom eaters of the virtual hunting ground. Nearly every person who wanted to converse with me either looked like a drug addict, a convict, or a lunatic. Another individual I chatted with was somewhat unique in their particular way. Although I completely forgot his name, his story is a bit noteworthy. He is a high-functioning autistic man who spent most of his adolescence and early adult life in either group homes or prison. Once he finally got out of jail, he thought it was a fabulous idea to get pregnant with three of his female friends. Not only did all these involved people believe it was a great idea, they repeated the process more than once. He has ten children with four different women. While repeatedly pregnant with all his female friends, he worked full time and got his ass in school to achieve a master's degree in engineering. Reading about his long, ongoing messages about his life's accomplishments and overcoming hurdles was utterly fascinating. However, when he shared that his older son tried to stab his grandfather for touching him, my reaction was, "Later, dude." I just don't have a stomach for taking on anyone's drama. Also, the pictures of this person's gun collection were a bit of an alarm. The Kik app wasn't working out.

After the Kik app failed, I returned to AM for the third time. Once again, the process was the same for me as before. Being on AM is like being on a great fishing expedition. You cast a great net into the mighty ocean. At first, the net becomes filled up extremely fast. The next step is weeding out all the undesirable fish and throwing them back into the sea. I bring the more exciting fish onto the deck for a closer look. Of course, they have the power to jump ship at any moment for any possible reason as well. Fishing works both ways. The small handful of aquatic life that wishes to stick around flops in the bucket as I examine each one closer. Who they are as people is either or not important to me. Not wanting to spread my legs for an asshole or a psychopath, I need some time accessing them through chats before agreeing to meet anyone in person. No one has to be a Nobel prize winner, as I try to settle on decent enough. As always, there are a few front runners that I message day to day to check if there's an actual vibe or not. The same handful of guys on this site always talk to the new girlie fish. Old faces pop up like Stan The Man and Alan as these men live and breathe on this site. I ignore these individuals.

It only takes a good week to go through what I call 'the process' of selecting a small handful of fish that I will continue communicating off-site. There is one fish that managed to stand out from the most. There was a nice chill vibe between us as our wants in all things discreet appeared to match. Half-Note and I wanted to be with someone we could connect with. Neither one of us was just looking for the singular fuck before quickly returning to our regular living situations. Having a chance to meet him for coffee, I chose a place close to a vacant lot by a gas station. It served coffee and other beverages. He kept mentioning that he had a massive truck with a mattress. Letting imagination play out with that scenario, this game we play is always a crap shoot. He could cancel. I could develop a yeast infection overnight. Half-Note might just want a blow job for his time before moving on to more extraordinary things. Sky was the limit.

Half-Note and I spent an hour and a half rambling in the back of his truck. My nerves and neurotic behavior proved that it had been a while since I had my first 'meet' with anyone. There was no indication of expecting a head or anything physical. Our conversation primarily focused on music theory, my art, and general life. Feeling comfortable, I allowed my inner neurotic self to slip out of the car. It's rare to have those 'be yourself' moments with a stranger in the back of an old truck. Half-Note's naturally easygoing nature allowed my inner butterflies to calm down enough to breathe, listen, and speak. Although I appreciated JS's down-to-earth spirit, my voice felt stuck in my throat as though it could not find its place in our conversations. I got my voice heard thanks to Half-Note's calm nature. Towards the end of the meeting, there were two kisses, which were inevitable and necessary in communicating our intentions. Not only did his lips feel nice on mine, but there was a lingering sensuality that needed to be explored more within private walls. With JS, the deal I was striking would not be pain-free. I laid out the shards of broken glass in the beginning with J. With Half-Note, there were no shards laid before me. However, the hunger of the creature inside stirred and screamed to feed beyond a meal of a backseat kiss.

And just like that, all romantic notions once had been pulled from under my feet. Half Note wasn't interested in whatever I assumed he was interested in. In a long-winded explanation of a long-ass text, he had chosen to have nothing to do with me simply because that was where his head was at. Whatever the fuck that was supposed to mean. Half- Note and I wanted to stay in touch, but that didn't last more than a week before it got boring. What probably annoyed me the most was that I prematurely deactivated my AM account. How fucken stupid was I to think that I struck gold or even slightly tarnished silver. It took forever for AM to reactivate my account, and by then, I landed back with the button feeders on Kik.

While waiting for AM to reactivate my account, I planned to have coffee with 'Buddha' after chatting back and forth for a few weeks on kik. I've learned to keep my expectations like a blank slate, and my nerves were in better check. Buddha could have been one of those individuals who know how to adjust their personality to achieve one goal, which is just fucking without strings. Some people can adapt themselves to be more likable to accomplish this goal. The one fundamental thing I just can't let go of is the basic need to simply 'like' the person. Fucking someone I just don't like is something I can't let go of. One thing I should add, from evidence from pics that he has shared, is that Buddha is no stranger to kink and alternative lifestyles. There's also the concern of too much liking where it becomes like walking on shards of glass. My feet usually get sliced up, but I don't foresee that happening with Buddha. From some of the language in his texts, I'm more concerned for his feet than mine. However, my concerns before meeting Buddha became compounded by his messages in one of Kik's local button feeder groups. He wrote how he missed his 'girl' who was in the Caribbean with her son for the week. Buddha was full of shit in one direction or another. Hoping there was a 'girl' he forgot to mention; my concerns about his feet were no longer as important.

However, another rug was pulled from under my feet with Buddha again. Not only did I get ditched, I got ghosted out of nowhere. On the day of our meeting, he pretended to be confused about the time. Then, he made up an excuse that his daughter was so sick she needed immediate medical care. Knowing this was complete nonsense, he didn't even leave his house. We were also chatting via Snapchat, which allows their locations to be pinpointed on a map if a particular user allows it. Buddha's avatar did not once move from his original location at all. Some people can go to the tundra in seconds. My "WTF!" feelings of anger and mild disappointment didn't last more than a full day. It only struck a curiosity about the psychology behind this behavior. One minute they are one hundred percent on board with their idea to drop you like dog shit on the street. Learning how humans tick has always fascinated me.

Finally, my AM account got reactivated, but none of the first ones intrigued me. There might have been one or two men to consider, but not enough for me to set anchor. Neither did the little nipples on Kik. Perhaps I was getting too old for this shit. Maybe it was time to dock the ship and disembark on dry land. Before I was ready to pack it all in, a post in the bi-sexual kik group I had just joined intrigued me. "Any submissive buttons around."

I responded, "Do girls count?" before receiving a private message from AB (AKA: The Major).

# Pieces of The Major- Summer 2023.

"Let it sink in" was what the Major's text read. Sitting on my sister's couch as her emotionally deprived cats fight to sit on my lap, I thought about how to respond. Trying not to let the side of dead roaches on the floor get to me, I "let it sink in." My route nearly every day was battling roaches to feed these cats. Doing my best not to inhale the odor of cat piss, I could only manage to be in the apartment for a couple of minutes before needing to run for air. During my daily battle for the past seven months, I felt bad for these two poor little creatures. How abandoned they must have felt. My quick feeding and head scratches were all they had going on in their four-legged life. Attempting to sit on the couch between pockets of cat vomit with them for a few minutes, those small triggers of childhood memories, where the grown-up pretended that everything was okay, were more challenging and more complicated to fight off. Maybe that's what I was doing as I was sitting on my sister's couch. I pretend everything is okay, but my self-delusions are challenging. My sister will never return to this apartment, no matter how much everyone else wants to delude themselves. She will always need twenty-four-hour care. It's time to discuss relocating the cats.

Letting the previous hour "sink in" without thinking about the need to clean the cat vomit scattered about the wooden floor. Even after mopping this place last week, no one could tell I'd made any effort. An hour ago, I was in the Major's car, in his backseat, with his hands between my legs. Allowing his fingers to wake up what had been stirring since mid-spring, a man I just met in uniform summoned my dark, innermost hunger. It had been a while since I felt my primitive instincts surface. It had been months since I was in J 's apartment, and my secret self-had no opportunity to stretch her legs. That time for inner reflection and dormancy, I only lasted a few months before the thirst emerged. Creatures of habit must follow their instinct to survive their environments.

Once, I met the Major through one of the bottom feeder groups, a local Bi–group in the Kik app. After toying in these groups for a few weeks, having someone click with me and follow through on their words was nice. Unlike Buddha's bullshit, where words turn into little bitch moments when his 'put up or shut' up moment came and went. No shows; ghosting is something I've just learned to expect anyway. I was over Buddha in less than twenty-four hours without involving any deep self-reflection. Posting in a local BI group on Kik, The Major posted that he was seeking a submissive bottom. I am asking if the girls counted in this particular request, respecting that everyone has their likes and dislikes. Lucky for me, he preferred girls over boys. Not knowing if The Major was fully bisexual or just having those moments of self-exploration, I jumped on board his private message request, fully respecting either road he was on. Our many roads, no matter the twist, how many turns they have, and how many cracks they obtain, tend to define us somehow. Through a night or two of chatting, it was clear that he wanted to be the ultra-dominant whatever arrangement settled on. He had particular kinks, and being the absolute alpha man was a massive part of it.

Our 'meet' was on a late weekday morning in a muddy and gravelly parking lot in one of the local parks on a day of many days plagued with thunderstorms and downpours. Getting there first helped me bring my head around another choice. The Major arrived on time and parked his car next to mine. We both got out of our vehicles to greet each other. The first thing I noticed was the mother fucken in a uniform. These are just his everyday work clothes for him or anyone else in a similar field. For me, I saw the absolute authority of this person in uniform. The second thing I noticed was his handsome face, intense gaze, and pure ownership of his surrounding space. Melting was impossible from where I stood. Without little to no hesitation, he kissed me where I stood. It wasn't a platonic 'hello' kiss either. It was 'I want to fuck you kiss". It was a kiss I wanted to feel. It was a kiss I waited to feel. That single kiss communicated the mutual dark need we both had. With little to no hesitation, we ended up in the back of his vehicle. The Major did not operate in the familiar shades of pure vanilla. The man was no fucken boy scout. He was a dominating bull daddy who was calling me " his baby girl." Hearing that title given to me in the back of his car was like being given the perfect pair of jeans. It perfectly matched my inner submissiveness that existed in dormancy, waiting to be summoned on hands and knees. I had no problem whispering, "Yes, Daddy as it was second nature. His greedy fingers explored my clit, my breasts, and my innermost darkest hunger. A fierce storm was setting its wrath outside and inside his car. As the rain poured down at its fullest intensity, I straddled and rode him until he fully released his thirst. As my hunger finally hushed, we sat there in silence for a moment as he held me as though he had found something special on the side of the road. Before 'it sank in,' a car came into the lot and began racing out of the new puddles like an excited puppy. We planned it, and we executed it. Mission complete in literally thirty minutes. "Let it sink in."

It had sunk in enough for the Major to 'meet' again the week later between 11 am and 1 pm at a motel. He's not a Major, but he did have rank and authority in his chosen profession. I could have easily called him a Captain, Officer, or even Chief. However, the name "The Major" fits like perfect jeans, which I never wanted to take off while writing this. I last did the motel gig with Anthony almost two years ago. That was, of course, a one-time done-and-gone arrangement. I wondered if that would be the same with The Major. Would he get his fill after one full-fledged meeting, and that would be all she wrote? During our ongoing texts, he liked calling me his 'baby girl' and liked when I called him 'daddy.' "Who owns you, baby girl"?

"You, Daddy,"

"Good girl". I have to admit I liked it as well. It felt like I had become tethered to something tangible and solid.

This type of role-playing is familiar to me, but only on a virtual level. There was never an opportunity to act out any scenes in person. None of the past "daddies" had the balls to play this game in the flesh. Playing the little girl role for the Major is nothing short of exciting for me, and I've even planned out a schoolgirl outfit with bubble gum, pink pedicures, and a manicure. Finding hair bands with bows and a cute Japanese schoolgirl blouse just seemed too perfect not to purchase. Dressing up is often a lot of fun. It's like preparing to take the stage, except this role came naturally to me, like putting on new skin that had been waiting for me all this time. Practice just makes perfect.

However, for the love of a fucking God, I got my period just a couple of days before the scheduled meeting. Even though I have an IUD, I still have irregular light cycles with the worst fucken timing. Light cycles or not, it always leads to cancellations with 'meets,' and I didn't want to postpone my meeting with the Major. Postponements often led to never happening. Having googled solutions like a magic pill to turn off the flow, I came across something called a menstrual disc that creates a barrier between one's flow and activities one wishes to engage in. It is a plastic ring that you fold up and shove up your lady hole to create a barrier between the bloody mess in your uterus and the outside world. The very first change I got, the first thing I did was to run to CVS and purchase a box of disks.

Of course, I needed to try one of these suckers out before even committing to even them during a fuck session. Running to my sister's apartment to battle the roaches and feed the cat, I used the opportunity of privacy. I was in the bathroom and shoved one of these disks inside my area. Being a small girl as I am, the thing would not go entirely in, no matter how much I tried to push the fucking thing up my woman hole. Maybe these things were buying shoes. Let me just walk around and see if my body will just break in this damn thing I just shoved up my privates. Throughout most of the day, I was not aware that I had a thing up my hole, except when I went to pee. The damn thing might as well stick out his hand and say, 'Hey, I'm here' every time I sit on the toilet. As a half-decent researcher, I looked up various reviews on these devices to see if a better-fitting disk existed. Coming across a much better brand and more, I ran to CVS to purchase a different brand of menstrual disc. This version came in two sizes, regular and small. I'm pretty sure you can tell which size I picked out. Pedicures, quick switch out of disks, I felt a difference. Perhaps this would work. However, knowing that some men like to use their fingers in specific ways, I was pretty sure the manager was going to quickly know that there was something not natural up my woman hole.

Reaching out the night before to The Major saying, 'Hey, just letting you know there might be a small plastic device in my hole. If you're down there, don't be alarmed. It's just, you know, a sexual health thing'. After divulging more details of the situation, my gut feeling is that he will cancel, and I probably will never hear from him again. No man wants a semi-bloody woman hole, but I might as well just be upfront with the guy. I did not expect his response after telling him about my female situation. Not only was he not turned off by a bit of blood, but he also welcomed the mild flow. He preferred I didn't use awkward devices or barriers and just came as I was. The Major had an openness when it came to general body fluids. Maybe after years in the military, a little blood on one's cock wasn't a terrible thing in comparison to various casualties of war.

What felt like the first time in my life was that I felt OK about the functions of my body. Soon after commuting with him, I could breathe a little better. The show was to proceed as planned.

As soon as The Major left the room, I needed to write and document the moment. Such were such rare moments that I needed preservation in the amber of the written word. Even though he was only here for an hour, it felt like I'd just experienced an eternity. The room was still mine for a good hour. Absorbing the reality of not just having someone I just met last week between my legs but this particular individual. It was his lunch break, and I had lunch again. For just an hour, The Major quickly demonstrated his talents of packing in many various activities in a short amount of time. He knew what to do with the dog collar and leash I provided. Unlike many men I've encountered, he was not a lazy fuck it at all. Maybe it's the training one had to endure in their particular profession., Giving me a little time to catch my breath or drink my vodka-filled iced tea, The Major parked his car within 10 minutes after I secured the room. Liquid courage is often needed when encountering someone in this capacity for the first time. Again, he was in his army uniform upon arrival, which was fucking hot. His uniform added to the moment. As soon as he opened the door, he took complete charge of the entire show.

I was his pretty little girl to fuck how he wished. My submissive nature complemented his total dominance. Towards the end, there was even a strange, awkward moment of silence as he held me in his arms as he did in his car last week. I needed to avoid this level of tenderness, but there was nowhere to go except in his arms. The shared tranquility after a raging storm felt peaceful, and threats simultaneously are where my detachment skills need to kick in. Enjoying intimacy without letting it "sink in" is like forcing oneself not to breathe fully. Having the room to myself afterward gave me time to gather my thoughts to reflect on the previous events. I was absorbing the moment, processing it, and digesting it. Run from it.

Having time to kill isn't always easy to fill. I took the entire day off when I needed a long lunch break. When my time in the empty room ended, I visited my sister. I wondered if she could figure out what I'd just done by looking at me. Did I smell of sex? Does having a severe stroke give one a particular awareness that they didn't have before? Would she be aware that an activity packed in one hour would be hidden in the memory under my skin and kept hidden in the marrow in my bones?

To avoid becoming close to anyone, I needed to seek the required balance to prevent myself from feeling anything. Once those emotions are set free, they will attempt to drown me to the point of suffocation. I need to continue to hunt for simple self-preservation. The abortion of these feelings from being held not long ago needed to be performed. I made further arrangements but not with the Major.

Soon after, at Willowbrook Park, I met Tom. This place was the same place I met the Major two weeks ago. By using the exact location, I decided to dilute that memory. I recently found Tom on Ashley Madison. With a down-to-earth vibe during our ongoing texts, I felt confident our meeting would at least help me think of the Major less. I expected to see someone resembling a laid-back grizzly bear desperate to feel someone else's hands on their skin. I'm unsure if The Major knows that other men might be in a rotation, but he wants him to ask his permission in our role-play game.

I didn't ask. If The Major asked why I wanted to be with another person, the answer is something I'm not prepared to say aloud. It had very little to do with a high sex drive. It is simply my defenses kicking in from having any attachments to anyone. Doubting the Major would understand the way my mind works or how it doesn't work? Honestly, I suspect there's any soul out there with any understanding. Tom was made aware in our conversations that there would be other men. As long as he had his opportunity, he simply didn't care. Turning off the noise outside these moments is not difficult for me, as though a switch inside me becomes turned merely on to perform as required. These actions are why I do what I do. I was simply just trying to silence things inside me. Although I did love J, I'm avoiding making the same mistakes I made a year ago of becoming attached to anyone at all. The drowning in those oceans of neediness is something I just don't want ever to repeat. However, I don't like just to have a lineup of guys I fuck in parked cars, never to see again after. Those one-and-done moments are too empty. Within the balance between the desert and the ocean, somewhere in a body of lakes and a pond, I may find a fragment of serenity.

Tom tasted like my childhood memories of sadness, mint, and cigarettes. Although his fingers left a tingling warmth of mint afterburn between my legs, the aftertaste was nauseating beyond compare. We 'met' at the park just after 9 am. There was no attraction to Tom. Maybe because I was able to turn off and on various switches inside me, I didn't care about opening my legs so Tom's fingers could claim me and make me forget everything outside the car. Whatever attachments I felt for the Major began to fragment themselves and peel away like ashes off a nearly burnt corpse. I could now embrace an emptiness and, therefore, achieve my goal. What I could not accomplish the day I met Alan after being with John last year has been done. I could stomach it as one tries to get through any medical procedure. Although I woke up with a mild migraine, my stomach couldn't betray me this time. Tom wanted to see me again, but there were so many menthol cigarettes and sadness one could digest in one lifetime.

The seats in the diner were warm and torn as the fake leather itself could tell a story of its own. I was sitting at a booth in a restaurant, hiding and waiting, hiding because I wasn't supposed to be there. Instead, it was assumed to be at work but left early, claiming not to feel well. Waiting for 4:15 to park in front of the Majors place of employment to snuck it like contraband. The kids these days refer to these moments as a bootie call. My bootie will be available in some unknown capacity for Major to use as he sees fit. I am still determining what to expect. I hoped the Major knew what he was doing, considering this is where he works every day. I do not want to stress him out; however, this is his idea, so I hope he knows what he's doing. Often, desire prevents us from making the best choices in life. To be in his office is a small invitation into his world. I'm hoping the French fries and coke will help delude the taste of mint and cigarettes from the other day. At 4:20, I parked near the Major's place of employment and waited to hear if the coast was clear.

As I sat on the couch, watching TV, I pretended that precisely an hour ago, I wasn't leaving the Major's place of employment. Within the thirty minutes allowed, The Major smuggled in through a back door of a large complex. Following him through a dark hallway, I followed him into what looked like an unused office. By the baroness of the desks and wall, there was no sense of any person ever using this space much. As soon as the door closed behind us, every molecule of my body was his to use as he pleased. He took complete control when he knew he had a green light to proceed. Commanded on my knees, I begged to drink him.

Commanded my ass on his desk to be filled by his thickness as well as being tasted from between my legs, I struggled to keep the emotions from surging from inside myself. The switches that turn off that part of myself refuse to operate how I need them to. As we make eye contact, I struggle not to feel any connection. The numbness I so depended on failed to itself be known. 'Fuck I don't want to feel!' the voice inside screamed. I stood, leaning forward as The Major took me from behind. Again, I am on my knees as he struggles not to release himself. I am placed face down on the floor as he covers my body with his. "I am his". The Major finally permitted himself that final release as I stayed still underneath. "I am his". I felt a tissue cleaning the crevice of my ass soon after The Major stood up. Allowed and guided off the floor, I think the carpet below scratches my knees. We dressed as I tried to regather my senses and desperately take in what had happened. My Major kissed me and asked if I was ok. I'm beyond ok.

"I am his". There were no immediate words I could communicate to summarize the current whirlwind inside that moment. If I weren't careful, the storm would burst out from me. Desperately trying to catch my breath and reassess reality, we left the office we entered thirty minutes ago. Following him back down the dark hallway and through the back exit, it's only 4:55 pm. I started the car and went home. The feeling of an overwhelming sensation throughout my body pulsed through my veins with revenge. An hour later, sitting on my couch with the cats, pretending not to be lost in this recent memory, the numbness has completely failed me. Where was the empty void?

### Pieces of a Day in NJ (Summer 2023)

Out of all the days the computers were down at work, it has to be when the written word is my only haven. They were the only lifeline I felt I had on a day when I needed a lifeline the most. Luckily, basic, sound, old-fashioned word-processing still works, carrying words of trauma into a flash drive. A fun day with work friends turns into an emotional rollercoaster. Maybe dissection wasn't the correct word, but it's the only word I could come up with that describes dissembling from within. The sounds of typing letters on the keyboard began to calm me enough to focus on each sentence. Each letter and word helps slow my heart down just enough to gather my thoughts.

Yesterday, I went to Red Bank, NJ, with three friends from work. Going out with people in this capacity, or much of any capacity, was often a rare treat for me. Our destination was an old-school-style arcade called Yesterday's Arcade, lunch, and a few thrift stores. Initially, we would go in separate cars because my nineteen-year-old son wanted to join us. Since he loves everything about video games, I thought the arcade would be up his alley. However, upon waking that morning, he mumbled that he hadn't slept well and apologized for bailing on us. So, instead of taking two cars, I didn't have to stress over getting lost in New Jersey. All four of us could pile in one car without air conditioning. My stupid ass thought it was a good idea to wear jeans on a hot summer day. Due to the lack of air conditioning, we drove with the windows down, causing a rapid breeze from the Garden State to make my hair as annoying as possible. The mild discomforts did not hinder the joy of being in the car and catching up with friends I rarely see. It was a small price to pay for the feeling of connection.

As we exited the car in Redbank, I loathed my choice of denim each step and each second. When we reached the arcade, I was highly grateful for the chill of AC. This place was fantastic. Small enough to fill an hour of entertainment. Pinball machines lined the back wall. I have an inner kinship with pinball machines from my time at Golden Acres. One day, when my mom and I were at Golden Acres, I fell ill. Once I felt up to it, I ventured out of our room to their dinky, sad excuse of a game room. There were a couple of pinball machines to choose from. I need to remember which one I picked, but once I put in one-quarter of the machine, it gave endless turns. The pinball gods above felt sorry that I wasn't feeling well. I think I played for about a good hour before having full entertainment. Yesterdays Arcade had at least twenty pinball machines. The Star Trek pinball machine attracted me the most.

Once I had my fill of Picard and 'making it so,' I checked my phone to see if anything was happening. My husband messaged me that his bank card became locked due to a fraud alert, and he was driving to Red Bank to get my card to do some food shopping. Even though we had enough food in the house to scramble up a couple of meals together, it seemed imperative to him to drive at least two hours to come and go grocery shopping. My friends thought this was a bit ridiculous and even intrusive of him. It was highly absurd, and I had a gut feeling that the day would slowly feel like an avalanche. As annoyed as I was trying not to look, my friends quickly learned that the situation wasn't good. One of my friends tried to occupy my mind by engaging me in two-player games. I attempted to take out most of my annoyance on old-school air hockey.

When my husband finally found me in the aisles of 1990s vintage arcade consoles, he didn't bother to say hi to me or acknowledge my friends' presence. He stuck out his hand for my card while one of the workers at the arcade told him he needed a wristband upon entering the faculty. My husband has a habit of just walking into places without reading any signs and has no regard for any business policies posted upon entry. Leaving a lovely first impression with my friends, he took the card and stormed out. After he left, I wondered if there would also be a problem with my card since we have a joint bank account. Here he is, driving for nearly hours to possibly discover he wasted time and gas. I tried not to think about bank cards, groceries, or him too much, and I was here to have a nice day with friends.

After leaving the arcade, we went to a low-key Tex-Mex for burritos, nachos, and more air conditioning. Checking my phone regularly, I wondered if I would hear any news on bank cards, groceries, or other things that would kill whatever fun I was enjoying. After we ate, we went to a fancy thrift store. Within minutes, I found the cutest and perhaps hot little purple dress. Soon after purchasing the dress and leaving the store, I got a message from my husband asking for my four-digit code for the card. Unfortunately, my dyslexic brain gave him the wrong numbers. About ten minutes later, the bombardment of messages began. Fun time was now officially over. Because of my dyslexic brain, he had to leave the store and all the groceries behind. Apparently, by attempting to enjoy my day, I have ruined his day beyond repair. I was a selfish fucken idiot who didn't give a fuck about family. Apparently, by not checking and responding within twenty minutes of when he initially called me about the card issue, I have no disregard for him, our son, or anything he deemed essential. Each felt like knives digging into my skin. This person had the power to cut through the walls I'd been building and repairing through all these years. My skin was not as thick as I had hoped it would be by then. If my friends noticed the tears I failed to hide, they did not say.

As we walked through a much lower class of thrift stores in a different part of New Jersey, I tried to repeat various matières to calm myself. If no one were around, I would whisper the words aloud as if they contained vital magic. "Major, military, office,"

"Major, military, office," "Major, military, office". For a short while, I felt like Arura Stark from Game of Thrones with her list of names of those she wished to kill repeatedly. "Major, military, office." I would add other words: "Major, military, office, J, strap-on," "Major, military, office, J, strap-on." For a few minutes, here and there, repeating these words helped silence the tears. It's impossible not to slightly giggle by repeating 'strap-on, strap-on, strap-on". I found a headband to keep my hair from annoying the shit out of me during the ride home and a cute little Japanese shrug. Before paying for the two items, one of my friends texted me an image of a bunch of signed Star Trek memorabilia somewhere else in the store. Among the memorabilia was a signed and framed photograph of Data, played by Brent Spinner. Besides Spock, Data is one of my husband's favorite Star Trek characters. As an attempt at a foolish peace offering, I purchased Bret for forty dollars.

The lack of air conditioning and traffic made the ride home nearly unbearable. Due to not being in any rush to get home, I readily agreed to be the last drop-off. The delay allowed one of my other friends to show me a tiny new house off Lighthouse Hill—this small yet delightful home located in one of the remote areas of Staten Island. Right now, I couldn't retrace our steps to find this house. Not enough words describe this tiny gem up on the hill. My friend recently dug into her finances and spent loads of time fixing it up and creating a delightful space for herself. It was as though she reclaimed her identity by polishing the house. As tiny as it is, the bottom floor contained a kitchen and a small living room. The circular staircase leads upstairs to her small yet perfect bedroom with access to the backyard. I even had an opportunity to meet her hyper yet adorable dogs. Wanting to stay longer, the thought of going home and dealing with what awaited me at home was nothing less than the weight of a boulder in the pit of my gut. Maybe Bret Spinner could rescue me, but I doubted it.

It didn't take long for the eruption to begin upon entering the door. My husband accused me of putting my friends first, emotional abandonment, and being ungrateful. The list went on and on and on. The only thing my husband accused of that rang true was acting as if I was dead inside. 'How nice of you to notice,' I thought to myself. 'You don't even know the half of it, dear,' I continued to say to myself. While he hurled the accusations of being a horrible human being at me, I sat as though I was a child scolded by an angry, disapproving parent. Being reduced to a child, I repeated "I'm sorry," "I'm sorry," and "I'm sorry" as an endless rain of tears poured from me. "I'm sorry," I said after being told I'd wasted his time in therapy. All the work he had done on his mental health was nothing but a fucken waste of time and money because of me. He was in treatment not to work on himself but on us. How horrible I was for not being aware and grateful for the hard work he has put into everything. If any of that is true, then it's true to attempt to claim that I am a walking, broken human. Many pieces of myself do not enter the house with me. Through the past fifteen or so years, they have broken off slowly. Having identified a few of these pieces, they now exist in their chapter. However, many pieces of myself are long gone. I don't remember their names, but they will not return soon.

If we agreed upon that night, it was that I needed to find a therapist fast. My husband believed that therapy would turn me into the wife he always wished for. After a few magical sessions, I will finally become this ideal that he had in his head. I agree to proceed in finding a therapist, not become his Stepford wife, but discuss my various options for changing this situation. Several paths became apparent, including the Stepford option. The other options before me included finding my tiny house on a remote hill. Leaving him has always been a thought lingering not so far in the back of my mind. Not wanting to disrupt my son's life, it had always remained a lingering thought with little substance to hold. He was nineteen then. Although far from being an independently functioning adult, he might not suffer as severely as one might think if I choose that path. Often, I thought of having an honest conversation with him. Maybe if I play the therapy card, I will make that thought of talking to my son more of a reality. As of then, I was used to being my casualty in this current path.

That night, it was challenging to find a second of sleep as my mind tried to explore each path and all the casualties each separate path contained. Knowing my husband would leave for work before I woke up would give me a couple of hours of peace to cry, think, and process. I waited eagerly for the salvation of the morning. However, when morning did arrive, he didn't go to work. Those couple hours I desperately needed to attempt to gather my thoughts were no longer mine to have. All I had left for any sense of respite was just leaving the house to go to work. As soon as the door closed behind me, I took several long, deep breaths before heading to the car. Hoping no one at work could tell I was crying only a couple of hours prior, and I craved the sound and feel of the keyboard.

Besides writing down the words, I'm supposed to meet someone called K-Rad from the Kik app. We are meeting for the first time at the same motel I was with the Major. The hope is that the act of adultery will assist in severing the nerves that can still be affected by unwanted outside forces. Or, if anything, be another temporary clamp to get me through these paths I will embark on. I also hope K-Rad will be an inefficient buffer to any potential feelings I have toward the Major I'm expecting to see on Friday. Luckily, they will provide a balance of emotional buffering from not just each other but from other factors I must begin facing head-on.

# Pieces of K-Rad

Since I've driven deeper into the various groups in the Kik app, Ashely Madison felt obsolete to me, unlike AM, where, most of the time, a certain amount of information is already given about each person, even before any type of communication begins. If anything, and if the person who created such a profile wasn't catfishing, their height, weight, and other elements were already established. Often, the process was no different than window shopping for shoes. If you see something you like, there is an option to try it on for a spell before making any purchase. Kik was utterly different. Each new dot icon of a person was someone new peel each time. AM, unless the person is a complete lying sack of shit, you give their age, weight, height, and sometimes a picture. With Kik, you have nothing to go on to stir you through the muddy backwaters. Each person who introduces themselves must slowly reveal their attributes. Each layer peeled determines if the conversation will continue or have a quick, painless death. There's also a little bit of fellowship among the regulars in these groups as though we are a little fucked family within this weird little app on our phones.

As of then, my favorite group is a Staten Island Bi group. As with the majority of websites or apps dedicated to "hooking up" to any degree, I found myself once again one of the few genuine females existing on them. You would never think being an average fifty-one-year-old would be so popular, but that's the harsh reality in these situations. As such a rarity, I was a Flying Unicorn. Knowing I was the minority to a majority of cocks, I had some wiggle room to be selective. Anyone who looked like they just got out of jail or a meth lab, I immediately eliminated. I eliminated anyone who appeared to have any bit of drama. I eliminated anyone who was not at all respectful. Anyone with a baby toe for a cock was eliminated. If you consider it, the above standards should be on everyone's list. In addition to that list, and hopefully on everyone's list, was a chill vibe and specific energy that drew me in. In this particular bi group, I feel a decent vibe from most of the men there. Here is where I first met The Major. To achieve some sense of detachment, adding to my dance card seemed not necessary.

Like the Major, K-Rad was also an on-and-off member of the bi-male member of our happy sludge water gang. Married, tall, and in his mid-thirties, his little freaky desires have brought him into this world of the down low. And just like the Major, K-Rad is one hundred percent secretly bi-sexual and has kindly shared pictures and videos of his cock getting sucked by another member of our fucked-up team named Tim. Tim became my virtual gay little brother and is one hundred perfect gays all the way. Tim and I were in the process of sharing K-Rad. Although Tim, I believe, had accomplished three encounters with K-Rad, I am still waiting for my turn, which was always tentative.

After still recovering from Sunday's emotional beat down at home, I wasn't sure if my mind, body, and spirit would be able to proceed in another that wasn't self-destructive. Partaking in double the amount of pot gummies and wine that I usually indulge in on Monday night, I would proceed with my plans. I would make my inner capabilities of destruction into a personal revenge day. As fucked up as they are, these were my coping skills. If I'm going to implode, I might as well make an entire day out of it.

Nearly every day, I must pass by the Major's place of employment to feed my sister's cats. Figuring it couldn't hurt to see what possibilities could come from "passing by," I inquired about them. According to the Major, any possibilities could occur between 10:30 am and 11:30 am on most days, with a 'heads up' notice in advance. Considering K-rad confirmed that I would be meeting him at the motel by noon, I could give the Major his 'heads' notice around 10:45. If this were going to be my revenge day, I needed to go full throttle. The cute dress I bought Sunday in Red Bank, New Jersey, was dubbed the official 'Revenge Dress'. Since K-rad and the Major enjoy daddy-dom play, I put my hair in cute pigtails for the day.

At 10:30, I made my way to the Major's place of employment. It wasn't clear what this 'meet' would entail or exactly where, but I put my faith in the Major's instructions on parking my car. Already outside waiting, The Major instructed me to park directly behind his vehicle. His car had much darker windows, and he placed a sunblock shield on the front window to give a decent amount of privacy for activities that require such privacy. Crawling past the backseats, which were down, I made my way to the back seats, giving me a bit more room and privacy to play. As soon as the Major got in and closed the door, I became utterly his to use in any way he saw fit in whatever time frame he had. Our hands were a welcoming invading force between each of our legs as the heat between us became an overpowering force we would gladly lose to. It also helped go commando underneath the revenge dress. The Major even put his military hat on my head, giving me an idea for future 'meets.' It was a handful of sweet gestures that were hard to digest.

"Whose pussy is this', 'he demanded to know.

"Your sir," I replied in a near helpless voice, even though I knew my privates would belong to K-rad within a couple of hours.

"Good girl," he said, confirming his approval. "I need to be inside you," he demanded.

"Yes, please, sir," I begged. I wanted him in any capacity I could get. Being in the back seat of the Major's car began to help serve the nerve that connected me to anything about Sunday. It was fast. It was delightful to allow myself to let go. Belonging to the energy that surged in these delicious moments, I was able to strangle the crying woman inside me from Sunday slowly. Her existence gradually began to fade into the collection of memories to file. Once he ejaculated, we got out of the car. The Major returned to work feeling a bit more at ease than he had prior, and I went to feed my sister's cats as I awaited to hear from K-Rad.

Waiting at my sister's nearly abandoned apartment is possible. I'm afraid to sit down because these poor, neglected little creatures will cover me in their cat hair. Also, the smell is unbearable. All I can do is feed them and give them water. Kicking the cat food bowls so everything crawled in them would scurry away. I still need to use the long claw stick to pick up the bowl and place it in the sink. Pouring in the dish soap, I turned on the hot water and stepped away because there would be roaches running out of the sink. Once the coast is clear, I retrieve the bowl from the sink and dump another can of new food. I haven't been able to change the trash bags from the bin because they are there, too. I dump what looks like poison in the trash, hoping I can leave the bag without anything crawling out. The trash bag is still there. These duties are all I can do, and all the time I can bear being there. I leave, locking the door behind me.

There's a Dunkin Donuts next to the motel, so I buy an iced coffee and wait to see which room number I will knock on. After waiting ten minutes, I got a text message to go to room 110. From one parking lot to the next, I park my car and grab my particular bag of props. The same dog collar, leash, my little toy, and a riding crop are inside the bag. As I knock on the door of room 110, my demeanor quickly alters to the little girl awaiting looking at 'bad things' on her phone and now has to face Daddy's wrath. The straw of my beverage lingers in my mouth as I look up with my not-innocent brown eyes. My eyes must look up further than usual because K-Rad is a few inches past six feet. I am a man, and it makes this role-playing situation feel more realistic, being over a good foot shorter than this Dom-daddy before me. K-Rad is a gorgeous giant with blues and knows how to play this kinky game. There's a bottle of beer on the nightstand. He must have been nervous, even more anxious than me.

K-rad doesn't bother to use the riding crop, but he has oversized hands that sting on impact. The collar and lease are soon attached to my neck, placing my entire existence under his domain. My job is to simply follow his lead and allow him to completely fulfill his dark needs as they now become my dark desires. My mouth and tongue remember Tim's advice on little things K-Rad likes. One thing is nibbling on his foreskin and circling my tongue around its opening. His uncut member opens me as I float in a spree of euphoria. He ejaculates twice during the hour and a half we are there, which confirms I played my role well. He allows me to use my favorite toy as he assists in bringing out an ultimate release from within me. Now, I am his "good girl." We sometimes talk and discover little pieces of each other's worlds. He's originally from Canada and only recently moved to New York City, which explains his non-New York dialect and chill demeanor. Knowing I can't stay the entire three hours, I leave him with a kiss, which begs for more—the revenge day ended with a calm numbness rushing through my veins. My walls felt reinforced.

# Pieces of The Major

Since I've been on cat duty, I've always passed near the Major's place of employment without much of an internal connection. Before the Major, it was just a place one could not help noticing when passing by. It was just a place we all passed by without any reflection on the interior and no connection to anything behind the walls, doors, or windows. But then, as I drove by and passed, I was overwhelmed with nothing short of an overwhelming reflection. Here is where the Major smuggled me in on Friday through a side door. An unexpected chill traveled through my spine as I passed by. I could not see the office window where the Major had me on a desk and a carpet because the window faces the back of the parking lot and not the street. On my left knee, there was slight evidence of rug burn. Unsurprisingly, I have not heard from the Major since then. It wouldn't be surprising if I never heard from him again. Here is the harsh reality of this lifestyle. No one ever holds onto anything besides memories. Even those slowly begin to weather away. Being prepared to let go of everyone you touch is just a reality. All one can do is hang onto the present for dear life.

Receiving messages from the Major tended to quiet down the storm inside me while making my blood simmer uncontrollably. The words on a device were far from feeling his intense wrath on my skin. Taking whatever, I could get, I slowly digested each syllable in each text bubble. The Major's sexual appetites are, by far, the most intense I've ever come across. The Major is a very, extremely down-low omnisexual. He seemed to favor women over men but had an attraction to trans-women as well. He preferred his male partners to be as femme as possible with dresses and wigs. As taboo as some might classify this, omni-sexuality was only becoming a social norm. He wanted to expand our daddy-daughter relations with either a brother or a sister for me to play with. I wouldn't have minded a big brother more than I'd enjoy a little brother playmate. The less sense of authority I have, the more enjoyable I think it will be for me. However, finding any type of third in any scenario such as this is difficult.

The tentative is not one of my favorite words. The word feels like walking on unstable ground. You might get to the other side or fall through. Tentatively, I was to see the Major again. All plans like this are always tentative, not just because of the realities of life but because one owes anyone anything. It is just the accepted nature in this self-created world of escapism. We are merely ghosting and phantoms that occasionally slide into and out of each other's worlds when choosing. The days and even nights of the 'tentative' brought out my insecurities, and I hated it. No matter how often I've walked on this unstable ground, it is nothing less than unsettling. Even if all plans go as planned, I would only have him in the room for about an hour, but I can't blame him. That's just the deck detail. Who are we to even ask for more? Who did I think was to wish for anything beyond the given? These were the feelings I wish I could permanently purge out of my body once and for all. Wanting something uncontainable has become a familiar feeling throughout the years. Why didn't I know better by then? Why did I have to relearn the same lesson over and over?

What was tentative had become solidified into another memory to store away. The Major returned to his post ten minutes ago. Like me, I assumed he was secretly rebelling against the socially prescribed normalcy we all agree to take on in life. Once again, I sat in the same chair the Major sat on to remove and then, an hour later, put his work boots back on. I sat and wrote about the events when he closed the door behind him to hold on to another intense memory. Having nowhere else to be, I'll remain in the sixty-dollar room until all three hours expire. I might as well get my money's worth.

Room 110 must have been the motel's room for adults like us. When I arrived early, two adults were leaving in separate cars. The Major didn't think it looked right for a man in his work clothes to request and pay for a room. So, I took on the responsibility of securing the room. Although being the one at the front desk at any motel was never comfortable, arriving earlier gave me time to prepare myself and the room. This time, dressing up like a Slytherin student, ready to engage in the dark arts. Preparing the tools, the Major may or may wish to use them on a round table by the chair he would sit at to remove his boots. I placed the dog collar, dog leash, toy, lube, riding crop, and a recently purchased black wine glass with a silver skeleton hand attached. In the glass, place a green straw. The Major said he was on his way, and I was hopefully ready for him.

I stood by the door, watching him enter before reclaiming me, his property. I never met anyone who quickly owned the space they existed in, and with no hesitation and no second to spare, my body became once again his. With no hesitation and inhaling each second as precious air, the Major becomes the intense storm that communes every molecule of me. The stinging on my ass cheeks from his hand was nothing but a welcoming sensation on my skin. I could tell he was restraining himself and probably could slap his palm harder down my ass. Maybe he was afraid to hurt me too much. He even teased my ass with the riding crop. As my body becomes nothing less than an orchestra for him to command, he tastes me from below, he enters me repeatedly, and his fingers know what note to play on my sensitive skin.

At some point, the Major takes the black glass and leads me into the bathroom. The Major had various dark and unique kinks that felt safe to share with me. There are certain things that no one would typically share with anyone. His kink was one of them. We were in the bathroom as he urinated into the glass. Standing right next to him, kissing his neck and ears, I welcomed this taboo. There felt like an almost secret closeness between us. The major was sharing something secret and even strangely personal with me. After filling the glass with his fluid, he ordered me to place the filled glass on the nightstand next to the bed. The Major commanded me to ride him while we both touched every sensitive spot on my body. These sensations experienced with him are no less than electricity running through each nerve in which I could easily drown myself. I was entirely his, and he was my air. The Major tells me he wants to one day feel my blood on his cock and his face. He forces me to thoroughly and repeatedly come apart over him. This action would disgust most people, but I wasn't. The thought felt primitive, wild, and even freeing. To share our innermost secret selves that we usually keep private and contained felt natural with him. Hearing that made me feel even more welcome to share something women typically don't feel welcome.

The Major then reached for the filled glass and handed it to me. Making direct eye contact, I sip and swallow this part of him. The feeling of disgust by drinking him never touches my mind as I drink him as though I am drinking a private potion that binds us. Instead, I only felt satisfaction upon seeing the euphoria on his face. Giving him something, although this was strange and taboo, I felt so tethered to him. He was in utter ecstasy as he kissed me while tasting himself and sealed the bond between us. We were bonded by this taboo, if not just our desperate singular rebellions.

Soon after, The Major finally takes the bottle of lube off the table. "Please, sir, fuck my tight ass," is repeatedly whispered into his ear. Another taboo to cross. Another piece of myself I gladly wanted to give. The tip of his stiff knees slowly opened past the restraint of my muscles. Any pain or discomfort I ignore as his thickness stretches me. Then he flipped on my stomach as he retook my ass. I think that was the Major's favorite position to release himself. To completely cover someone's body from behind while penetrating their ass. Having him side me like that made me feel pleasantly owned as he finally allowed himself to release his seed into me. The Major nearly roared as he came in long abandoning strokes.

He held me in his arms for the little time we had left. The tenderness was still the most challenging part as I fought the desire to melt into him completely. Feeling the present slip into another past, I tried to hold on to each second as though attempting to hold onto dry sand. The breeze of reality doesn't allow for such things. An hour was not enough. Finally, we broke our silence because he had to get back to work, and I had to try to return to life's prescribed normalcy. As he showered, I put on his official work hat, folded my Slytherin outfit, and began packing the last sixty minutes away. It's impossible not to melt inside when he smiles at the sight of his hat on my head. Standing there naked with just my Slytherin knee-high socks and his hat, I took in his movements as he dressed. Trying to capture each basic movement, he put his clothes back on. Studying his movements to capture them in memory, I think my heart broke when he finally buttoned the last button on his jacket. That meant I had no choice but to return his hat and repeat goodbye.

While I had less than thirty minutes left of the room, I allowed the prior hour to sink in as it sank into another memory. There's always the chance of never seeing him ever again. Life itself has consequences that steer us to and away from each other. We are particles in space colliding with each other and then separating. In secret relationships, there's always the frightful chance of turning moments into distilled memories. I had to prepare never to see him again and tried to allow the detachments to take their natural place.

Detachment became even more unfathomable, if not disquieting. All I had to keep me from drowning in emotions before they completely overwhelmed me was writing it all down and drawing fragments of memories. As the Major might have felt I tolerated his most unusual desires, he seemed to tolerate my lyrical words and abstract drawings. A strange match we were as we continued to collide and separate in the vast space of the universe.

The last thing I needed was to be in love with the Major. A peaceful, detachable love was something I could handle, as we were often able to love a particular day or a particular smell in the air. For the past couple of weeks, he's shared his innermost sexual desires with me, and we've only known each other for a bit over a month. These desires wouldn't be safe to share with one's chosen life partners because social taboos shroud them. As long as consular adults are involved respectfully, shame should not cloud our inner needs. I truly believe the major loves his wife and never intends to hurt her. However, due to this shroud of taboo, I assume there is nothing less than terror to make this part of him known. The feeling and fear of rejection often lead us to the strict compartmentalization of ourselves. In those past couple of weeks, I've tried to be a safe space for him to explore these kinks because who am I to judge anyone? Just because the Major's kinks were somewhat unusual, he would describe himself as a freak. I often assumed he often judged himself harshly. Reassuring him that I saw him as beautiful, raw, and unique might bring a little piece of needed acceptance. Perhaps when he goes home to his wife, he will feel released from his fears and fall at ease in his shoes. Assumed that the Major had fully mastered the art of compartmentalization, I was nearly just another blimp in his already vast radar. These were all just assumptions that brought me peace until my insecurities took over. Once my insecurities take over my interior spaces of thought, rationalizing becomes an ongoing battle. Some days, I lose.

Time was my ongoing enemy. The Major and I had only been able to 'meet' for quick stolen moments in the back of his car parked near his employment. However, we managed to find time on a Sunday. In all my life, I have never had an opportunity to 'meet' anyone in that capacity on a Sunday. Sundays always felt off-limits in this secret life. Also, cover stories were hard to fabricate. Fortunately, I had the excuse to feed two poor cats. Once again, he smuggled into his place of employment, through the red side door, and into an office. I assumed it was just an empty and unused office my first time here. However, it was his actual office, and it was his actual desk that I was placed on as he fucked me. To be on his desk, in his office, a place he enters and uses nearly every day, feels connected to his world. Although grateful for every stolen second to absorb his intensity, these brief moments leave me even more hungry. This hunger was not solely sexual but a simple need to disconnect. Maybe it wasn't hunger but my ongoing need to disappear in my self-created voids. The disconnection helped to create the void, and the voids helped to keep my walls unbreakable. This need to detach was a strange motivator that led to seeking out unorthodox ways to escape any tangible emotions toward the Major or anyone else.

I struggled to avoid these feelings last summer of 2023, although I had experienced them to some extent before, and they had a unique quality. The unique textures one experiences once an individual's layers become slowly peeled away. My need to feed a curiosity was the culprit, as was my profession of finding things most people don't bother to look for. All one needs is a name to enter a search engine. Sometimes, these results are limited, and occasionally, they are an array of so much information. The Major's world was not limited to results, as I was able to dig up brief moments of his timeline. Those moments that I've unsurfaced were far from current. They are approximately a decade old, if not older. These beautiful rare gems contained a multitude of multimedia. Finding these precious treasures was when the Major voiced his opinions of the current world. The overjoyed sensation of hearing this man's voice in my ear at night made the detachment even more difficult. Embracing fragments of his past of him allowed me access to an unexpected layer. When listening to his thoughts on the world, my new word that describes the Major became 'fierce.' If anything, this man was nothing short of beautifully fierce and primitive intensity.

In a leap of faith, I confessed to the Major my ability to dig up his past ideas of the world. He should have easily turned off if I had placed his name in a search engine. It would have been a normal reaction and a reaction I was terrified of receiving. Instead, he sent me a link to something he wrote about a traumatic work experience. The fact that he offered a tiny bit of information and included some level of emotion was beyond the unexpected reaction but made detaching from him much more challenging. I read his words several times to get a more profound sense of this individual. There were even a couple of pictures of him at age twenty-five and holy fuck; he was cute. There is one picture of him gazing up at the camera, and I see a hint of that boyish grin he often has before saying goodbye. It was impossible not to melt where I sat looking at him. Of his willingness to share his story while not feeling freaked out that I had a tiny scrapbook of pieces of him, it's impossible to feel disconnected. I'm sure the Major's opinions have not shifted too much these past years. However, I am curious why he stopped. What does one experience wanting to speak one's mind to silence? Perhaps this is a question I will be brave enough to ask him another time.

Detachment has always been a lifeline I've clung to, but it was becoming a thin line of string to hold onto. The concept of letting go and being let go of for any reason is a reality. It should not be considered a threat of cutting off someone's air supply. I am no one who has any right to hold onto anything or anyone. This revelation is not just my opinion but a pure fact. I'm merely a collector of experiences I feed off to feel and not feel simultaneously. I just wish the fucken insecurities would fuck off already.

**A Letter to the Major:**

Hi, The Major, aka Daddy, aka sir, and feel free to include any other Aka,

*I'm currently hiding in a Panera bread as I write. Before you read any further if you are stressing out over whatever you could be stressing out over, close this for now. Come back to it when you have a moment to breathe. And if that's not today or not the next, so be it. However, my intention in writing is not to stress out and add to the stress. Hopefully, the results are the opposite, but it's easier to take in words when the mind can better have some stillness. This letter is just me putting words onto paper because this is the form I communicate best in. Essential verbal communication is not my strong suit and probably never was since I could remember. The written metaphors feel like home, even though most don't understand what I'm trying to say. Also, I have gained a slight anxiety to speak through the years. I'm usually not saying the correct thing or relatively ignored. So, I would rather stay as silent as possible. I haven't planned what to write here. I think I'm just going with it and letting you in my mind.*

*You once and recently asked me if I was crazy. That question is a double-edged sword. Society says if someone says they're crazy, they're not because they know their actions. However, those who say they're not crazy at all are. They live and drown in the currents of denial. So yes, to some point, I'm crazy and aware of it. To quote you, 'You are a product of our experiences.' I have written over 150 pages of experiences to understand the product I am becoming. I'll include these words within the growing pages because they are based on experience and are part of the story. Most of my experiences lead to the need for detachment from certain feelings. I'm not saying I don't feel. I often overthink; luckily, I can draw those emotions out of me. Writing helps, too. I've been secretly rebelling for maybe 16 years.*

*I will share one particular and current experience that I am struggling to detach with. About eight months ago, my older sister, by six and a half years, suffered a severe stroke. She had some underlying health issues she ignored, as well as some mental health issues she even ignored more. We both have similar demons. Unfortunately, those demons have attempted to eat her alive, and I've learned to name a few of them. The day after her stroke, I went to her apartment, which looked like a crime scene with all the empty bottles and medication. There was a strange powder on the counter meant for withdrawal. I think the chemical she put in her body that day or night made her blood pressure pop a pre-existing clot to shoot in her head. She's now recovering at a Nursing Home. She's mostly paralyzed on her right side and lost most of her use of speech. It's her cats I've been feeding, but after Thursday, they will be surrendered because they have fucked up her apartment, and she can't take care of them anyway. Crap, this got depressing fast!! But I've always had an unwanted front seat to her imploding life. Hence, it is an experience I'm a product of.*

*As you might have noticed, I've been an active voice in the Bi group. You know the group I met you in. I find bisexual men very intriguing. I think because they seem a bit more in tune with their Sexuality than straight men. There's a bit more awareness of self. At least, that's my current perspective with those I've encountered. However, there is another dimension to them, which is a bit sad. Married bisexual men appear forced to live in two worlds: fear and shame. And being a person who also exists in two worlds, I think I understand what it is to hide a part of oneself—the compromise we make to live in that forward-facing world.*

*This world sees most of us but not all of us. The required balance is to keep everything in its proper place because that's how trained we are. I just don't think a person should be ashamed of who they are in this aspect. It must be somewhat painful. Shit. I got depressed again! Fuck! Anyway, I've come to care about these guys (the regulars) in the group. I'm now the co-mod and feel I must look after the guys and make sure they stay safe and have a safe place to communicate without being fucked with or taken advantage of. I'm like their bizarre den mother.*

*I hope you're dealing with the stress of late tapers off and that you don't need to 'double up on blood pressure meds,' as you once said in one of those podcasts. You, sir, have a vast digital blueprint or at least had one. I'm curious why the podcasts started and stopped abruptly. What changed? Finding them was a surprise that just gave more texture to my perspective of you. It's like noticing various line strokes and shading in a painting. Or like walking in a park and noticing the details of a path. Anyway, I hope it does not add to any of the stress. I'm sort of just going with the flow of whatever this is. I see this as another experience I'm becoming a product of. It's just another piece to the story that I'll one day organize, edit, and maybe have something to put in the world. Perhaps those who read it will connect to some parts and even feel a bit seen in the world. Or possibly use it as fucken Toilet paper. By the way, "The Major" is about 11 pages now. It's not the longest chapter.*

*So I apologize that this is somewhat long and perhaps a bit of an over-share, but fuck it. I felt like doing it and did.*

*Yours truly,*

*Aka Little Girl, Aka your Property, Aka* **crazy person**

The Major's response a couple of days after:

*I love your writing. I wish we could drink wine and tell our stories. You are unique (in a good way) and don't add to my stress at all.*

*PS- I love stress.*

After a couple of weeks, the Major became less available due to what he calls 'chaos' at work. My insecure self was on high alert. A loud part of me believed he was losing interest in me. After experiencing being blown off countless times, I felt this was just his subtle approach to blowing me off. As painful as that was, I accept that people just move on in this life choice. No one owes anyone anything when it comes down to it. The process of fully detoxing from the Major will eventually occur. The man will run his course through my bloodstream, and I'll probably sweat him out of pours. It's unavoidable and can happen as soon as today, a week from now, or a month. Nothing in this secret world ever lasts. This reality is a simple, rational fact I often need to be reminded of because I do not want to become attached to anyone. Reverting into an insecure child is a familiar pattern I recognize in myself. Placing various fail-safes helped to buffer any attachment. There were always available options to explore to help sever any nerves that dared to threaten my sense of want and need. This existence is simply survival.

# Pieces of A Bad August

The beginning of August started with COVID-19. All three of us took our turns with high fevers and brutal coughs. The worst of it started with my husband, simply because he turns into the biggest fucken asshole when he's sick. All men become the essence of douchebags during illness. These are the moments when he reminds me how I never do enough, as though I had magical powers to transport him to a specialized medical facility. "You don't give a fuck if I'm dying, do you!" His words didn't penetrate my wall much. They might have found a small crack to seep in, but that was all. All I could do was make a special chicken soup and keep Advil and other medicines at hand. Soon after the worst passed for my husband, our son began his downward cycle as COVID-19 made its rounds. Luckily, my son, in this aspect, does not act like a father when he's ill. The nineteen-year-old gathered his needed self-care supplies and hunkered down in his room. Every few hours, our son would report his status after taking his temperature and taking two Advil. While the male adults were amid fevers and coughs, I knew it would soon be my turn. However, each take-home test resulted in a negative for COVID each time. As soon as both of them began to recover slowly, my symptoms kicked in. Still, the take-home test resulted in a negative. No longer having any faith in the take-home test, I went to the local urgent care, where not only was I diagnosed with COVID-19 but a wicked sinus infection to boot. That was the first two weeks of August.

Cleared to return to work, I went back to work for one week before having an actual week off. When I scheduled my vacation, I thought this was my son's first week back at college. Being available for him to adjust to a new schedule seemed important. Unfortunately, I got the week wrong; his first week back would be the following week. Having a week to myself, I chose to keep the week to myself. While my family thought I was at work, I was not. I would become 'missing in action'. I spent most of my time at a local Panera Bread, where I could write peacefully. My goal was also to attempt to try to detach from Major emotionally. After a deep dive into his digital blueprint, I began to drown in this man's existence more than any person should ever in these situations. In the task of detachment, I made arrangements with other men.

The week began with meeting Mike at a park. After only talking online for a couple of days, I invited him into my world of a part-time rebellion. Our conversations were descriptive enough to understand each of our expectations clearly. Mike was currently separated but was hoping to work things out with his wife at some point. He was also bi-sexual. Wearing my 'now-known revenge dress,' were well I communicated my intentions. Mike was tall but not all my type. Yet, he would do with my mission of excavating a chunk of emotions. As he enjoyed the cleavage that the revenge dress provided, we took a stroll around a not-so-private park. We ended up in the back of my car. It only took a few minutes and just some effort to get most horny men off. Mike hoped to meet again later this week at a motel to take full advantage of my week of rebellion, but that wouldn't happen.

While I was trying to get some writing done, Frank, another bi-sexual, had been bugging me to meet him. Frank is, without question, not my type whatsoever. Frank eventually became one of the most annoying people in the local apps. The man was like unfix dog who needed to hump everyone's leg upon their arrival virtually. He's a retired detective who not only tries to whore himself out but his poor unexpecting wife as well to anyone, man, woman, or in between, he comes into conversation with. We were all broken toys, and this little toy met Frank at High Rock Park that week. My experience with Frank was not short of cringy and triggered childhood memories. Strangely enough, I learned that Mike and Frank had hooked up the week before. Oh, what broken toys we all were.

Like an abrupt, sharp set of claws, the pain in my lower abdomen began on the last Sunday night in August. Sitting on my spot on the small couch in the living room while watching TV like any other night, the first wave of pain hits like an unwelcome friend. Over a year ago, I had the same episode of razors trying to push through my guts. Although that episode lasted no more than an hour, it was an hour of screaming pain. After seeing my Gastrologist soon after, he prescribed a muscle relaxer to help prevent any future episodes. As soon as I felt the abrupt pain of planning to visit, the medication would prevent it from overstaying within fifteen minutes. It had been a while since I felt that discomfort or refilled that prescription. I hoped, like before, the pain would end after an hour, but it didn't. Instead, it continues in endless waves as Freddy Kruger himself is about to pop up. Requiring assistance to even go to the bathroom to vomit, I could barely move off the couch. Being known to endure pain on various levels, I could no longer endure this.

Crying for 911, I remained screaming and praying to be put out of my misery on the small couch as the two family members looked on with their powerless concerns. Hoping the pain would vanish upon the arrival of the EMS, it continued to havoc as they transported me from the couch to the waiting ambulance. The ride to the hospital seemed endless and tortuous as the pain of internal blades resumed its onslaught on my intestines. Thinking of S's stories of the horrors of infinite body fluids in ambulances, I vomited again and again into a hazmat bag provided upon request. Again, I had the false hope that as soon as my body was in the ER, this pain would finally depart. My screams continued as I was waiting in the entranceway, hoping for an insertion morphine drip into my veins. Instead, a nurse reprimanded my endless screams of F-bombs. "WATCH YOUR LANGUAGE!" and as a dumb ass, I apologized. After they took blood work, a doctor attempted to make his assessments. After being there in horrific pain for almost two hours, a nurse attached the IV drip and inserted the morphine. I was finally diagnosed with Colitis and sent some to recover from the worst August ever.

Some euphoric moments burn brighter than most. I hired an exterminator and someone to help clean most of the horrors from my sister's apartment. The task, minus the bedroom, where I've locked up the cats, to make the apartment look livable took five hours. Once we finished, it no longer looked like a place of dread, sorrow, and horror. Summoning my inner Sara O'Conner, I went through a can of raid alone, killing every small crawling living thing that managed to survive the exterminator's grasp. However, it was an exhausting yet most needed experience. About a week later, the dread, sorrow, and horror held within these walls became replaced with a new memory. Having the Major in a piece of my reality made the walls know something new and secret. A month ago, I cried in overwhelming despair over the overwhelming horror. That morning, as I lay quietly in the Major's arms on my sister's couch, I cried silently in reclaiming that space, in pleasure and feeling a different sense of connection with this person from whom I was trying to separate myself. Being with the Major, there was now part of the collection of memories I tried to hold onto before time eventually dissolved into an afterthought.

### 2nd Letter to The Major

*With the varied experiences that create the ongoing products we become, our detailed memories shape and weave the fragments of such experiences. The afterthoughts are pieces of thread stitching the scraps of fabric. They are the adhesive of our coming goings to create scrapbooks, which we initially become. Memories alone are fragments that, with time, dissolve into the shadows. Yet still, they can be our secret road map to our endless roads. Invisible time machines we chose not to share with another living being. The representations of these recollections are in solid forms, like red side doors of brick buildings and a car racing through puddles like an excited dog after a downpour.*

*Some experiences can alter the perspective of these locations. Before July, a door went unnoticed as the brick, concrete, wood, and mortar details held the structure in space. It was a random door attached to a random building. Now, it invokes longing, need, and all things delectable. The door and the circular scar from a mild carpet burn on my left knee are a new description of a place and a thing reshaped into a euphonious memory. It is something my fingers can touch and my secret time machine. Before today, my sister's apartment was a place of collected sorrow. The walls only knew my dread. After today, they now know of a sweet secret absorbed by a brown leather couch. Those walls have something new to say, meant for my ears alone. It is a new yet tiny peace thread weaving the fragments shared between us that will soon, with time, dissolve into the shadows of an afterthought. However, this particular door will always remain a door, and a couch will always stay a couch.*

*Most people simply write, "Hey, had a great time.. Can't wait for it again". I must overthink, get over absorbed momentarily, and write an essay. Yet, there go I.*

*What would an evening of shared stories over wine even look like? It is one of several collections of wishful thoughts. However, our realities will keep such wishful thoughts as such. Most daydreams never materialize past those tiny pieces of thread. However, with that said, this bitch prefers Pinot Noir. After this week, my schedule will become more rigid and not as bendable as it has been due to those pesky realities and responsibilities. My time to overthink things and over-internalize becomes slightly hindered.*

**The Major's response a few weeks later via kik:**

*What would an evening of shared stories over wine even look like? I want that.*

Taken back by the intimate response, my emotions needed a moment to process his words. Then he wrote that he missed me and asked, 'Is that ok.' Speaking of emotions, he wrote that he was emotional and "I don't do emotions." The Major was somewhere out of town and was not having the best weekend. After what is one person's lifetime, he was leaving his field of work because 'too many straws broke the backs of camels.' Also, the fact he was chilling with a bottle of Jack Daniels and was very drunk while he was writing to me. Even though he was probably very intoxicated, he was sharing thoughts and feelings beyond sex with me. Maybe I should have taken his words lightly as the drunken ramblings as they were, but my inner irrational self-refused to digest that basic logic. The next day, I reached out to him to see if he was at least alright, and, of course, he said he was. I am unsure if he's leaving his agency after over a quarter of a century. If he actually 'missed me,' I wasn't sure either. One thing was for sure: he was leaving out a massive chunk of information. Information that would have been a basic courtesy if shared promptly. Maybe in his mind, I wasn't worth that civility. Some truths enjoy punching us in the face.

It has been a month since I've seen the Major. Being sick throughout August only allowed me to see him once. That was on my sister's newly-cleaned couch in her apartment. The privacy of the couch seemed like a better option than the back of his car. Even though the Major was his usual dominating self, having a candlelight room set a different mood. Since then, but briefly, our communication seemed to have an affectionate tone. One could even mistake the tone for actual love. The Major even wrote in a text, "I adore you on many little levels." Certain words can easily cause a heart to melt as it melted mine even further than it had already become liquified. This level of expressive closeness might have scared him because the sense of him backing off was evident. Cracks in the well-structured walls within his years of mastered compartmentation he found and quickly sealed. Painful or not, It wasn't difficult to understand. Emotions during these situations do not absorb well without them slicing hearts. Things that become liquified can easily and quickly evaporate and disperse into the atmosphere.

Lighting candles around the living room as I set the mood in my sister's apartment. Pushing down any guilt over using her living room for my private moment with The Major, these actions, although sinful, helped clean out all sorrow contained within these walls. Plus, the couch is cheaper than a motel room and more private than the back of his car. How many times had my sister cried on that very couch or drunk herself into oblivion? I'm erasing all that painful energy off the leather surface of the cushions and replacing it with something more decadent.

The Major was a militaristic prompt upon arrival. He texted that he parked outside the building, and I hit play on my phone. I wanted to control the mood slightly with a variety of music. After opening the lobby door for him, I led the way into this new temporary sanctuary. Fiona Apple's "Smooth like Honey", played as he pressed against the door. His mouth communicated his need as mine communicated in like while my left hand struggled to lock the door's bolt. With a natural ease, we sunk into the mood of music and onto the couch. As our bodies entwined, our clothes fell onto the floor. Metallica's "Lover Man" played as he feasted on me, demanding my release with his mouth. We were not fucking. I didn't feel like I was being simply fucked. I'm not sure it was safe to refer to it as lovemaking, but it was primal and sensual. It was passionate. It was us capturing forty-five minutes. It felt like forever. The Major finally allowed himself to release as he laid his body fully on top of mine from behind. Being his vessel of his intense release brings nothing short of my final escape to let go as Fiona Apple's "Hot Knife' ended.

After cleaning himself up, we lay together in the tranquility of the music. It is impossible not to feel a connection or an illusion of such between us lying in each other's arms. Permitting ourselves to submerge into a closeness that never felt like a game of pretend nor of any malice. Listening to The Major's breathing lull, I fought not to fall asleep in such peaceful calmness lingering. Could we have fallen asleep if the demands of our actual lives would allow it? This brief moment of sanctuary was only a cruel dream in which I would awaken. Soon enough, he would have to get dressed and return to his world. But in those brief minutes on that couch, it was easy to pretend we belonged to each other. Eventually, the Major needed to go. The reality of ourselves returned like an unwanted friend. He said he enjoyed the music selection and appreciated that I hand-pick each song for us and this moment. My heart broke a bit as I could hear his feet go down the stairs and through the door. Because I never know where life will take us, I tend to digest these moments like the last cool drink of water. Keeping them secret in my heart and under my pillow, all I know is that this will end.

*Sep 22, 2023, 8:46 AM*

*Dear Sir, Maj, Daddy, and the reason my Dopamine levels are skyrocketing,*

*Currently, I'm hiding in Panera Bread by the mall, waiting to hear what our later plans will involve. This place overflows with people all over the age of 65. Don't worry, I will stay here all day waiting to hear from you. Although I admit, it's unsettling not knowing where or when one will be and for how long. I wonder if this is how an untethered balloon feels as it floats to an unknown destination for an unknown time. So here I float, waiting for your grasp to take hold. Like it or not, untethering is part of the course in these situations. Everything and anything are uncertain in the shadows of the down low. This existence is nothing new to me and not to you, either. Again, we are products of our experiences and have consciously chosen to wear different faces. We are merely a tiny slither of a piece of our current worlds. However, that tiny slither, small enough to hide in our back pockets, embodies the most intensifying sexual experiences I can remember experiencing.*

*What shall we label this 'thing'? It's autumn, so we can no longer call it a summer fling. Plus, the word 'fling' seems too small, like a shoe box. Is it an affair? Did the fling graduate to an affair? 'Love' 'affair'.*

*So, what will we experience today? I'm hoping for at least 90 minutes in the seclusion of a room where you can fully release your edgy velocity onto me—full green blinking lights. Challenge me. Dare me. Attempt to break me if you can. Use your dark, war-like witchcraft on me. Make me the most vital tiny slither and vessel for every little intense kink you have. With the privacy of a room, I can create a stage for almost anything to celebrate your elegant, twisted desires. I don't know how much I enjoy the theater. To dress into a character for your pleasure is my pleasure. I hope to be your little piggy that tastes like a gold shower today. I want to ride your cock while torturing my clit with that toy so my fluids can release themselves all over you. And then lick you clean. Or you can take my ass as you pull up my legs and knees in front of me. Again, I would torment my clit with my toy and see where the juices flow. Then, you can be on clean-up duty afterward.*

*Although the apartment is available, it is limited in releasing body fluids. So, I guess I do have some limits. That couch has absorbed an extremely passionate energy from the last time. That living room has a new vibe and a secret. Trust me, it needed it. My mouth is watering, remembering, and waiting to feel more of you, for I have become addicted to you. I walk around daily with a growing storm deep within me, waiting to release its thunder. This small slither is sometimes unbearable and overwhelming. And each day I don't have you, it grows into a near-raging typhoon trapped inside my gut.*

*Are these just merely overactive hyper-dopamine levels? After we are together, a sense of calmness gently drapes around me as though I can finally catch my breath. However, soon after, maybe a couple of days after, the cycle repeats itself. And here I sit and wait to hear from you as the blood in my veins boils over. I need you. Only you. God damn mother fucken dopamine!*

*However, my feelings towards you, dopamine or not, will always have a notion of detachment. Years ago, some prior experiences trained me to let go when needed. Even the present isn't particular. I believe I've made my feelings for you a bit evident. You are the downpour I crave. Often, the skies are clear, and the air is dry. Like it or not, storms do end. Chapters get their final sentence. However, I would be lying if I didn't admit I hope it rains a bit longer and the sun stays behind the clouds for a couple more days.*

*I'm not sure if I will send this now or wait. You probably won't be able to read it until much later. And you'll likely read it in less than two minutes. I'm heading out of Panera Bread soon and taking care of some things as I desperately wait to hear from you. A group of ten old guys arguing about limbo has been here longer than I have.*

*In the uncertain present, yours with overloaded dopamine,*
*me*

Sep 22, 2023, 3:50 PM The Major's Response:
*There is a lot here. I don't know what this is, but I'm having fun. You're a great person.*

Sep 23, 2023, 11:48 AM My Response:
*I was overthinking again—bad habit. Fun is an understatement. I'm going to use the word "accelerating" ...and you're pretty fucken incredible too.*

*I love hearing you say my name. Have a peaceful weekend.*

Since the above communication, there hasn't been much communication between us. Opening up to The Major as I had is something I'm now regretting. I've said way too much for anyone to want to digest in this situation. Leave it to me to misinterpret all the mixed signals I thought I was picking up. Allowing myself to become swept away like this was foolish. Along my way, I lost my inner voice of reason. No, I didn't lose it. Instead, I purposely tied it up, gagged it, and threw it in the back of my closet. I'm a fucken idiot. For the past few days, I've been grieving whatever fairy tale I created after repeatedly trying to set it on fire. His chapter will have to come to a complete close soon enough because that's just the nature of chapters. I eventually turned that last page. I always knew in the back of my head that this would hurt like hell in the end. Still, I proceeded. It hurts more than I bargained for.

Like the ongoing emotional yo-yo that I've allowed myself to become with the Major, he did not disappoint when he came to the apartment late Wednesday afternoon. I purchased an air mattress as an alternative to the couch, which held up wonderfully. Even the major commented that this was probably one of the better air mattresses he'd been on. Lately, I've become accustomed to playing set music lists when we can share these rare, unrushed moments. Taking time to create each list, sometimes with the same songs but often a few different ones, I try to build a mood in the room and, in some way, convey my feelings. Fiona Apple's "Shadow Boxer," Eddie Vedder's Breath, and Wicked Game by Chris Issacc are on it with other Fiona Apple songs that communicated what my heart needed to say. If he could comprehend whether these song selections have an actual meaning to how I feel, it is beyond me. To him, we are just two grown adults with excellent chemistry who have agreed to have fun. If I could control the insecure adolescent lurking inside me, I would be in absolute agreement with the Major's conclusion. My inner adolescent typically gets confused because when and if we have time, the major always wants to hold me in his arms.

Sex is one thing, but mixed with these moments of intimacy; it makes my inside squirm in emotional disarray. I was whispering in The Major's ear. "I'm addicted to your cock. I'm addicted to your cum" was the final nail to his intense release. When our time together ended, and we dressed, I saw a different, playful side of him as The Major helped deflate the air mattress. Imagine a grown man in civic uniform on the floor helping to get all the air out of this thing. We two adults, rolling on our bodies up and down, forcing the air out. However, we could have been two kids giggling at a brand-new invented game. There was a brief calmness embedded inside me after he left. That calmness never lasted long as all my childish insecurities, like an unforgiving tidal wave, came rushing back in total, relentless force.

# Pieces of a Stoned Lyfe

Because I cannot deal with various situations like a functioning adult, my invented fail safes needed to kick for what felt like survival. The best possible solution to diminishing someone's impact on your life is to find some tangible distraction. The ever-growing void, with the poxed cavern of my heart, the Major was leaving would be temporarily filled to some capacity by 'Stoned Lyfe.' That's not his real name. It's just his KIK handle. Stoned-Life and I were chatting through that god-forsaken app for maybe a good week, if not more. The chatting quickly becomes flirting and then becomes entirely something else. These online conversations typically fizzle out and go flat like old soda after a day or two. The vibe usually loses momentum and disinterest sets in on both parties. Or they can easily take another turn, which, in this case, it had. This situation was not the case.

Having one of my off-the-radar days with little to fill up my time besides hiding somewhere with free Wi-Fi just in case I wish to write or revise these pages, starting my day at McDonald's because I've been craving pancakes for a couple of days. With little pocket money to spend, it was the best option. The local diners would've been okay, but I didn't want a waitperson to rush me out by placing a check on the table. I need places to chill, think, and possibly create. While shoving food down my face, I was chatting within my regular Kik groups and the 'dudes' that seemed to exist in them 24/7. The regular guys on there seemed to have accepted me as the weird artery chick that often keeps the conversations alive and helps weed out the fakes, hookers, and creeps on a good day. For a brief moment, I became a den mother of some of these virtual sex groups. "Stoned" was part of the morning conversation along with "Angel," "Gramps" and myself.

"Stoned" and I were getting that vibe again that makes one want to turn words into actions. Taking the first steps, I privately messaged 'Stoned' to investigate the vibe further. Having my brave girl pants on, I asked if he was interested in meeting somewhere. He could have quickly jerked me around and made up some excuse that he was too busy. Instead, we placed plans in motion. We agreed to meet near the railroad around the Dongan Hills area. Not being familiar with that part of Staten Island as a typical car fucking location, I got to the area a little early to scoop it out. It's not like I know every inch of this Island to get laid, but I like to feel comfortable where I tend to go. Getting the layout of the land just seemed like the thing to do. However, driving around, I noticed a few pockets, here and there, at the end of the street that could work if someone had tinted windows.

The location "Stoned" wanted to meet didn't seem too private. Maybe this would be one of those quick, boring hand jobs deals in someone's car. Honestly, those feel like I'm milking a chatty moaning cow. This scenario ended up not being the case. Stoned shared a garage with some friends in which they stored their motorcycles. He wanted to get his bike out to take somewhere. We flirted as he retrieved various equipment needed to transport his two-wheeled vehicle onto his huge pickup truck. Not knowing what to expect from our flirting, I even helped him load some stuff onto his truck. I might as well be helpful just in case nothing else happens.

Once he had completed his task, the situation could have gone two ways. We could have shaken hands, said it was nice meeting each other, and then gone our separate ways. The problem did not go in that direction. Instead, as we stood outside the garage, Stoned put his arms around me as I wondered if he could sense me slowly melting where I stood. It was, if not a sensual gesture, it was intimate. As his mouth found mine, we entirely communicated our inner intentions. These clear intentions lead us back into the garage. The mutual need and hunger were apparent as our hands explored what was underneath our clothes. Our mouths continued to hunt each other's needs as our fingers and hands explored beneath the fabric of jeans, t-shirts, and shorts. As my hand tormented his hardness, his hand managed to make its way down and past the opening of my jeans. His fingers punished me so sweetly that remaining standing was different, but I kept my ground.

Then 'Stone' phone rang. It was impossible not to have the Cheshire cats grim as I heard Stoned wife's voice coming out of his iWatch. Never in my life would I have imagined having a man's cock in my hand while hearing the voice of their wife as if all three of us were sharing the same space. There's a first time for everything, I guess. As I listened to her asking him to do her a big favor and the tenderness in her voice, I probably should have felt like a piece of shit. After so many of these encounters, any shame I should have felt has been long gone, or I could simply not touch it. After years of finding numbness, I have squashed guilt, shame, and disgust. My main intention with 'Stoned' was to achieve absolute internal paralysis. Hearing his wife's voice just confirmed my achieved lack of feeling. It did not hinder Stoned much, either. As soon they hung up, our actions continued and quickened in velocity. I was being nearly stripped naked, 'Stoned' turned around with my back facing him. How he managed not to fall entirely on my face as his erection plunged inside is beyond me. Balance and coordination are not my strengths by any means. The fullness of him quickly brought me over the edge as he emptied himself. We stood in this garage filled with tools and motorcycles for a few minutes, allowing the blissfulness to drift through before I claimed my discarded t-shirt and bra.

Before parting ways, our mouths stole a few more breathless kisses. 'Stoned' made it clear that 'Stoned' wanted to see me again soon. 'Stoned' asked about tomorrow, which I knew was impossible, but I promised sometime next week, hoping we could pull something off my lunch break. 'Stoned' has access to some sort of clubhouse not far from work and a great deal of availability to go along with it. We'll see, I thought. My body is already on board with the idea. It's just the mind that needed to follow suit. As I learned through the years, months, and even weeks, things constantly change. 'Next' can never be fully promised. Our encounter would be just another collection of one-and-done moments.

As I drove off, my eyes began to tear. My sorrow had nothing to do with what happened with 'Stoned.' It was a strange sense of grief. The sadness was a particular type of mourning. Whatever connection I had with the Major was served and shot at point-blank range in that garage. I was no longer "the Major's." I wasn't 'Stoned', either. A familiar numbness began to wrap itself around me. Whatever tether held me down to a notion of deluded connections was cut. If I were to be completely honest, I don't think I felt much of anything then. And if I were to be even more honest, I welcome the emptiness and the clear hallowed void. Who knows. I might see the Major again down the road, but that hold he had on me became temporarily removed along with "Stoned's" bike from that garage.

# Pieces of The Major

The repetitive patterns of running away from raw feelings have been part of my survival. Unfortunately, the mob of emotions is often relentless. After days of attempting to avoid the Major and allowing my insecurities to believe he was avoiding me, he finally broke the silence between us. Allowing the numbness to its job, I tried to be detached. It didn't work. The Major questioned if I was mad at him without explaining why he felt any hostility from me. Trying to seem indifferent but not angry at him was my weak attempt at any detachment. The Major was drinking. It's difficult to rely on anything he was saying or take it too seriously. He shared a link to a poem called 'Ithaka" by C.P Cavafy, stating, "I have referred to it for a couple of decades now. That one just seems to nail it. It sums up the journey of life. The destination isn't the point. It's the journey." Sometimes, this man dropped these words of wisdom on my lap only to give me pause. Without much effort or knowledge, he breaks through my defenses, and I am back where I started again—overwhelmed and looking for a direction to run. Little did I know that the poem and wise words were just preludes to what would come.

On a Sunday, the Major asked if we could 'meet,' but it being Sunday, I had no excuses or cover stories to explore his request successfully. To make matters worse, the Major was to be out of town for a week. It would be another week, if not more, of being unable to have him to myself. At some point in our conversation, I casually mentioned to him that I might require strict discipline to remember my place, in which he asked, "Did you stray without permission?" Before admitting my actions, I needed to explore the reality of the consequences of this behavior. "For being a dirty whore without permission, you deserve to be slapped, choked and spat on." As depriving and violent as those sounds, these are typical disciplinary actions between a sub and a Dom. I felt I was getting off lightly for my actions. For some reason, knowing I would feel the Major's wrath helped me feel somewhat centered. Except I didn't understand when I would ever actually get this opportunity.

Then, I had to take my confession to the next level because I'm an idiot. "Strange as it may seem," I said, "Such actions just numb me. The satisfaction is just a void. A serving of nerves and something I don't think you can fully understand. I never told anyone that before"., which is true. Besides these typed pages, I've never revealed to anyone how broken I am inside.

"You can tell me anything. I own you." I wondered how sincere that statement was. Could I pour out my broken heart as though it was an expected regular occurrence between us? Could I lay out, in complete illustrated detail, how fucked up I was? I would have loved that to be true if I were honest, but I knew it wasn't.

"However, I'm not numb with you," I continued. "It's the opposite, and sometimes it's overwhelming," as if I believed The Major understood me like I desperately wanted to be understood by anyone who would listen.

"Good", he responded,

"Overwhelming is sometimes not good. I probably don't have the tools to digest that. Hence my actions". I tried to explain further.

"So, the things you were worried about that I would feel, you are feeling," the Major asked. Maybe he sorts of did get it.

"Yes, I think so," I answered.

"That's not good."

"I know, and I apologize. Maybe that didn't fall under the 'tell me anything.'

"I did mean that." And that was the last of the conversation, leaving me on the cusp of believing The Major's words. The Major now knew how screwed up I was and had a weird way of dealing with any range of emotions. Not hearing from him since then, I wasn't sure if holding my breath for an extended period was even in the cards anymore. Maybe I just played my last hand.

Unexpectedly, I heard from the Major one morning in the form of a simple text. "Hi". The Major was still away, and out of curiosity, I asked where he was.

"Back and forth between one state to another." I was even more curious, so I asked him why he was going back and forth. "My future," was his response. I invited him to explain what 'The future' means in some context. "Maybe another day," was his response which meant none of my fucken business.

However, like a dog with a bone, refusing to let that go, I asked, "OK, but when you say future, is it like this month, years, future nursing home, or something to do with time travel?"

"Months". The Major plans to move down south within months, which could be in two or three months.

Trying not to seem taken aback by this information, I asked, "Is this a good thing for you?" He did not respond and never did. The Major is supposed to return on Sunday, but I doubt I will get any information about the 'future' and 'month.' The whirlwind that entered my life was simply leaving almost just as abruptly. Having no choice but to digest this reality, I quickly realized that this 'new' information was far from new to him but only to me. It would have been information and an act of kindness if shared initially. Maybe people like myself who exist in this manner do not deserve the bare acts of courtesy. That would be new information I would learn to digest like a shard of broken glass.

After days and days of silence, I finally knocked on The Major's virtual door. He could easily have ignored me. "I'm hoping the plane didn't crash and you survived your trip." Having gone into the habit of waking up in the middle of the night almost every night to check my messages, he had responded. "Lol, I'm alive," which was quickly followed by "When can I fuck you?". Reminding him of my previous transgression, which I confessed before he went seeking his so-called southern future, he owes me a session of severe, relentless punishment. Not only was this upcoming season to include the reddening of my ass, but I was to bring a marker. Since the beginning of this arrangement, The Major has constantly threatened to write on my ass "Property of (however he wished to write his name)." The only question I had was what color maker I should bring. He also requested that I wear a blonde wig, which he claimed to have purchased as we spoke then and there. I was to be his blonde whore.

Considering that the Major was up late and might have been drowning in a bottle of Jack, he might be regretting and inquiring about claiming a refund for that late-night purchase. He also required me not only to cum all over my face but to walk me to my car with remnants of it still on my face. So, The Majors' current requirements were a maker, wig, cum-walk, and also once again partake in his urine. In response to his dark requests, I would be fully prepared, including a couple of tiny jars to collect samples of all his fluids if and when they become available. They would be my parting gifts. Also, let's not forget the hard spanking and possible slapping. I would take my chances in leaving with bruises on my body. If I sensed the Major holding back, which he often does, refusing to say goodbye to him forever without experiencing his full wrath, I would egg him on with varied disobedience.

The night before the scheduled punishment, the Major and I texted late, going through little details. Instead of utilizing my sister's apartment, he had a room elsewhere. Considering what The Major had in store for me, a room that would fit our needs was a much better stage for what would possibly be our final performance. However, instead of getting a room at the usual motel on Hylan Blvd, he wanted me to go to a more excellent establishment where ordinary people stay. Also, he mentioned 'he'd be getting the room,' which is unusual because this task has always fallen on me due to him always being uniform. Does this mean I will see him out of his work uniform? When we met briefly in late July, on an early Sunday at this place of employment, it was the only time I'd seen him out of uniform. All of this, as always, was up in the air. All I could do was carry on with my day as I anxiously awaited details and confirmations.

Luckily, I had emergency vodka because I was meeting the Major in a new venue and wasn't sure what I would be walking into. It was either the anticipation of experiencing his inner fury or the different location causing violent butterflies to attack my stomach. Room 638 at five thirty was the where and when. What he had planned in Room 638 will be revealed shortly. My noisy brown paper bag contained a few markers, the leash, collar, lube, my toy, a cup to drink his piss from, and a paddle. These would be tools offered that the Major may or may not use. My only honest regret was swapping my boots for the heels hidden in the car. Forgetting they were half a size too big, I felt like I had just traded a little piece of my identity for struggling to have these heels fall off as I walked from my car to the hotel. It was the second upscale hotel on the island, the Hilton being the first. Room 638 and 30, regretting using the noisiest brown paper bag for the tools. You could hear the crinkling of the paper bag crinkle and crinkle as I walked off the elevator to find room 638. In front of room 638, after taking a few breaths, I knock with a light-medium knock.

At five thirty-one, the door of room 638 opened, and the spell became automatically cast on by the quiet intensity of this man's eyes. All my planned disobedience and rebellion dropped onto the floor with my car keys and phone as he took the bag out of my hands. His free hand drove me to the couch by my neck. The show was to begin immediately. His ownership was instant. I was his, and

I was happy. Direct onto my knees between his legs, and my mouth becomes his to enjoy as though I was a feral cat to tame. First, I was ordered on my knees in front of him as he released his hardness and my instant reward to take into my mouth. Soon, he instructed me to undress and to lay over his lap. It was time for punishment and to test my limits to withstand the force of his bare hand. The Major's palm took turns coming down hard on each cheek. The blows were rough but not enough to make me scream but wince repeatedly. The Major had me count to three as his palm connected with my skin. I wished the number was higher. Hearing the rustling of that bag, the Major fished out a black maker to claim ownership of me in writing on one of my ass cheeks. Then I heard the familiar sound of the leash as he placed the collar around my next.

Like a trained pet, The Major ordered me on all fours before him and placed a plastic bag in my mouth to carry as he led me to the sink and mirror. The bag contained the blonde wig he purchased the other day for that exact moment. He ordered me to stand as he took the plastic bag out of my mouth and left me alone in front of the mirror to put this wig on. Besides a couple of Halloweens, I have never worn a wig before. Underneath the wig were two clips that looked like they required connecting to something, but I had no idea what. The thing was a bit bulky, and I had a terrible time adjusting it on my head without it looking like it was taking over my head. Wearing piggy ears and the snout was far more up my alley than this monstrosity of blonde hair.

I thought I looked fucken ridiculous, but it seemed to please The Major as I approached him near the best. As ordered, I was back on my hands and knees and led to the bed like a favored pet. More blows came crashing down onto my already reddened ass. There was no way this wig would stay throughout the entire hour. Ordering me to straddle him within what felt like the entirety, my body crumbled into pieces repeatedly as he orchestrated my movements for his enjoyment as well as mine. As promised, he removed a pillowcase from the adjoining pillow and placed it over my head. He slapped my ass and my tits, and so was my face. We agreed that only marks were allowed, but only where I could hide them under my clothes. The Major then led me back to the bathroom and ordered me into the tub. Noticing the tub was recently wet; I had to remove my socks. Usually, I like to keep my socks on. Luckily, The Major did not notice my left ankle. People rarely look down anyway. It was time to drink straight from the source my mouth couldn't capture poured onto my chest. The Major then peed in the cup that I had brought. Back on top of him, he ordered me back to the bed to drink the contents of the cup. I drank. The Major finally permitted his release as he regularly does. With me lying flat on my stomach, he filled the inner cavities of my ass with his seed.

There were a few minutes to spare for him to hold me in his arms as we were silent. Sometimes, I wonder if he had always timed our encounters perfectly so there was time for him to keep me. This part was always the most difficult for me. I can be spanked, slapped, dragged, and pissed on, but to be held by someone that I knew was eventually leaving my life was the most difficult. Holding my breath underwater would have been far more manageable. We remained silent as I felt my tears linger on my face. My hands tried to capture all his different textures in memory. The feeling of his soft chest hair, his arms, and whatever parts of my hand and finger could trace. Then he motioned it was time for me to hit the road; I did have to be home at a specific time. However, I would have wanted to stay so much longer with him that night if I had a choice. No matter how tightly we shut our eyes and wish, some options are never to have.

There was just one of many handfuls of moments when there was no choice but to turn another page. The first thing I did before dressing was to collect a small sample of him remaining in the cup. I brought a few tiny mason jars that could hold no more than half an ounce of fluids. "Mine," I proclaimed, showing I had captured some of his DNA as a keep-safe. Whether he thought this was weird or not was of little concern to me, considering how it originally got in the cup in which I collected it in the first place. Honestly, who was he to even judge my bizarre little actions? Even though it was urine, it was still a part of him.

As I collected my clothes on the floor, I noticed the suitcase and a couple of drawers stuffed with clothes. It didn't take me long to see that this room wasn't meant just for this moment or just for a night. He was living here. I inquired about the suitcase, the stuffed drawers of socks, and the lived-in look of the room, only to be told that the only information I got was he was planning to be living there for a few weeks. "A story for another day" was all I got from him. Before me, I could see those solid walls of compartmentation solidify. He never gave me any reasons why this room had become his current living arrangement, so he kept me out of any personal information. He might as well have said, "Sorry, it's classified," or handed me a retractive statement. Did a few weeks equal the previous answer of 'months' until he settled into his 'future' in "Nowhere near" states?

The Major sat next to me on the couch as I put my socks back on. With sincerest concern, I asked, "Are you okay?"

"Yeah! Are you?" was his defense response. By his closed-off body language and high reflection in his voice, the response was just another wall he had placed between us. I was in the 'need to know' category of his life. Therefore, I didn't need to know anything. The Major wanted what was happening close to his chest, but I wish he hadn't. Again, even if my eyes were tightly closed, it was just another empty wish.

**A Letter to the Major:**

*When approaching the computer keyboard, I sometimes wish it would magically turn into a piano keyboard. Then, with the same magical force, I would know what keys to tap and which chords to play that would speak when the primary language fails me. Unfortunately, I don't understand how to play piano or any musical instrument. All I know are words and on paper and sometimes, with luck, create a series of lines to form an image. Drawing is a personal language unto itself. The ability to draw, what I find challenging to put into words, has brought me some form of tranquility and internal release. For me, keeping thoughts and feelings bottled inside for too long only results in some form of collateral internal damage. Therefore, I have become accustomed to the serenity of words and lines because my verbal voice often fails me. Lately, I've combined writing and drawing to solidify the entire concept.*

*As of now, I have written close to two hundred pages representing pieces of myself. The project is, in part, a piece of personal narrative I've written in sprouts throughout the years and a documentation of a current series of events told in a broken timeline. Some, but not all, of the series of events I've written about emerge from ugly places I've passed through and how those places tend to stir the direction of one's path. "We are products of our experiences". Like opening an elaborate jigsaw puzzle, I needed to connect as many of these pieces as possible to see a bigger picture of myself, hoping to understand various patterns I tend to repeat. I've summoned demons of the past and called them into a meeting to weave these pieces together in some aspect of self. All that is left is to revise a couple of chapters, find a trusted person to do a final edit, and possibly, in some form, send it anonymously into the world. I'm leaving your chapter toward the end, not as a final destination, because I know my road will continue past you.*

*Speaking of puzzle pieces, you've become the most complex one I've encountered. Some pieces don't seem to fit, as though there are more than four corners to guide the border. It's as if there is more* than one puzzle in the box, with a blurring and fragmented picture as a reference. I'm aware that I will never be able to see all the pieces and won't even find all the pieces to create the border. Why you are living in a hotel room after returning from the Southern States, where your 'future' will begin in 'months' is perhaps a huge question I have. Months could mean two to ten before it becomes almost a year. Maybe it's just me, but it's hard to swallow little details with some clear context.

Expecting never to have the string needed to sow a somewhat clearer picture will never be offered, which is something I'll have to deal with. I'd like to know how long I must say goodbye. Perhaps you are wondering why I want to understand your story. I find you the most elaborate and complex individual I have encountered whose stories might offer wisdom and reflection. I am not a person who can just walk the path without looking under the rocks and inspecting the ground's surface. It's just who I am. Plus, it's no secret that I care and feel for you if you've stated, "That's not good." Good or not, and probably 'not,' they seem to exist, and I will deal with them either poorly and carelessly or more constructively. As I've written my story, I see a clear pattern of how I deal with any overwhelming emotion of attempting to either violently rip them from which they came or finding ways to dull the sensation of feeling. It is a pattern I'm in the process of understanding better. So please permit me to feel quiet, if you don't mind, to see myself more precisely and not seek the numbness as I usually do. I expected nothing to feel in return. You'll continue to be my simple muse.

This morning I woke with a blotchy pink ass and very mild bruising on the left tit. There is some sign of carpet burn on each knee. While showering, I tried to be mindful of the ink that would eventually disappear. I failed with wig-wearing and producing a significant amount of phlegm. My legs are overall a bit sore and stiff from riding you. Maybe you threw out the cup used and left it by the sink, or room service has cleaned it. The tiny jar of you now sits by my pillow. I know it's probably an incredibly bizarre thing to collect a person's urine into a small jar, but I'll take whatever tiny pieces I can get as a parting gift. In the few months that have passed, last night was only the second time I've seen you in non-work clothes. Seeing you in everyday clothes and in this strange element of 'living in a room' was like finding new little pieces of the puzzle of you. The pink flip-flops included. Honestly, I didn't want to leave but to be an observant fly on the wall. Hopefully, I will have another opportunity to return to room 638 next week to find a couple tinier pieces and the week after that.

Last night, I wrote this song, which summarizes what I've already said above:

Allow me to scratch the surface
Permit one-time access behind your breath
Just a second to sink into your depth
Lose myself in you in the blink of an eye
I've been collecting pieces of you on the sand
Catch loose remnants that float past
But I have no string to connect
The fragments I've collected
Stay loose in my hand
I promise not to stick around past the hour
I only take the crumbs scattered
I won't sink my teeth into deep
If you offer up a taste of your identity
I've been collecting pieces of you on the sand
Catch loose remnants that float past
But I have no string to connect
The fragments I've collected
Stay loose in my hand

*As you said, maybe two weeks ago, I can tell you anything. So here I am, with much guidance, continuing to tell you anything. However, I hope the 'telling' isn't a one-way street.*

Without fail, whenever I hear from the Major, even if it's just one word, there is a blazing sensation along my cheeks that eventually spreads through my entire body. My breath quickens like a bolt of electricity has struck my existence. In our last communication, he asked if he was too rough the previous time, and I reassured him that he was absolute perfection. This man's effect on me was nonsensical and was exciting my life. Although he never responded to the last email, The Major had confirmed he had read it. Sometimes, the simple knowledge of being heard or reading brings me peace. Just having him aware of my thoughts and feelings without having him want to give him pause is enough to sustain me. Only being able to be in his presence again when we can is all I ask in return. If, by any chance, I had the opportunity to hear any fractions of his story, I would be nothing but honored to listen to any parts offered.

Last night, The Major allowed me to ask a few questions about this "future," which would begin in a few weeks.

**Me:** And can I ask you something, sir?

**The Major:** You can ask

**Me:** But if you'll answer?

**The Major:** Not a fan of questions

**Me:** Why are you leaving?

**The Major:** It's time to leave. Start over. I never liked New York.

**Me:** I get that and envy that you can find a new one. Will you be alone in this new beginning?

**The Major:** No

**Me:** Good. Will you still be working in your field? I'm trying to keep asking yes or no questions so it's easier for you.

**The Major:** No, that chapter is coming to an end.

**Me:** And that's going to be a huge transition

**The Major:** Yep. I thrive in chaos

**Me:** Do you know what you might do?

**The Major:** Nope, Maybe sell hotdogs. Doesn't matter

**Me:** Can I still write to you?

**The Major:** Sure

**Me:** Will you attempt to write back?

**The Major:** of course

**Me:** Will you still dabble in devious ways? Never mind, you've answered the important ones. Thank you

**The Major:** LOL

If I would have an opportunity to The Major before he headed off to greener pastures was known to me. It's not my way to force the issue. As he transitions to his new life, I, too, will be transitioning parts of myself away from him. Having already felt we were parting ways, even before becoming aware of his actual move, I had jump-started the grieving process. Sometimes, you can feel loss and distance occurring in your bones. It would have been nice if you told me from the beginning of our arrangement that he was soon relocating. This information might have saved me a lot of tears. The keyword in the sentence is 'might.' Maybe I wasn't worth the simple consideration. Perhaps if he had told me on day one that he was planning to move far away, I could have had a nice chunk of detachment prepared in my back pocket. Either way, his chapter is ending. Yet I've been rattling my brain about why it seemed one of the more essential pieces I've collected throughout my life. What caused me the most significant emotional and dysfunctional deep dive about this individual? Maybe the rationale will become more apparent as I continue to type. Perhaps I have already answered this question repeatedly but haven't found the sense to comprehend it in complete understanding of its context.

The Major has mentioned a few times before that he thrives on chaos. This statement made me think about what I thrive on. One I know I thrive on is creativity. Yet part of my creativity thrived on its chaos. Chaos for The Major was similar to a mammoth disorganized Lego set in which he could still create the final masterpiece. My chaos stems from these situations and arrangements. Instead of completing the so-called Lego project, I would make my masterpieces while hiding the remaining Lego bricks under a rug or in the back of a closet. Therefore, I have been the conductor of all my chaos to invoke creativity. Even if I had transformed the chaos to various degrees of heartbreak, still, there is art in such sweet sorrow. The question I still had to answer was, 'Why?' Why did I create these cycles repeatedly? Have the demons been winning all this time, and I've been so naive to believe that I've struck a deal with them?

At 1 pm, on a Wednesday afternoon, I would have lunch with a man I met on Fetlife. Let's see if my inner chaotic cycles continued. I already attempted to be upfront about the current transition away from someone, leaving out the emotional impact I was struggling with. If anything, I hoped this person would be an acceptable replacement on the sexual level, if not on a mental level. Anything remotely emotional was to be off the plate, ultimately. So far, this person appeared to write intelligently enough to keep me interested. If he will spark a whole new chapter in another story, that answer will remain for discovery.

# Pieces of Battery Acid

As The Major slammed one door on my face, my inner adolescent became buried in its average abandonment. Knowing I won't even receive a simple text saying a simple "Goodbye" hurt more than I bargained for. Needing to dig myself out of the pile of unwanted emotions, I did what came naturally: I hunted. For a few weeks, I was exploring a new site called Fetlife, which is not for the faint of heart but for the people. The feeling of ownership needed placing, and what better place to hunt for that? Trying to weed out the selfish and sadistic and the ones I found undesirable, being my age, doesn't leave much left to consider. Personally, becoming band and gagged by someone's grandfather didn't seem appealing. Most men just want a text sex buddy, which I found as dull as watching paint dry. Immensely few people even bothered typing complete sentences. This detail was probably the reason why I found Mathew appealing.

Using the correct language to strike my curiosity, he wrote intelligently. Could I find a replacement or someone to bring to the gentle void of nothingness? If I could have an opportunity to rip out the internal mess, then moving forward in life would be less rocky. The razor-sharp ground I walked that Major left behind would feel more like blunt knives sticking up. With little hesitation, I agreed to meet Matthew at a diner down the street from work. Through testing to see if I would follow directions, he directed me to park next to his car, which happened to be in the far, far back of the lot. By this maneuver of parking cars far from most of the others, there was no doubt that he was expecting something to happen in the back seat at some point. I might be emotionally immature as fuck, but I'm not stupid.

Once I got inside the diner and found Mathew at the table, I knew this would not work for me. My inner adolescent wanted to run back out the door and not swoon. There was no attraction for me whatsoever. I like to eat my grilled cheese and go as soon as possible. The subservient in me ordered me to be polite as I picked on the crust and sipped the diet Coke. All I had to do was get through the hour. Not even an hour if you factor in travel time. We talked, and I could tell he was into me. Saying the feeling isn't mutual directly to anyone has never been my strong suit. Now that I think about it, I should have excused myself to use the bathroom and just made my getaway then and there. If only I did. If only I had that type of inner survival skills.

We finished eating with, unfortunately, time to spare. As we walked to our distantly parked cars, my heart raced as panic joined the grilled cheese in my gut. 'Whatever it is, just get it over with,' the compliant voice whispered from within. That voice might have been similar to the one I heard in Camp Sussex and Author's apartment. I wonder how many times I hear those words in my head. 'Be a good girl and get it over with.' Somehow, in some fucked way, I have equated survival to compliance during these situations. I compiled; I got in the back of his SUV like a child listening to a grown-up. Matthew got in at the other side of the car as he took on his natural dominance and pulled me over his lap. With a hard slap, it was impossible not to wince as he had me over his knee. His fingers then probed me for inspection as I lay silently, trying not to breathe. 'It will be over soon,' my inner voice consoling me. Unzipping his pants, I saw my only escape was to make him cum as quickly as I possibly could. Pushing my head toward his uncut and unimpressive cock, it didn't take long to quiet him from completing the required action. Leaving the car, I politely said goodbye and tried not to look as if I was racing to the safety of my car nearby. As soon as I got to work, I wanted to wash my mouth with battery acid if not drown.

Instead of having the desired void, I felt gross on the outside as I did on the inside. If I could burn off a layer of my skin, I would without any hesitation. The ability to turn me completely off to allow anyone to do anything they wanted to me just didn't exist. Unfortunately, I needed to feel something that resembled humanity. Sinking into a dark place within myself, I tried other ritualistic options to focus the pain outward rather than inward. A healthy person would have deleted every app and account that provided the required escapism to 'feel better.' There was no AA for the likes of me. We are just creatures of unhealthy habits, with bare feet, existing on roads covered in broken glass. Eventually, some of our roads will cross over, and I could create a new chapter with a bit of luck, detachment, and a lack of moral judgment.

# Pieces of The Major

I found out where the Major's new home will be. Correction is his new home. He probably had left New York City already without saying a word. This information I managed to find out on my own without even looking for it. I have fucked up boundary issues. It was an unanswered question the very last time we texted. All I knew was the state and town. The actual address was unavailable due to various reference databases needing to be fully updated. Unknown to him or most people, I have ways to find a bit of information even without searching. However, a magician never gives away their secrets, and neither would I. Let's call it a skill set I've obtained throughout the years. The Major's new town looked like one of those slices of old America still preserved through a rapidly changing world. Although it looked like the area had the essential Starbucks, Walgreens, and Popeye's chicken, it looked surrounded by lush greenery. Farther from the center I looked, more apart the homes and structures appeared on the map.

Maybe because I still had a touch of pride left, I wouldn't reach out asking to see him again. There's no reason to hold my breath. If that moment were to happen, it would have happened. The man is gone. To be honest, I felt him leaving before he left. It was something I had to force myself to take in. The Major was just another piece of myself that came and went like any other storm. His dent just happened to be much bigger than fully bargained for. This idea means I'm full of various dents. Unfortunately, I've failed to find an adequate distraction to occupy and quiet my inner thoughts. Swimming too far from the shore and forgetting to bring the needed floating device to keep my head above the surface is where I've gotten myself. Not The Major, not another person but myself, had created this inner ongoing chaos. However, I wouldn't call this thriving or anything close to that word. I was ending chapters before. I never felt this sad. Maybe because I allowed this one to get closer to the pieces of myself that should have stayed hidden, let's just call it another lesson learned or even failed with no make-up exams offered.

Call it part of the closure process or the downward spiral. I drove by the Major's 'old' house on Wednesday night. I'm not sure what to expect; I just wanted to see the last scraps of this meteor. The house looked vacant and dark. A bit of envy surged through me, not from what was once there, but the actual vacancy through its dark windows. Empty inside, with only the scars of memories, hung on the surface of the walls, I wanted to be like that house. Vacant.

Thinking he was gone entirely from life, I got a message from the Major. "I miss you". If I could figure out how to digest it, I'm not sure if I could. By responding, I'd open a window with no context of what was on the other side. The Major could have been messaging from his new home or, if I was lucky, room 638. Each location held a separate emotional path. I don't know if I could face either. 'I miss you too' is what my heart wanted to respond. Either way, this chapter needed to seek some closure to end in some form of peace. ' I thought you were long gone by now' is what the voice who lived behind defensive walls wanted to say instead. Instead, both voices spoke at once.

**The Major**: I'll be back for a couple of weeks at the end of the month

**Me**: Oh, so you are long gone.

*(But he missed me, and I might have one final opportunity to say goodbye to him.)*

**Me**: Hopefully, I'll have a chance to say hi and bye in one shot

**The Major**: Stop being so negative. Let's see each other.

*(At least he can sense my inner adolescent was sad, but I tried not to sound too negative)*

**Me:** I would like that.

**The Major:** good

**Me:** How is (*the new far, far away State*)

(He never told me where he was going but didn't question how I knew that information, considering the only bit of information given was limited. Maybe he thought I was just a good guesser)

**The major:** I hate NY. So good

**Me:** I get that. I hate NYC or any city.....I need mountains and forests. So, the end of November, then?

**The Major:** yes

**Me:** We will be able to arrange something without limited hiccups. Will you be staying in the hotel again?

**The major:** Yes. Stay the night

**Me:** I wish I could do that, but I cannot. I could call out of work, but that's all I got

**The major:** Lol. Ok. I knew it was a long shot.

**Me:** Couldn't hurt to ask. You can have me for almost a day if the sun is up.

**The Major:** K. I'll try something

**Me:** I'll leave the situation in your hands then. Just try to stay away from Wednesdays if possible.

**The major:** OK

**Me:** And I do miss you, sir. it appears unavoidable

**The Major:** 😊

I don't know how to interpret that smiling emoji as I left the conversation with that. That was the first emoji The Major had used in our discussions after months of texting back and forth.

Maybe a week after

The rhythm of my heart changes when I see his little circle icon pop up. Each conversation has a risk of going badly simply because of who I am and my inability to deal with much of anything as a functioning adult.

**The Major**: hi

**Me**: hey

**The Major**: How are you?

**Me**: I'm good. How are you?

**The Major**: Same

**Me**: Good. How's _______.....?

*(Not a smart move on my part to name the town I'm not supposed to know of)*

**The Major**: Why are you taunting me? It doesn't make sense.

**Me**: How am I taunting you? I've sort of been letting you be in your new environment.

**The Major**: You know what you're doing. I just don't understand why.

**Me**: What exactly am I doing? Some details would be nice

**The Major**: Nothing. I'm just crazy, I guess

**Me**: Nightmares?

**The Major**: Which I am BTW. But that's another topic

*(I think he was referring to his level of sanity)*

**Me**: So am I.

**The Major**: Lol. Cool

**Me**: I'm in the process of understanding the crazy, though; it's rooted. It's a process to look under our layers. I'm still curious about what you are accusing me of doing!

*( I should have left it alone, but I'm a fucken asshole sometimes)*

**The Major**: Nothing. I'm just crazy

**Me**: Tell me about the crazy then. I speak the language.

**The Major**: You don't. I asked you not to look deep. You continuously ignore that request. That's not healthy for me.

*(Was he referring to the actual location of his psyche? Plus, how was my unhealthy behavior unhealthy for him? Maybe we're just cut from a similar fabric)*

**Me:** How have I looked deep? If I have a better understanding. I know where you are on the map; everything else is slightly blank. And how is it not healthy for you?

**The Major:** I'm asking for privacy.

**Me:** That you have.

*(well, to maybe some extent)*

**The Major:** Then why lol things up and put it in my face? Look things up. It only makes sense if you're trying to provoke me.

*(Holy fuck! I poked the bear and thought I'd done it on purpose. Was I trying to provoke? Maybe out of anger for not telling me he was moving from day one, I needed to display some power or an upper hand. Perhaps I just have a weird way of displaying anger)*

**Me:** Like anyone could provoke you. But I'm confused

(Play dumb)

**The Major:** I'm very competitive and will win anything I want. It's just not something I'm interested in doing. We went into this with boundaries.

*(Did we? Honestly, I don't remember having this conversation. I recall being brushed off and closed out when I asked specific questions. But he never said, 'Hey, no, don't try to find me.' As far as I was concerned, there were never any conversations on boundaries. Maybe he had me confused with someone else)*

**Me:** OK. Where exactly is this coming from?

*(Still playing dumb with my poking stick hiding behind my back)*

**The Major:** We'll talk in person.

*(Will we? I know he mentioned he'll be around by the end of the month, but I have little faith that I will ever see him again)*

**Me:** OK, and I apologize if in any way made you feel what seems cornered. I'm entirely sure how I've accomplished this by not even communicating with you. It is strange how silence is almost a declaration of an assumed war. I have avoided the urge even to say hi.

*(So many times, I've wanted to reach out to him but thought better of it)*

**The Major:** You know it's not the silence. You're brilliant.

*(So much for playing dumb)*

**Me:** Then what is my weapon?

**The Major:** I don't care. Not looking for a fight. But I don't lose

**Me:** But you thought it would be entertaining to suddenly be confrontational for something I'm not even sure I did? Gee, that makes perfect sense. That's sort of painful to digest, but okay.

**The Major:** Did I look up where you live? I haven't, BTW. That's out of bounds.

*(Except for not wanting ejaculation in my hair or visible bruises, we never discussed what was strictly out of bounds or not. However, when it came to actual ordinary people's boundaries, after our second or third encounter, I took a deep internet dive into this person's world. Call it pure fascination or even the brutal reality of temporary obsession, but I wanted to peel the layer of this onion. I knew more than where he lived on Staten Island. I knew where the iconic villain hung in a room. I learned of the oval coffee table near the couch. I knew of the photo of previous presidents hung in a small office. Beyond the pictures they hung in the living room, this office appeared to have a wall of photos. I knew of the Yahtzee box that lay on top of the DVDs. I came to learn more than was intended for me.)*

**Me:** I've known where you lived for months. I didn't see it as a big deal, but assumed it was incorrect. I apologize. I would never use my knowledge of your location will never be used against you.

**The Major:** I don't live in fear. So, don't sweat it. I would do whatever is done to me tenfold to the person who did it. I just don't see the point.

*(He doesn't know how self-destructive I am. However, I would never have him in a fearful situation. Unless a person fucks with me, I will make it my project to set their world on fire for the first week or so.*

*After that, revenge gets boring. The Major has never fit that category where I've wanted to bite down on his world like a relentless pit bull.)*

**Me:** Just to see a small dot on a map and know that a dot exists in the world. I guess it's my weird way of making peace that you left.is perhaps the point: nothing more, nothing less, no less or more than looking up at the sky at one particular star each night just knowing it exists so I won't sweat it.

**The Major**: Lol. Turn the page. Let's hang out when I'm back in town. Deal or no deal?

*(I wanted to draw turning pages. I'd probably draw the red side door where The Major once smuggled with a hand page turning. The only thing is I wouldn't be sure about what would be on the other side of the turned page)*

**Me:** Let's, but do you have a better understanding now?

**The Major:** Nope. Just respect boundaries. I promise I will. And have.

*(If he doesn't understand me now, it simply means he has never understood me and will never understand no matter what words I write, images I create, or even attempt to say aloud things I struggle to say)*

**Me:** Noted.

**The Major:** Physical and psychological

*(Does this mean I'm living rent-free in a small part of his brain as he lives in mine?)*

**Me:** again noted

*(It was time to let him go and turn a page)*

Like a ghost who can penetrate the walls, The major gently touches me with soft words that weaken me, confuse me, and sadly delight me through one of the less active groups I co-admin. I never asked to co-admin one of these smaller groups. One day, when I opened a Kik app on my phone, I saw a random person I'd never had a conversation with who made a co-admin. When I messaged him, 'WTF?!', this person simply said he trusted me to do a good job keeping out 'fake people' and 'sex-bots.' The group grew a little with some help and influence, but like any unattended child, it eventually died. I would test and practice various Rage Bot Commands toward the end of its short little life. By typing in the word "Usage," a list of regular lurkers and their time stamps would appear. Those who resented talking in the group and the 'Talkers' would generate a similar list. The Rage Bot tool pretty much brought to light that this group was barely on life support. However, I would notice the Major (aka AB) name would pop up as a daily lurker. I also co-admined one of the local Bi groups and ran the same Rage Bot commands to generate the lists. Again, on what seemed like a daily basis, the Major was lurking in there as well. Maybe I assumed he'd eventually remove himself from these groups since he was no longer local.

While playing with more advanced Rage bot commands in the nearly-dead group, I saw the Major's icon pop up out of nowhere.

**The Major:** Don't boot me

**Me:** *(really trying to keep my cool and my head on straight)* We could be taken in so many ways.

**The Major:** Of course, you would say that

**Me:** As if you know me so well

**The Major:** I don't know anyone

**Me:** I believe

**The Major:** Of course, you would say that *(with an emoji sticking his tongue. I could see that mischievous boyish grim in my mind. Oh, how I admired that grim)*

**Me:** Touché, my love

**The Major:** I always had a crush on you

*(That made me think of those High School lost loves. Usually, they get buried in time; occasionally, the breeze of life lightly uncovers*

*them. Maybe in some previous life or another universe, this could apply to us)*

**Me:** Oh, hush before you break my heart

*(too late)*

And about ten minutes later, I added 'more'. Letting The Major go is something I should have been doing, but how easily he makes the task impossible with a straightforward emoji. At least he seemed no longer angry for invading his privacy. Knowing where he was on the map was so desperately needed. It is no different than needing to find that distant star in the sky, knowing they will never get to space. Maybe he finally understood my intentions to have a tiny dot to hold onto or just drunk.

The following day, I got a message:

**The Major:** I still fantasize about you. Is that OK?

**Me:** Well, it's mutual. So, if it's ok with you, it's ok with me

**The Major:** Good

*(We are both holding on)*

Later, the same day, I got a message from him, "I need to feel you". From someone over 628.8 miles away, I don't know how to respond without opening the doors to the turmoil of feelings that can easily drown me. Spending the last couple of weeks struggling to keep myself above the surface, I want an opportunity to feel the major one last time. Although he did say he would be back at the end of November/ early December, I was terrified to hold onto any hope of being in his presence. The hesitation to respond was overwhelming. It was impossible not to feel, and I'm tired of finding attempts to purge these feelings. I wanted to reply, "We need the same thing," and let Pandora's box do what it can.

I knew the major read my last message as I'd known he'd read them in the past. When the D in the Kik app message changes to an R, the person on the other end has read your message. Waiting for a response, if there would be any, was never easy when it dealt with him. As part of my soul lingers in limbo, again, I sometimes wonder why he had this effect on me and if, at all, would either of us finally. 'Turn the page'. Maybe his non-response was due to not wanting the same thing. Maybe our things are not the same after all. Perhaps he was just drinking and regretted the day's series of messages. Pandora's box hurts, but so does trying to shut it.

Speaking of lurking virtual ghosts, my inability to let go, I became a ghost in a southern state trans kik group. This Kik group was the Major's new hunting group. Out of all the variety of groups, this is where he would make his fresh start. I've known the Major was into femme men, so I wasn't surprised by his virtual choices. Allowing my ghost self to have a tiny bit of connection with him, I poke fun at his device's autocorrecting 'woke' or 'people.' Trans-women, at least in this group, seems to feel much more accessible to share various sexual pics in the group in which the Major had commented as 'hotties.' Hopefully, man won't do anything stupid with his abundant freedom in his new location. I knew what I was doing was far from the actions of any stable person. The letting process had become the most challenging yet. Not long after, I spotted his black and white circle icon in one of the gay groups of his new area. Perhaps he is using this fresh start to explore this part of him within his new beginnings. Exploring this aspect of oneself could be a lot in a crowded and overpopulated city. Weeding out the undesirables to uncover precious gems could be a bit much for some. The Major might have a less exhausting experience in a less populated area. Again, although I'm sure he's skillful, I genuinely hope he stays safe in his explorations. If anything, this is the barest nature of my love for him.

Every time I'm about to take steps to detach from the Major functionally, I get a text. The text was a simple question, "Monday or Tuesday possible?". My response, which lingered in my head as my heart did its usual procedure of racing a mile a minute before typing out the word on my phone, would be "Tuesday." So much for turning pages.

After trying to wait as long as possible, I finally responded after fifteen minutes that Tuesday would be best. His response was 'okay'. Of course, the blazing sensation along my cheeks eventually spread through my entire body and didn't fail. Now, I had a whole week to contemplate 'Tuesday.'

**The Major:** What time are you thinking

**Me:** I will be available from 12-7, so within that time frame

**The Major:** OK

The next day:

**The Major:** Fuck. I Want you

Not because I don't want him just as much, if not more, that I didn't respond immediately but because I need a little time to process. 'Let it sink in.' What capacity did he want me? Did he want me on all fours with a pig's tail thing up my ass? Did he want me to whisper "Yes, Daddy" in his ear?" Did he want me badly to have the conversation mentioned above? Probably the first two considering the use of the word 'Fuck".

After about two hours, I responded, "Never stopped wanting you," which was the absolute truth. It is impossible to let The Major go right now. He was my addiction.

"Can't wait," he responded as though those two words instilled hope that I would feel him one last time. Some chapters take longer to end. Would he take advantage of the seven hours of my availability when that Tuesday arrives, or will it be another sensational euphoric hour where my tears become hidden as he holds me one last time? Will we have a heart-to-heart conversation in which I would struggle to produce words like an average human?

Maybe it was finding one of my sister's cats dead. Perhaps it was finding the colony of roaches in my sister's closet while attempting to clean it. Maybe it was not knowing where I would be working due to a car crashing into my place of employment. Perhaps it was the wine extra glass of wine consumed to help digest all the mentioned events that had a tiny need to fuck with Major. While trolling his newly found Kik trans-bi-gay groups, I wrote in several of them, "Any sad members of the military, or is that pushing it too far."

Most of his responses were basic "??". In one trans group, he wrote, "What do you mean?".

To which I kindly responded, "??".

I was allowed to have the final words with, "Maybe it's me. I'm not understanding your question above.". I could have responded and enjoyed the back-and-forth banter, but I enjoyed leaving The Major wondering. However, on the way through my second glass of wine, I finally put on my big girl shoes to reach out to him under my regular Kik account. Because I hate leaving any plans up in the air, I needed to know what the deal was that coming Tuesday. "Am I still seeing Tuesday or?

"I hope so", he confirmed. "What will we do this time?"

"Depends on the amount of time given, location, and insurance policies"; however, the insurance policy statement might have gone over his head. We were to meet at the same hotel as last time, and I would have him for at least two hours. Considering how packed our regular one hour was, two hours seemed extraordinary.

Again, he asked, "So what will we do this time?"

"Hopefully fuck, talk, depending on the time of day, drink, play, but I'm sure Daddy has his wicked needs."

"Less talk. Ok? Why can't you live in the moment and enjoy the now?" which was probably a question to think about. "Because I enjoy the now."

After some back-and-forth banter, I thought about what I wanted, which was vindictive sex. "I can hold my own in a fight."

"Hope your ass is ready to get bruised," asked the major.

"Can I 'attempt to' to hit back? I have loads of pent-up hostility."

"You willing to suffer the consequences of those actions?

After finishing the second glass of wine said, "Yes, I can be fearless and dumb at the same time but bring it bitch. You might have the strength and the training, but I have the nails as well as some special skill set".

"Gonna use the belt on you and choke the shit out of you."

"Promises. Promises. I didn't tap out last time."

"We'll see," he said.

So, on an upcoming Tuesday at noon, we had planned on some level of sexual carnage. Although I don't have the ounce of training as a person who spent the last twenty-seven years in the military, I did plan to be highly feisty. One of my skill sets is picking pieces of a person apart enough to piss them off enough to want to react. I hoped to verbally draw a little blood while tasting his moment of vulnerability. These tiny, violent thoughts bring a strange sense of calmness for some bizarre reason. Perhaps the solution to exasperating the Storm within was to create my own tiny living, breathing nightmares. Maybe I was planning to physically and cruelly express my anger for leaving, making me feel so intransient that I felt a little calm within my violent inner storms. The trick will be to own my mouth, finally. I allow my words to be whatever random colors they will be as they drop from my mouth without any concern of reaction or look of nonconcern. The actual trick might be not to give a flying fuck and enjoy it no matter what? Is this what 'enjoying the moment' means? Could I ultimately turn off a certain piece of myself to fully achieve this? Maybe the secret to this was simply to draw blood internally or externally.

Soon after the last message between the Major and myself that night, I felt like something was left off my chest, "enjoy the moment." If I can finally allow myself to be harsh and brutal in my twisted, submissive way with the Major, I would find the opportunity to let out all this pent rage I've collected through all these pieces. This story is not a victim's tale. I am not a victim of anything. Neither am I a survivor. What I am, though, is surviving. Find little pieces as I go to create a great weapon with myself. Yes, I want to draw a little fucken blood and not just my own. Through all my emotional turmoil over this Major person, I need to figure out what was so fucken special about him that got me all twisted up inside. I'm not entirely sure I've completely understood it myself. He was a series of so many choices I've made only to deal with or avoid dealing with all the fucken elephants in the room. Maybe it's time to say fuck you, elephants. Even better yet, I think I want to bitch slap all the elephants.

During my time with S, he had a bear tooth that I wore around my neck for a few years. After the velvet cord broke, I added the tooth to my keychain. It's been there ever since. Upon request, S also gave me a t-shirt saturated entirely in his order. The shirt reeks of his scent, and I used to sleep with it each night. The smell and its soft texture soothed me at night. Over time, the shirt lost its scent, and I'm unsure where the t-shirt is now. J gave me an old travel bag that sits unused in my work locker, fresh pesto fed to the family with the salmon pasta dish I make almost every night. I also cook the dish with pesto, which is not fresh but improves the flavor. J also gave him a Mr. Clean magic eraser sponge the last day I saw him, which I lost somewhere in the house. As for the Major, I stole a work T-shirt from his suitcase while he was in the shower. Unfortunately, it's an immaculate shirt, but I can smell him slightly.

Sitting at Panera Bread, reflecting on previous events, I wrote words to capture the detailed textures of the current memory of room 306. Before my arrival, I had enough time to feed the surviving cat and get some most needed wine for the house and the approaching encounter. The wine helped me to summon my inner savage self because I wasn't going to be the usual passive submissive. Whatever fierce velocity within me needed to emerge in this final current call with the Major. Before I texted him that I had parked, I probably consumed about a good glass of wine. I wasn't drunk but more in tune with hostility reaching the surface. If I was to "enjoy the moment," the feral demon needed to make herself own. I was partly angry for him leaving and, in part, for leaving as much of an imprint on his brain.

The Major grew a soft salt and pepper bread during his new life. He looked even more beautiful than I remembered. Like a perfectly trained zookeeper who can handle and tame a poisonous snake, the Major attempted to calm and tame this animal who he just left. Biting his lip as I repeatedly struggled so hard not to draw any blood, God knew the taste of his red fluid on my tongue would have been delicious. An aggressive submissive who only obeyed because it suited her needs and wanted to claw and bite through his clothes and possibly his flesh became a welcomed guest of room 306. Every inch of me was fully received by every wanted inch of him as I allowed myself to release this wild storm that had been existing in my soul. I didn't ask for permission to touch myself in ways I wanted while riding him. The Major introduced me to Erotic asphyxiation. As my orgasms would begin to emerge, he would cover my mouth and nose. He only allowed the air into my lungs when he felt it was time. "Breath. Good girl," he gently whispered while his hand controlled the oxygen entering my lungs. He would also on and off apply mild choke holds as well. As violent as this sounds, it calmed me while my body would convulse in the purest pleasure. Sometimes, a little violence is like that welcoming hot shower on a cold day. The enjoyment of slightly touching death's fingertips was a sensual secret kiss that I only knew. "Breath. Good girl". I would only trust experiencing this particular thing with him. A trained zookeeper just knows how their selective crafts are. The old and new marks hidden under my left sock went unnoticed when The Major took off both socks. Neither were the small, newer ones on my left shoulder any cause for alarm.

I felt the sting on my breasts as I rode him, another delightful sensation I experienced. I wondered if I would find new bruises the next day. Turning to my stomach to receive his slaps on my ass, "You can do better," I taunted before I fought off the screams as well as the devious giggle. This vicious hedonistic dance continued for approximately seventy-five minutes before the Major released himself. Then, the more challenging part of the afternoon followed, where I often got lost. To lay quietly in someone's arms who had a bit of impact on your existence in a short time is difficult. It's fucken difficult not to feel what I felt, had felt, and I don't give a fuck, will feel. Our bodies fit together perfectly, and he spooned me. That was only the second time he helped me from behind. The first time was when we used a room at the motel on Hylan Blvd. 'Enjoy the moment' as I allowed my body to sink into him. There was some sort of morbid actual crime show on the TV. Hearing words like death, murder, and other words about killing was a strange comfort while I 'enjoyed the moment.' For the first time with him in these moments of tender silence, I felt like I could easily drift into his arms and forget about whatever existed outside of room 309. 'Breath. Good Girl. 'Breath'.

Then, as always, time refused to stay still as I wanted to remain there. The Major had to run to Brooklyn before 5 pm. However, it was impossible not to briefly get lost in each other's skin. To feel this beautiful creature inside me one last time was beyond necessary. It was my last breath of perfect air before saying 'goodbye.' We took turns showering. On my way to the bathroom, I saw his uniform hanging up. Brushing my hand across it, 'Hello and goodbye, my dear friend',. When it was his turn in the shower, I desperately needed to have peace of him to keep. Something solid and tangible. As his suitcase sat there, I saw the T-shirt on top and stuffed it deep in my bag. To be fair, in this non-requested trade, I left my crotchless underwear under one of his pillows. The bizarre exchange of objects gave a sense of peaceful closure. There might be a slim chance of the Major traveling back up here occasionally. I know he has family up here. He might want his shirt back, but I doubt it. "Keep it," I can imagine him saying.

I wondered why this person affected me these past few weeks. Maybe I saw parts of myself in him. Perhaps I saw what I wanted to visit. Maybe finding someone you feel you can trust to explore various sexual experiences is something not easy to let go of. The offbeat experiences I shared thought they should stay sacred with the Major. Trying to find his 'replacement' isn't going to be easy. The mother fucker left considerable shoes to fill, and the goddamn bar appeared to be set a bit fucken high for anyone else who might come after. The possible candidates have fallen short as of now. After completing the advanced level, these novices were boring to me. They were mere cliff notes to a masterpiece. Anyway, winter has always been my off-season. My inner sexual demon has a habit of hibernating in the winter. "Enjoy the moment". I should ask him about these in-between moments and where the "enjoy " can be found. Maybe people come into your life at this fierce velocity because there's an important lesson you need to learn: "Enjoy the moment." If anything, The Major was a massive hit-and-run in which I found it rather challenging to get myself off the pavement soon after. I think I even liked the gravel. Maybe I envied his ability to live as I do without overthinking, feeling, just "enjoying the moment." We might be a similar product. Still, the collective experiences of which we are the product might be vastly different. Hence, there's a bridge I cannot even begin to cross. Perhaps it just got lost in the rubble.

However, I had to figure out how to smuggle a t-shirt into the house and under my pillow. Also, I liked the act of smuggling. That night, I secretly held the Major stolen shirt as a child would hold onto a security blanket. Finding the small pockets of his scent, I clung to each memory before time could begin its decay process. There are pockets of knowledge I discovered in those past few months. The one pocket I became desperate to find is the lesson of 'turning pages.' To allow the series of secret delectable moments to be what they are and as they are. Maybe I just need to learn to eradicate my feelings before they have a chance to grow into thick-rooted weeds. Perhaps that is the main lesson to conquer.

*The Last Letter:*

*Like some of us, I have to debate various crossroads before me. Often enough, these crossroads are frequently self-invented with too much energy involved. I've written these three lines with too much thought and consideration involved. It could be because I spend too many hours planning out the context due to its true intent. My intention right now is to share a bit more than just your chapter finally, but the part in which the events of the previous become woven in. Therefore, it is a decent-sized part representing a fourth of a much larger picture, which is nearly complete. It's basically about the ongoing need for survival through various experiences, which I'm partly the product of. The next step is attempting to get published before just simple self-publishing. Before that next step, I'm giving you and a couple of others an opportunity to review the content. I would be open to negotiating various adjustments to ensure privacy for all.*

*Although I wonder if this will even have an audience, I feel it's best to take certain precautions to avoid lawsuits. I should warn you that some of what I've written in detail about various activities, thought processes, and pesky things called emotions. I hate having them. If I could, I would take a scalpel to cut them out. I should also warn you that there will be a handful of things that will differently piss you off. Including was often a debate. I'm not even entirely comfortable sharing it. However, not including them, the risk of pissing you off, felt like lying. So, with risk, I'm attempting not to give a fuck about your reactions. However, attempts can quickly fail. Therefore, allow me to apologize in advance. Perhaps I was destined to be that tiny thorn in your side to the small pebble you can never excavate from a shoe. Or maybe I'm just a bit of chaos that is difficult to thrive in fully. Perhaps these 70 pages can fall under the "you can tell me anything" clause. If you wish to just go to where you begin, jump to page 6, but then be woven in and out of this part like a string. I also adjusted the font size to accommodate your vision needs. And I apologize for some of the content and am prepared for the consequences.*

I sent the above letter on Saturday afternoon with what became Part IV of the project. One about shared document is that you can tell when someone has opened that document. On the top right corner of the screen, that person icon or often and, in this case, anonymous appears. The icon changed several times, indicating the person logged off and on again.

Upon waking up the next day, I check for any messages. It's a typical morning habit to look for any signs of life out in the world before my eyes can entirely focus and process the words. At 1:57 am, there's a message from Major "Hi." 'hi' is often benign, like a head nod from across a crowded room. In this case, however, this 'hi' could be radioactive. While attempting to wake up, I knew I had responded in kind with a 'hi' of my own. I had to deal with the dread of cutting open my hands upon opening this box. I created the box, so I might as well deal with it. Lou Reed said best, "You're gonna reap what you sow."

How long would it take that (d) to switch to an (R)? In this case, it took about ten minutes. Now, just wait for the words that should follow. I wondered if they would have sharp, piercing words or words of concern. They could even be atomic and bloodier. They may become thoroughly thought out like a script, or there may be no words. However, there were no words at all. He may have already hired a lawyer. Possibly, he just needed time to let the seventy-five pages 'sink in' awhile. It's not every day that we have someone's mess electronically delivered. It would be beyond reasonable if I never heard from him ever again. I am more than anyone could bargain for during the basic routines of 'hooking up.' The best way to deal with my chaos is to bury it deep in the backyard.

As I was losing faith in getting a response, the following Monday night, "We need to talk about your book" was the beginning and probably the end of any future communication. To sum it all up, I have unexpectedly but yet successfully become just like the demons I have been surviving for all these years. The Major had become a causality of my inner chaos. The raging storm in me had become a threatening devastation to another human. He has seen the product in which I have evolved, and it is disturbing and understandable. He should hold absolute regret in meeting me. Maybe those who know the entirety of all parts might come to a similar conclusion without bothering to crack through the rational understanding that is clearly beyond me. A monster in words and actions is what I've become. That was now the realization.

**The Major:** We need to talk about your book

*(All the blood rushed out of my face. This conversation wasn't going to be pretty. We have opened the can of worms, and these suckers are about to bite.*

**Me:** This is your opportunity to tell me how you hate it. The floor is ultimately yours.

**The Major:** Don't hate it. But it is instead exposing. I can't condone that. Not sure why you would either

**Me:** You are welcome to highlight within the shared document any portions you wish to change or become less exposed, and I will consider them.

*(How cold I must have seemed as though the word 'consideration' could be easily translated as 'not concerned.'*

**The Major:** Ok. Interesting. Thanks. I'll respond soon. I didn't know I was signing up to be part of a tell-all book. If we're playing this game, I'm not authorizing my image, likeness, or any intimate details of my life to be published. And I didn't appreciate you stealing the shirt I needed for an event. But whatever. I trusted you. Fuck me, I think. The story is just as good with adequate protection in place.

*(There's no answer I could give to justify my actions. I deserve The Major's anger and his disappointment; I deserve everything)*

**Me:** Again, as though I know the word 'apology' carries no weight when one becomes a casualty in another's dysfunction, including garments. Again, please highlight any particular details you wish to alter.

(Hoping the word 'dysfunction' could be seen as an umbrella excuse for my ability to destroy things. Isn't that what monsters do)

**The Major:** My heart asks why. But ok

*(His heart? His heart! Because I'm a little monster with teeth and claws. I take no pride in it)*

**Me:** Your heart? I am a product of my experiences (part 2). I don't understand or comprehend 'normal.'

**The Major:** We all are. You're not any more special than any other soul.

**Me:** Trust me, the word 'special' is a word I will never apply to myself ...ever ....

**The Major:** I never tried to harm you. I didn't get it even when you gave me the green light.

*(He didn't do anything wrong. It was me. It was always me)*

**Me:** No, you always held back. That was always clear.

**The Major:** When we started chatting, you said you were in a similar situation and didn't want anything to change. That is the only reason I met a woman.

**Me:** As for separate situations, nothing will change, at least for you. We both live our secret lives for whatever reason, and we must pursue them; I needed to write mine down. And there are plenty of emotionally needy heterosexual men out there.

**The Major:** Yes. But your words completely expose me. Anyone who knows me will know who you're writing about. And you robbed me!!! Who does that???

**Me**: Again, use this opportunity to highlight any threatening words, and they will be adjusted.

**The Major:** I didn't do anything that caused you to go on your revenge tour.

**Me:** No, you read past or missed a few things. If you did, you would see that. You skipped "Pieces of NJ."

**The Major:** What the fuck does that have to do with you writing about me? And my house? And my location, and taking my stuff without permission?

*(The shirt was now a tangible reminder like the scars under the left sock)*

**Me:** What the fuck does that have to do with you writing about me? And my house? And my location?

**The Major:** And taking my stuff without permission?

**Me:** No, there's no justification for those actions in your perspective

**The Major:** Cool. Let's do this. Goodnight.

Instead of a planned thin one-inch incision, I pressed the razor with all emotional force, and even with the tissue crammed into my sock, it bled throughout the night and onto the morning. The inward scars were now slowly and steadily becoming outward. The other lurking Kik account, and I deleted my existence in most of my actual accounts. If only the delete options and delete keys carried more force. Scars and stolen property were not just bitter reminders of what I had become but taggable evidence of what I probably had always been.

When I reread this chapter, it's like witnessing one's decomposition from the delusions of internal control to the inward crumbling. One would be greatly disappointed if one hoped for a happy ending where we can find finite clarity and rationality would be achieved. It might take some time for them to get the taste of battery acid out of their mouths. Yet, there was an awakening in the process of writing and revising this part. The demons I assumed I had control over were in the driver's seat more than should be allowed.

After a week since The Major first read this part, he reached out with complete sincerity on how I was. My response was nothing short of regret for invading his privacy and that my detailed descriptions were nothing invasive. I promised to revise this so his identity would be vague where a reader might believe or might not believe he was a head cop, fire chief, ferry boat captain, or even a high-ranking mailman. Everyone needed to know that he held authority within his world, even without work clothes. Also, he became an influential force of nature so quickly that it was impossible not to record in as much detail. Writing about him was my strange way of keeping him. There are just some pieces we encounter that are impossible to forget. Hopefully, I have respected his wishes of anonymity. I only wish him peace in where his journey towards Ithaca leads. I was now ready to turn the page.

I stole your shirt

Like stealing fragments of time

An act of desperate compulsion

Because I could not simply say goodbye

Like an average person
I unjustly claimed your property
To absorb memories
tears
a heavy breath
Because I could not merely move forward
My feet never learned that motion
Without some texture of joy
I took what wasn't mine
I took it with regret
I took it for survival
A piece of you
That will never be mine
No matter how much I attempt to fold it
Crumble it
Hold it
I stole your shirt.
I'm sorry you won't be able to get back
There is no excuse for such an act.

**Epilogue:**

When I started this project, my goal seemed simple. It began as a collection of the old fragments of myself to understand my current actions in a better light. The entail goal was to see all the broken pieces of the past to put me better together in the present. If I described the train crash fully, I could find the tiny bits and pieces to fix to get back on track. The assumption that I had control over my demons proved to be false. They appear to pull my strings more than I was willing to admit. Maybe I was already aware of their control but didn't want to realize I was losing this battle.

There are a few things I learned about myself during this process. One was my capacity to self-harm in various ways. My first memory of trying to hurt myself was when I was either eleven or twelve, but I think it might have started even before that. Part of my job was going to schools in the area. There was an incident During my visit to a middle school. A boy was strangling himself. The teacher noticed he was turning purple and passing out. As soon as the teacher addressed him, he quickly regained conscience and returned to a standard shade of pink. Reckoning myself in his action, I was about the same age when I would choke myself repeatedly. People like us aren't always suicidal, but we also don't feel fully alive in our skin either. Tip-toeing between life and death is sometimes a balancing act for us. Living on the 17th floor in Brooklyn, it would have been easy to take a step ladder and place it next to the railing on the terrace. One, two, three steps, and over and over, so much would have been. However, I would find access to various, not-so-high areas and linger on the edge of the vast difference between the ground and myself. I never jumped but existed in that lingering feeling between the living and the non-living.

Instead of death, I had lived in a world of various ways of self-harm. The cutting is just a visual form of it. Fucking the random strangers over the years was another. When I began this project, I only knew of the various starting points that would direct me down a varied path. Opening the drawers and scattering boxes of memories to collect the required pieces opened parts of myself; I lacked the preparation to be recognized. The overall picture of all these pieces weaved in is not pretty. If I am a product of my experiences, then I am a toddler with sore and bloodied feet. I am a child with tangled hair and dirty underwear. I am unaware of baby roaches in the cereal in the morning. I am a repetitive nightmare of a man in my bedroom. I have spitballs in my hair and a cord twisting around my neck. I am the sexual bargain made to boys to stop hurting me. I am a tiny object that secretly penetrates my skin. I am volutation. I am rage, words, and lines. I am a wife, mother, and a monster. I am a librarian, a wannabe writer, and an artist. Maybe I'm even you or at least a fragment of your reflection.

Anonymous or not, exposing myself to the world by writing this reminded me of when I was seventeen. There was a criminal justice class in my high school. Maybe it was another act of self-harm, but I volunteered to tell three classes of about thirty students each about the rape and the hospital process of a rape kit. To be honest, no adult or teacher should have allowed me to stand in front of these classes to repeatedly and repeatedly tell the tale of being raped and nearly strangled a death. However, a couple of students in these classes had experienced some form of sexual violence as well. From keeping their experiences, a secret, they found a safe place in Frank Casa's office. They were no longer alone. Without a doubt, I know several adults exist in this world, living with shame and guilt as though they, too, are living with a raging storm inside them. If anything, if anything alone, they are not alone.

There are still more tiny fragments lingering in the draw of memory that didn't share. There are still patterns I may or may not repeat. There is still a razor and bandages hidden in the bathroom. I hope to make a healthy choice, repair most of the missing and broken pieces, and get back on track. There's always book #2.

December is an officially depressing month. It's the month my mother died. It has been a month since my sister had a significant stroke. The month of words and actions stabs the Major in the heart. It's the month of my birthday. I hate this month. It's a month of depleting your wallet to feel loved. December is destruction. Soon, it will be a year since my sister had her stroke. She still lived in the nursing home facility with no idea if and when she would be able to return home. After having her over on Thanksgiving, my nephew finally realized that her mobility outside of her wheelchair is minimal. As I kept trying to tell him there were stairs leading up to her apartment, he eventually concluded that that was not the best living arrangement for her. I guess seeing is believing because what the fuck did I know. Where and when she will end up at this point is anyone's guess.

Being in my sister's apartment held a cascade of emotions. Although most of the roaches and the smell of cat piss appeared pure eradication, the memories within those walls were beyond overwhelming. Every other day, I avoid looking into the living room when I'm there to feed the one surviving cat. It's too much like looking into someone's eyes and feeling nothing but regret and guilt. It's strange how the emotions of one area of one single place can rapidly change within a week. Those walls contained so many casualties. First my sister, then the cat, and now the Major. All in one place, I couldn't stop my sister's demise, I failed to keep the cat alive, and I exploited and violated the Major trust.

Soon after I eliminated my existence in every kik group, The Major did the same. If he did so because I created an unwelcoming space for him, it is something I had to own. We are both now shadows of an imprint on the app. Although we were still attached to it, we remained in the distant, unseen background. The bottom line is I got involved with someone from here and ended up being very destructive and possibly hurt them beyond any repair, so I removed myself from all the sandboxes because I couldn't play nice. There would be no apology for me to convey because no apology would be acceptable. "Sorry for exploiting your personal life and most sensitive and trusted details, but I managed to keep it anonymous."

Throughout this journey, I tried therapy a couple of times. It didn't take. The last time I went through the therapy road was in Fall 2021. It lasted no more than a couple of months. Maybe due to my insurance, my therapist was a newbie PhD student who couldn't handle my shit then. It was virtual, so I would see this kid's bewildered facial expression when it came to just touching the surface of self-harm. I probably owe that particular agency a few dollars on co-payments. If I'm lucky and this book gets off the ground, a few therapists and psychologists will be kind enough to lay on a few diagnoses. From various internet searches, I believe I have borderline personality disorder due to the trauma I endured as a child and an adolescent.

www.ingramcontent.com/pod-product-compliance
Lightning Source LLC
Chambersburg PA
CBHW050315160726
48002CB00001B/40